# The Politics of Past Evil

FROM THE JOAN B. KROC INSTITUTE
FOR INTERNATIONAL PEACE STUDIES AND
THE ERASMUS INSTITUTE

*Kroc Institute Series on Religion, Conflict,*
*and Peace Building*

# THE POLITICS OF PAST EVIL

*Religion, Reconciliation, and the Dilemmas*
*of Transitional Justice*

*Edited by*

## Daniel Philpott

*University of Notre Dame Press*
*Notre Dame, Indiana*

Manufactured in the United States of America


*Library of Congress Cataloging-in-Publication Data*

The politics of past evil : religion, reconciliation, and the dilemmas of
transitional justice / edited by Daniel Philpott.
p.  cm.
"From the Joan B. Kroc Institute for International Peace Studies."
Includes index.
ISBN-13: 978-0-268-03889-2 (cloth : alk. paper)
ISBN-10: 0-268-03889-9 (cloth : alk. paper)
ISBN-13: 978-0-268-03890-8 (pbk. : alk. paper)
ISBN-10: 0-268-03890-2 (pbk. : alk. paper)
1. Truth commissions.   2. Reconciliation—Religious aspects.
3. Reconciliation—Political aspects.   4. Restorative justice.
5. Crimes against humanity.   I. Philpott, Daniel, 1967–
JC580.P653   2006
303.6'9—dc22

2006008039

∞ *This book is printed on acid-free paper.*

# Contents

# Contributors

### Mark R. Amstutz
Professor of Political Science,
Wheaton College

### R. Scott Appleby
Professor of History and John M. Regan Jr. Director of
the Joan B. Kroc Institute for International Peace Studies,
University of Notre Dame

### David B. Burrell, C.S.C.
Theodore M. Hesburgh Chair in Philosophy and Theology,
University of Notre Dame

### A. James McAdams
William M. Scholl Professor of International Affairs
and Director of the Nanovic Institute for European Studies,
University of Notre Dame

### Daniel Philpott
Associate Professor, Department of Political Science, and Faculty Fellow,
Joan B. Kroc Institute for International Peace Studies,
University of Notre Dame

## Alan J. Torrance

Professor of Systematic Theology, St. Mary's College,
University of St. Andrews

## Ronald A. Wells

Professor of History,
Calvin College

## Nicholas Wolterstorff

Noah Porter Professor Emeritus of Philosophical Theology,
Yale University

# Acknowledgments

The idea for this volume was hatched in 1999, when James Turner, then director of the Erasmus Institute at the University of Notre Dame, provided the inspiration and resources to form a working group on reconciliation in politics. The authors subsequently met together three times, developing their ideas on the theology and politics of reconciliation through argument and discussion, criticism and encouragement. Professor Turner merits the authors' abundant gratitude for this unusual opportunity for collaboration. The editor and the authors also thank the staff of the Erasmus Institute, especially Kathy Sobieralski and Terri O'Brien, for logistical support, as well as Professor Turner's successor as director, Robert Sullivan. We thank Lowell Francis and Rebecca DeBoer, our editors at Notre Dame University Press, for their conscientious support, Elisabeth Magnus for her excellent copy editing, and two anonymous reviewers for their helpful comments. Finally, we thank R. Scott Appleby, director of the Joan B. Kroc Institute for International Peace Studies at the University of Notre Dame, for including the volume in the Kroc Institute Series on Religion, Conflict, and Peacebuilding.

# Introduction

## DANIEL PHILPOTT

Over the past two decades, all over the world, newly emergent liberal democracies with long, dolorous pasts of injustice—under communism, under military dictatorship, under apartheid—have sought to confront and to overcome these persistent legacies. From these episodes has emerged a concept relatively new to the vocabulary of liberal democracies, but now the subject of a global conversation: reconciliation. Scholars, mostly philosophers and social scientists, have also begun a conversation about reconciliation and the justice of political transitions. While their perspectives are competing and diverse along several dimensions, the majority of them share an outlook that is not at all preponderant among actual participants in transitional justice in South Africa and Northern Ireland, in Argentina, Germany, and Guatemala: secularism.[1]

What unfolds in the following pages, then, is a conversation about how theology and politics are related in the theory and practice of reconciliation, situated in the context of transitional states. What place does reconciliation have in the politics of transitions? What are the warrants for it? Four theorists, two theologians and two philosophers, draw explicitly from theological perspectives in answering these questions. The answers are fresh angles in today's debate. Our conversation, though, also recognizes that reconciliation's credibility as an approach to politics depends not only on a theoretical foundation but also on an account of its place in the tug and haul of actual political transitions. Two political scientists and a historian, all sympathetic to the theological perspectives, then chart the path of reconciliation, sometimes tortuous, sometimes propitious, in South Africa, Northern Ireland, Argentina, and Germany. The divide between the two sorts of inquiry is not neat. The theorists are cognizant of contemporary political transitions; the empirically oriented scholars are theoretically conscious. Explicating theological warrants, mapping the texture of actual political transitions, echoing debates within these transitions, our conversation addresses a wide variety of interlocutors, both scholarly and generalist, both with and without theological commitments.

The context for our conversation is the historically unusual concentration of societies that have passed from authoritarianism to democracy or from war to peace over the past quarter-century or so. In what political scientist Samuel P. Huntington calls the "third wave" of democratization, states in Eastern Europe, East Asia, South Africa, and Latin America have sought to progress from one or another form of regime that denied human rights—military dictatorship, communism, or apartheid—to a constitutional liberal democracy.[2] In Northern Ireland, the former Yugoslavia, East Timor, Guatemala, and elsewhere, states have settled long wars. Among the most difficult dilemmas that all of these societies face has been their own past. Particularly, how ought they to treat perpetrators of egregious violence and human rights violations? Try them? Grant them amnesty? Leave the problem alone and continue onwards? Stage public hearings? Might forgiveness be appropriate?

In fact, transitional states have responded to their pasts in a variety of ways, often combining elements of different approaches. One alternative is *pragmatic compromise*. Here, no authority, international or domestic, addresses past injustices in any meaningful way. There are no trials, no punishment, no truth commissions, no procedures or rituals for reconciliation. The parties to the transition—usually the representatives of the old regime and their ascendant opponents—may choose this solution because they are concerned about peace and social stability, because the outgoing regime is powerful enough to prevent any official examination of the past, because a constitutional court rules against such an examination, or simply because there are no strong advocates for governmental solutions to transitional justice. In chapter 6 of this volume, for instance, Mark Amstutz describes how, in Argentina, President Raúl Alfonsín's efforts to prosecute senior military leaders of the previous junta ultimately came to naught due to the resistance of powerful military factions and their public supporters. In Northern Ireland and Poland governmental solutions have thus far been weak to nonexistent.

Approaches to transitional justice that do involve official institutions are divisible into two broad approaches: punitive justice and reconciliation. Each, of course, has its variations; often, states combine elements of the two. East Timor, for instance, adopted a sophisticated hybrid approach combining trials for perpetrators of the most egregious human rights violations with a truth commission and local community reconciliation forums.

In states where the punitive approach is dominant, an authoritative court, international or domestic, puts to trial perpetrators of past injustices and punishes them when found guilty. The Nuremberg and Tokyo trials conducted by the Allied powers against leaders of Germany and Japan after World War II are the classic examples; today, tribunals for Rwanda and Yugoslavia have resurrected these innovations in international jurisprudence. In the recent wave of transitions to democracy, some states have conducted their own trials for top officials of their former regimes. Unified Germany, for instance, placed on trial former communist officials like Egon Krenz, Erich Mielke, and Erich Honecker. Trials, though, in Germany as elsewhere, are typically few, highly publicized, and mixed in their ability to secure convictions. Chile has only recently made progress in securing the right to try General Augusto Pinochet, who was electorally defeated in a referendum in 1988. But trials are not the only form of punitive justice. In the Czech Republic and unified Germany, it has taken the form of "lustration," translating roughly to "cleansing," in which past perpetrators of human rights violations are disqualified from holding future office.

Reconciliation is different. The concept essentially means "restoration of right relationship." But its political forms are diverse, as different as the dilemmas of the societies in which they are found. Reconciliation need not even involve official procedures and may take place in civil society. Ronald Wells's essay describes how, in Northern Ireland, leaders of Catholic and Protestant churches and members of ecumenical communities built friendship and significant cooperation with one another both before and after the Good Friday Agreement of 1998. Similar efforts took place in Bosnia during the late 1990s, many of these sponsored by faith-based nongovernmental organizations. In Brazil in the early 1980s, the Catholic Church and the World Council of Churches conducted the equivalent of an investigation into the past abuses of the military regime prior to the onset of democracy, involving the surreptitious gathering of documents from courts and other sources.

The most innovative forums for reconciliation, though, have been the sundry truth commissions that have emerged in recent political transitions. As

Priscilla Hayner describes in her thorough study of them, truth commissions are officially sanctioned bodies with temporary mandates to investigate a pattern of abuses that occurred in some specified period of the past. Generally, their final aim is to publish a comprehensive report that makes the injustices public. Since 1974, over twenty-one such commissions have been established across the globe, the most prominent ones operating during the 1980s and 1990s in South Africa, El Salvador, Argentina, Chile, and Guatemala.[3]

Now, the mere occurrence of truth commissions, the mere revelation of past events, is not necessarily restorative. Commissions may be little more than a mere prelude to trials, one faction's instrument for exposing another faction's evils, or a process that succeeds only in reopening the wounds of the past, creating instability and deepened bitterness. But recent proponents of truth commissions tout their restorative promise. José Zalaquett, a Chilean lawyer and truth commissioner, for instance, insists that, "from an ethical position, the ultimate purpose of dealing systematically with past human rights abuses is to put back in place a moral order that has broken down or has been severely undermined, or to build up a just political order if none existed in historical memory."[4] Truth commissions acknowledge the suffering, hence the dignity, of victims; they crack the carapace of anonymity behind which perpetrators hide and expose them to public shame; they reduce all parties' ability to use the past as a political weapon; they sometimes lead to repentance and forgiveness. At least, these are the arguments for their restorative value.

It was South Africa's truth commission that most strongly made reconciliation its goal. Although healing, repentance, forgiveness, and other elements of restoration were not explicitly, legally mandated by the constitutional provision that established the commission, they were openly extolled by the commission chair Archbishop Desmond Tutu, the other members of the commission, and sundry proponents of it. The South African body openly used the label "Truth and *Reconciliation* Commission," borrowing the name from the Chilean commission that had just preceded it. It was unique in its use of hearings that gave voice and visibility to victims, offenders, and family and friends of both, along with the commission, who represented the state, and a public of millions of South African citizens who watched the hearings on television and read about them in the newspaper. Since the commission published its report in 1998, a lively debate over its successes and failures has continued among South Africans as well as scholars and commentators elsewhere. Clearly, though, the commission stands as the most robust attempt to bring reconciliation into politics among all of the recent transitional states.

What is striking about the states that chose reconciliation as their approach is the strong involvement of religious communities—mostly Christian churches—in both the formation and the conduct of truth commissions and related proceedings. In South Africa, Christian churches and theologically minded leaders, as well as Muslim leaders, urged a truth and reconciliation commission. The commission itself was led by Anglican Archbishop Tutu, who famously brought religious rituals and discourse into the hearings, eliciting both praise and criticism. Religious communities helped to host and conduct the hearings as well. As already mentioned, religious communities in Brazil courageously conducted an underground inquiry into the truth. Similarly, Chile's Catholic Church was instrumental in investigating abuses under the rule of General Pinochet; after Pinochet's departure, President Patricio Aylwin explicitly drew on his Catholic beliefs in calling for a truth and reconciliation commission and national repentance for the torture and disappearance of thousands of Pinochet's opponents. East Timor's Nobel Prize–winning Bishop Carlos Belo was instrumental in calling for reconciliation (but in a way that also involved accountability through trials) after his country achieved independence in 1999. In Guatemala, Bishop Juan Gerardi, unsatisfied with his government commission's failure to name perpetrators, even formed and conducted an entire separate commission; a day after releasing its report in 1998, he was assassinated.

There are also many cases where religious communities have not contributed to reconciliation. Argentina and El Salvador formed truth commissions with little help from the Catholic Church in their countries. In Rwanda, churches hardly contributed at all to transitional justice solutions after the genocide of 1994; many church leaders and religious laypeople were in fact implicated in it. Neither Ireland, Poland, nor Bosnia has yet formed an official truth commission, despite having strong religious communities within their borders. Analytically, such negative cases are just as important as the cases of demonstrable influence. Together, they call for attention to the complex and significant relationship between religion and reconciliation in the politics of transitional countries—attention that few scholars have yet given.[5]

Reconciliation, truth commissions, the restoration of right relationships in politics—these recent entrants into the discourse of liberal democracy raise a whole host of conceptual controversies. Are they even appropriate for politics? Do they involve a sacrifice of retributive justice? If so, is this justifiable? Are truth commissions more justifiable when they seek mere social stability and refrain from promoting reconciliation? In what sense is knowledge of past evils restorative? Does discovery of the truth conflict with retributive justice?

Is forgiveness appropriate to the political order? If so, should states practice it? Or should it be confined to citizens, churches, and other groups outside state institutions? Is it possible to combine reconciliation and forgiveness with punishment? If so, how? If reconciliation is to be defended, then on what basis? What warrants it? Can it be realized in political orders as we know them? What is the appropriate and just involvement of religious actors in transitional justice?

A theologically informed answer to these questions will indeed be distinct. This is my own argument in the essay that follows this introduction. There, I seek to fill out the concept of political reconciliation, examining the many dimensions along which relationships can be both broken and restored in the political context. I then argue that a deep tension exists between reconciliation and the liberal tradition of political philosophy. Unsurprisingly, many contemporary liberals are critical of reconciliation. The tradition contains few conceptual resources to ground it and several venerable orthodoxies that evoke skepticism. It is rather theology that provides a strong warrant for reconciliation. Ultimately, possibilities may exist for liberalism to accept a theologically based concept of reconciliation, but only if liberalism is configured in a significantly different manner than it usually is today.

Chapter 2, by the theologian Alan J. Torrance, most strongly challenges conventional Western conceptions of justice, particularly their retributive features. Reconciliation, for him, begins with the addressing of past wrongs through "evangelical repentance," a practice that models God's covenant with humanity. As revealed in the Jewish Torah, then in Jesus Christ, this covenant is one of unilateral forgiveness, which evokes in its recipient *metanoia*, or a change in heart, that leads to repentance and reconciliation. This logic, rather than the balancing logic represented by "the scales of justice," ought to govern human relationships, even in politics. Though Torrance does not reject punishment as a social practice, he calls for its subordination to the logic of repentance. In the contemporary world of transitional justice, he finds evangelical repentance best expressed in South Africa's Truth and Reconciliation Commission.

The philosopher Nicholas Wolterstorff (ch. 3) then addresses the question of whether states ought to practice forgiveness, one of the vital components of reconciliation. He answers in the affirmative. Drawing upon New Testament Scriptures, he first puts forth a definition of and philosophical argument for forgiveness. Then he shows that it is both intelligible and defensible for states to forgive and offers several grounds on which they might legitimately do so. Though Wolterstorff shares with Torrance a sympathy for political forgiveness, he adopts a contrasting defense in certain salient respects. For instance, he views forgiveness as a victim's foregoing of his right to see an offender punished, whereas Torrance rejects the logic of retribution altogether. Through his argument emerges a philosophical warrant for the decision of states like South Africa to grant amnesty to the perpetrators of past political crimes. Though the commission, like many of its analysts, did not express its amnesties as forgiveness, Wolterstorff insists that this is indeed what they were. What is more, they properly belong in the politics of transitional states.

Both Torrance's and Wolterstorff's essays highlight most strongly what is true of the entire volume—that it is informed not only by theology but by Christian theology most distinctively. The relationship between a Christian perspective on reconciliation and that of other faiths or a secular perspective remains an open but important question. In chapter 4, the theologian David B. Burrell looks at the other Abrahamic faiths—Judaism and Islam—not only asking what their texts and traditions have to say about reconciliation in politics but commending conversation between the faiths as a source of insight. For him, reconciliation is powerfully enacted when believers of one faith enter into a dialogue of "mutual illumination" with believers in other faiths, who in turn illuminate, enhance, and confirm their own faith. He sets his proposals in the Holy Land, where each of the three faiths is inextricably involved in a political conflict that has distinctly eluded reconciliation.

The conception of reconciliation in *Exclusion and Embrace: A Theological Exploration of Identity, Otherness, and Reconciliation,* by the theologian Miroslav Volf, frames A. James McAdams's discussion of transitional politics in unified Germany (ch. 5). McAdams agrees with Volf that reconciliation is double barreled: an "inclusionary" strategy of accepting the wrongdoer must be accompanied by a "victim-centered" strategy of justice for the wrongdoer. But as a political scientist McAdams is acutely aware of his fellow social scientists' objection that transitional societies cannot have it both ways. Usually they are constrained to choose either justice or inclusion and will most often adopt inclusion as the least costly option. Yet Germany, he shows, ended up adopting a mishmash of both strategies that ended up being closer to Volf's theological conception than to the supposedly more realistic conceptions of social scientists. It arrived at this solution not by following an abstract theoretical blueprint but through the response of leaders to the competing demands of multiple audiences. McAdams's account of how the shape of reconciliation emerges from complex political contingencies is best captured by the aphorism that he quotes from Marx: "Men make their own history . . . [but] not just as they please."

Mark R. Amstutz (ch. 6), also a political scientist, conceives reconciliation as restorative justice, a set of practices that contribute to "the healing of victims, the restoration of community life, and, most importantly, the consolidation of rights-based democracy." Like Torrance, he contrasts reconciliation with retributive justice and favors reconciliation. Central to reconciliation, he argues, is political forgiveness. He agrees with Wolterstorff that states may appropriately practice forgiveness and argues that it may contribute to rather than detract from justice, at least when conceived in restorative terms. Like McAdams, though, Amstutz is eager to trace his concepts through the exigencies of transitional politics. He contrasts the case of Argentina, whose "truth and justice" approach was comparatively retributive, with South Africa, which embodied restorative justice. South Africa's approach, he argues, was not only more normatively attractive but also more successful in bringing about a stable transition to an inclusive, rights-based democracy.

Northern Ireland, as Ronald A. Wells (ch. 7) describes it, is a study in how warring parties can be powerfully reconciled, but in a manner that contrasts vividly with reconciliation in the other locales described in the volume. Here, the parties—Catholics and Protestants—voice reconciliation and forgiveness more strongly, more directly, and in more explicit theological language than anywhere else. A second difference, one that may well be the cause of the first, is that the state plays very little role in reconciliation. Northern Ireland has not yet staged a truth commission, and there does not seem to be any prospect of one soon. Rather, reconciliation there has occurred over several years through friendships within and between religious communities. As a historian, Wells describes these relationships, how they developed and what obstacles they encountered, through narrative analysis. He shows how openly theological concepts fare in the exigencies of politics, thus drawing together themes from the other essays.

R. Scott Appleby closes the volume with an essay that not only synthesizes the foregoing essays but poses a question for the entire project: How is reconciliation to be forged in political settings where Christians do business with practitioners of other faiths, of no faith, and not infrequently of a "realpolitik" that views religion and reconciliation alike as unfit for politics? It is an important question. Although the political transitions discussed here, like the vast majority of the past generation's truth commissions, have taken place in predominantly Christian populations, even these involve non-Christian minorities as well as influential figures who balk at Christian politics. How to bridge the ravines that separate worldviews is a question that Christian scholars must confront—and by and large do not confront here, with the exception of Burrell's essay and to some extent my own. It is a question, too, whose magnitude and complexity requires exploration elsewhere. Helpfully, Appleby begins such an exploration by suggesting ways in which the present interlocutors might address the interwoven problems of pluralism and realism. In so doing, he also advances the central project of the volume—namely, to discover how a conception of justice whose roots and warrants lie in theology can become meaningful in the realm of politics—and models what the essays together offer: a unique conversation between theologians and philosophers on one side and analysts of empirical politics on the other, between perspectives that begin with the transcendent and ones that begin with the tug and haul of political struggle.

## Notes

1. For instance, see the excellent collection of essays, mostly from secular perspectives, collected in Robert I. Rotberg and Dennis Thompson, *Truth v. Justice: The Morality of Truth Commissions* (Princeton: Princeton University Press, 2000).

2. See Samuel P. Huntington, *The Third Wave: Democratization in the Late Twentieth Century* (Norman: University of Oklahoma Press, 1991).

3. Priscilla Hayner, *Unspeakable Truths: Confronting State Terror and Atrocity* (New York: Routledge, 2001), 14.

4. José Zalaquett, "Confronting Human Rights Violations Committed by Former Governments: Principles Applicable and Political Constraints," in *Transitional Justice*, ed. Neil Kritz (Washington, DC: U.S. Institute of Peace Press, 1995), 45.

5. Exceptions are the recent book by Mark R. Amstutz, one of the present authors, *The Healing of Nations: The Promise and Limits of Political Forgiveness* (Lanham, MD: Rowman and Littlefield, 2005), as well as Raymond G. Helmick and Rodney L. Petersen's *Forgiveness and Reconciliation: Religion, Public Policy and Conflict Transformation* (Philadelphia: Templeton Foundation Press, 2001) and Lyn S. Graybill's *Truth and Reconciliation in South Africa: Miracle or Model?* (Boulder, CO: Lynne Rienner, 2002).

# CHAPTER ONE

# Beyond Politics as Usual

## *Is Reconciliation Compatible with Liberalism?*

### DANIEL PHILPOTT

It is not obvious that anyone should reconcile with anyone at all. Timothy Garton Ash recounts the story of a black African woman at a hearing of the Truth and Reconciliation Commission (TRC) in South Africa who, after listening to the confession of the man who had abducted and murdered her husband, was asked if she could forgive him: "Speaking slowly, in one of the native languages, her message came back through the interpreters: 'No government can forgive.' Pause. 'No commission can forgive.' Pause. 'Only I can forgive.' Pause. 'And I am not ready to forgive.'"[1] If agents of law and order have silenced, quelled, murdered, tortured, terrorized, arbitrarily confined, brutalized, mocked, or denied jobs, public facilities, or freedom of movement to one or one's family, all of this because of one's skin color or ethnicity or dissenting political stance, then it is not crystal clear on the face of things that one is called to reconcile with those agents.

Why bother with the point? Because over the past decade or so, within both venerable and fledgling liberal democracies around the globe, the concept of reconciliation has sashayed—sometimes escorted by euphoria—into political addresses and debates, stump speeches, sermons, editorials, and now, the scholarly writings of liberal political philosophers. Rooted in biblical texts and ancient languages, reconciliation is an old concept. It connotes the restoration of relationships—in the context of the polity, their restoration toward *shalom,* a peace characterized by justice and wholeness.

But in liberal political discourse, reconciliation is new. Its most dramatic lexical debut occurs in "the third wave" of democratization, the transition of sundry societies away from communism, military dictatorship, and apartheid during the 1980s and 1990s.[2] Chile was the first to use the term prominently— its TRC was a prototype for attempts at political restoration. South Africa has used the term most famously—its TRC is the most ambitious socially restorative effort yet. In dozens of other new liberal democracies in Latin America, Eastern Europe, East Asia, and Africa, reconciliation now shows up regularly in political discourse.

Is the ancient concept of reconciliation friendly to a historically new form of political organization, liberal democracy? The question is important, for reconciliation may hold great promise for sundered political orders raw with memories of recent injustices. It is also important because a spate of liberal political philosophers has, of late, come to see promise in practices of reconciliation in South Africa and elsewhere. One set of these philosophers recommends it as a "second best" solution to the problem of past political injustices when criminal justice is not feasible during transitions to liberal democracy.[3] Another set agrees to reconciliation's instrumental value but further asserts its intrinsic worth for political justice: it acts as a therapeutic process for healing victims of human rights abuses, and it instantiates deliberative democracy.[4] Can either liberal case for reconciliation persuade us?

In fact, reconciliation does not mesh easily with liberalism. Still another set of contemporary liberals expresses skepticism toward reconciliation, a skepticism that draws from traditional liberal themes and resonates with the plaintive protests of victims like the one Timothy Garton Ash describes. In recent writings, they draw upon four of these themes in expressing skepticism toward reconciliation. Most vigorous is their argument for retributive justice. Where reconciliation substitutes for or minimizes punishment, it shortchanges retributive justice, allowing offenders literally to get away with murder. Liberals argue, second, that reconciliation is personal, not political, and properly confined to individual relationships. Closely related is a third objection, namely that reconciliation is a religious concept and not a suitable desideratum in secular liberal discourse and laws. Finally, reconciliation is charged with divisiveness. During the delicate seedling phase of democracy, uprooting old injustices and stoking already bitter memories may well undermine social unity.

Fortifying this skepticism is liberalism's own paucity of conceptual resources for demonstrating reconciliation's normative intelligibility. Its stress on individual rights, liberty, autonomy, equality, and participation leaves it with little warrant for incorporating the restoration of relationships and personal transformation into politics.

Against these objections, those liberals who favor reconciliation face a difficult challenge. Instrumental justifications, consequentialist in character, are hard pressed to demonstrate that the positive consequences of reconciliation outweigh the negative consequences. The weakness of the substantively principled justifications is their lack of clarity as to why they trump liberal objections to reconciliation. Such objections, after all, are rooted far more deeply in the tradition than therapeutic healing or contemporary renderings of deliberative democracy.

Here, I seek to describe what I will call "political reconciliation"—as a concept and as a set of institutional practices—and explain why it is in tension with liberalism. I then examine liberal arguments in favor of political reconciliation and aim to show the weakness of their grounds. In the end, though, we should not abandon hope for the prospect of grafting reconciliation into liberal thought and troubled transitional politics. Its promise is too great to give up easily. But the medicine of reconciliation will be accepted only by a favorable liberal physiology, a liberalism constituted so as not to pose its usual objections and so as to be open to incorporating warrants that lie outside its own concepts. Reconciliation goes beyond politics as usual. Such warrants are available in a "comprehensive conception," to borrow the term of John Rawls, that itself offers deep grounds for reconciliation and that is also favorable to liberal democratic institutions. Political theologies of reconciliation of recent vintage are examples of such comprehensive conceptions. The essays that follow this one then take up this very project.

## What Is Reconciliation in Politics?

If it is not obvious that anyone should reconcile, neither is it obvious that reconciliation is appropriate for liberal political orders. The concept is virtually absent from the liberal tradition of Hobbes, Locke, Kant, Mill, Dewey, and Rawls, the tradition that poses individual liberty, civil and political rights, equality of citizenship, democratic elections, distributive justice, and punishment for criminals as central values, even despite its proponents' differing philosophical foundations: natural law, natural rights, utilitarianism, and pragmatism. Is this tradition now ready to receive reconciliation?

Any answer depends on how reconciliation is understood. Like many words that become common political parlance—think only of *multiculturalism* or *pluralism*—*reconciliation* enjoys no tight consensual usage. But unlike these more recent terms, *reconciliation* is blessed with ancient meanings, whose pedigree commends them as initial definitions. Common to all of these meanings is the concept, "restoration of right relationship." In Hebrew, reconciliation is expressed by *tikkun olam,* meaning "to heal, to repair, to transform." In Greek, its derivatives are *katallage, apokatallasso,* and *diallasso,* meaning "adjustment of a difference, reconciliation, restoration to favor," "to reconcile completely, to bring back a former state of harmony," and "to change the mind of anyone, to be reconciled, to renew friendship with one." In Latin, the word *concilium,* meaning a deliberative process by which adversaries work out their differences "in council," expresses the concept, while in Arabic, reconciliation is denoted by *salima,* meaning peace, safety, security, and freedom, and *salaha,* meaning to be righteous, to do right, settlement, compromise, restoration, and restitution. All connote the restoration of relationships between persons.

To restore something is to return it to a lost condition. Without an understanding of the meaning and content of this condition, to speak of a return to it is unintelligible. To what state of affairs, then, do a community's relationships return when they are restored? This condition ought not to be conceived of temporally, as something realized at some lost halcyon moment, some Golden Age, Year of Favor, or Garden of Eden in the history of an actual society. Partisans who propose and laud such eras will rarely be joined in unanimous consensus upon their sweetness; disputed histories are indeed a notorious source of violence.

Instead, we should understand restoration as a state of perfection toward which reconciliation moves. The Abrahamic religious traditions describe such a state as *shalom (salem, saalam).* It is a state that is realized fully in heaven. As heaven comprehends all time and exists prior to war, violence, and injustice, a movement toward it can properly be called a return. But what is *shalom* like? The term broadly means peace, understood not simply as the absence of violence but as the realization of justice and even more so as a condition of mutual love, one in which a community's members actively and constantly promote one another's good. Enmity, revenge, and anger motivated by hatred disappear. Erstwhile estrangement is resolved in embrace, Miroslav Volf's metaphor for reconciliation.[5] *Shalom* is the telos of reconciliation, the condition to which relationships are restored.

To speak of *shalom*'s peace and perfection together with community, and even more so with politics, will instantly evoke cries of utopianism. But what is the place of a state of perfection in political analysis? Surely it is not to deny the typicality of its absence or to invoke the prospects of anything but its radically imperfect attainment. Rwanda, Kashmir, the former Yugoslavia, and Sudan dissipate these expectations. Reconciliation comes in parts, peace in pieces — limited, fragmentary, in glimpses, as thin rays of light shining through broken clay vessels. The purpose of a concept of *shalom*, rather, is to set forth a standard, an essence, whose presence, absence, or partial realization we can then assess. It tells us, not how much we may achieve, but what kind of ideal we are moving toward, albeit asymptotically, in the first place. Theories of liberalism, describing human rights, democracy, and the rule of law, after all, often proceed much the same. They offer standards for aspiration and for criticism, even if societies remain distant in practice. This distance, however, does not discourage proponents of the ideals from advocating and working on their behalf. The most pertinent question to ask about *shalom*, the question of central concern here, is whether this kind of ideal — restoration, reconciliation — has a proper place in politics at all. Or should some other ideal — political liberalism as traditionally understood, for instance — guide our efforts?

As will become apparent, it is the restorative essence of reconciliation to which liberals object. But in exactly what sense are political orders restored through reconciliation? It is in fact reconciliation's far more familiar absence that best reveals the meaning of its presence; the character of its compromise suggests the substance of its realization. In the political order, *shalom* is compromised in two ways. First, it is diminished through the legal and social structures that create and perpetuate injustices — the laws and ordinances of apartheid, the Jim Crow laws of the American South, the laws of any state that prohibits free speech and political participation. Second, it is diminished through acts of violence, both legal and extralegal, some of which sustain the unjust laws and structures, all of which are themselves unjust. These two forms of compromise work hand in hand. Violence itself implies injustice — one party's proper and true good is violated by another person — and is to be distinguished from the just use of force, either in war or in the apprehension of criminals. The nature of justice, of course, is a disputed matter; so, then, are the criteria for what counts as violence. Although a particular view of justice cannot be defended here, the basic human rights enumerated in the international covenants provide a working standard that is widely agreed upon and that will serve the present argument adequately. If it does nothing else, violence violates these.[6]

Not all acts of violence are political. Human rights can be violated by a brother against a brother, a gang member against a gang member, or a Mafia hit man against a hapless debtor. What sets apart political violence is the affiliation and cause of the perpetrator. It is committed by an agent of a state or a movement opposing a state, and it is committed in the name of that organization against a victim whom the perpetrator deems an enemy. The agent's act may not always reflect the state's laws or the movement's proclaimed ends—states and rebellions often claim that they do not kill innocents, even when they do. But it is done in the name of a state, of a movement, whose true and proper end, whose genuine basis for legitimacy, involves safeguarding human rights. Murder, torture, interrogation, armed attack, unjust imprisonment, racist discrimination, and denial of the franchise and other human rights are familiar examples. Once agents have committed such acts, there exists a new state of affairs in the moral universe of that political order. Not only has an injustice taken place, but an act that has not been rectified, recognized, punished, or addressed, an ongoing rift in the just order, now lingers on in memory.

Unjust systems and acts of violence leave their victims' dignity wounded—not extinguished, for dignity inheres in personhood, but violated, in need of restoration. As the injustice is promulgated against a victim or set of victims by a political system or an agent acting in the name of a political organization—that is, by one party against another—it also violates a relationship. Now, *relationship* may connote the intimacy of family or friendship; on this understanding, relationships are broken when this intimacy is lost. But the term is in fact open-ended. Here it involves varying combinations of parties—victim, offender, elite superiors, publics, and even international authorities—who are bound to one another according to some set of obligations. A citizen of a state, for instance, may properly expect the agents and members of a state to protect and respect his human rights. That is the nature of his proper relationship to them. In wounding dignity, political violence severs a proper relationship, breaks a set of justified expectations. This severing occurs along at least six dimensions, ones that vary according to the mode of relationship, the kind of expectations involved. These dimensions of woundedness will in turn reveal the varying senses in which reconciliation is restorative.

First, and most simply, violence involves brute harm—physical, psychic, economic, or emotional—to the victim's personhood. In the hearings of South Africa's TRC, victims who were blinded and wheelchair bound by injury and grieved by the death of loved ones exemplified only a sampling of the results of political violence. The psychic damage and economic deprivation caused by the myriad injustices of apartheid were wounds wrought by systems of laws. Even this brute harm is significantly relational, as there is an important moral difference between this sort of suffering and that which results from a natural disaster or a single car accident, where there is no perpetrator.

Second, victims suffer from their ignorance—often willingly sustained by the perpetrators—of the source and circumstances of their wounds. Who was behind the gun that night? How was my son abducted seven years ago? Not knowing the truth of one's past, especially the most traumatic parts of it, is itself a form of torment.

Third, when a victim has suffered violence or other injustice at the hands of an officer, a bureau chief, a rebel commander, or the state at large, he has been violated as a subject of justice, as a member of a political order from which he is entitled to respect for his human rights. Instead, at the hands of both the offender and his responsible superiors, he was treated as an enemy of the order, as an outsider who was threatening it. This dimension of woundedness is compounded by the ongoing failure of offenders, superiors, and even knowledgeable members of the political order at large to regard him as a legitimate member. Imprisoned, in hiding, on the lam, disenfranchised, in continual danger of arrest, or denied any other of his rights as a citizen, in the eyes of the political order he is still an enemy outsider. Paraphrasing the sociologist Orlando Patterson's concept of "social death," the political philosopher Rajeev Bhargava calls this condition "political death."[7] As long as the political order fails even to recognize this injustice, emitting silence or official denials, the victim continues to be politically dead.

Fourth, the wound of withheld regard is deepened through the failure of the same parties not only to recognize the victim as a legitimate member but to recognize him as a victim of suffering in the name of the order. Conceivably, after all, his citizenship, but not his suffering, might be restored, leaving one dimension of his woundedness unhealed.

Fifth, the perpetrator has not been held accountable for the wound inflicted. Here, severed relationships attain additional complexity, for it is not merely victims to whom perpetrators of crimes are accountable but the political community that promulgates and upholds the law. When political violence is committed under a regime that generally condones it, it may be only the representatives of a successor regime or even an international body—a criminal tribunal, an intervening force—who provide accountability.

A sixth dimension of suffering outlives and outsizes the acknowledgment and accountability of offenders, elites, and publics. It is their failure to confess, apologize, atone for, and make amends for their perpetration and condoning of political violence. Even if the other dimensions of suffering were palliated, this one would persist. The relational dimension of suffering is not alleviated by recognition of suffering and restoration of rights; it persists through the failure of perpetrators to take responsibility for and seek to make amends for suffering. Conversely, victims will continue to suffer from the anger and resentment that accompany their failure to forgive.

These dimensions of woundedness reveal the complexity of political injustice and violence. Not only are they sixfold, but they involve several sorts of relationships. Among the relational goods that political violence thwarts are knowledge of suffering, acknowledgment of suffering, rights of citizenship, acknowledgment of citizenship, confession, responsibility, repentance, and forgiveness. A further sense in which the woundedness of relationships may vary contributes yet another layer of complexity: the number of agents involved in an injustice. As Nicholas Tavuchis points out, wrongs may be committed by many against one, by one against many, by one against one, and by many against many.[8] When many commit violence or injustice, they may be guided by a leader who acts in their name, raising even further complexities involving agency and collective responsibility. Heretofore, the analysis has assumed a collectivity or an agent of a collectivity acting against a single victim—the many against one. But violence and injustice, indeed any of the six dimensions of woundedness, can vary according to the size of the party involved. Collectivities may commit them against other collectivities—Japan against the United States, the United States against Japan, Germany against Poland. Over time, the lack of acknowledgment of these injustices and their attendant suffering, the absence of reparations of brute harm, of repentance and forgiveness, will amount to a historical wound. All of these variations, all of these dimensions together suggest the manifold forms of brokenness, injury, severance, suffering, and denials of *shalom* that political violence and systemic injustice elicit and the manifold respects in which reconciliation must restore.

The dimensions of this reconciliation correspond to the six dimensions of woundedness outlined above. In some respects, the first dimension, the brute harm of political violence, will be the most difficult to restore. Lost sight and the dead loved ones are irreplaceable. But again, when caused by political violence, brute harm is relational harm, implying appropriate restorative roles for offenders and official bodies: reparations, recognition. The second dimension, victims' ignorance of the circumstances of their wounds, calls for restoration through revelation of the truth about these circumstances. The third dimension, victims' violation as subjects of justice and the ongoing failure of the political community to acknowledge them as legitimate subjects of justice, calls for their "resurrection" from "political death"—reinstatement of their full citizenship, of their full rights before the law. Both state authorities and fellow citizens must view their opponents no longer as people to be subdued, apprehended, "disappeared," tortured, and killed but as people to debate, campaign against, argue with, deliberate among, and refute, as people who are entitled to all of the basic human rights. Fourth, reconciliation demands that recognition of victims be deepened beyond their citizenship to their suffering. The fifth dimension of reconciliation is accountability—the offender's confession and his sanction. But as all of these dimensions could be fulfilled while offenders remained defiant and victims vengeful and resentful, full reconciliation demands a sixth dimension of repentance and forgiveness.

These, then, are the ways in which relationships that have been sundered by political violence must be restored if a community is to move toward *shalom*. But if this is the substance of reconciliation, then what are the institutions, procedures, and practices by which it is to come about? Several facets of reconciliation point to the legitimacy and necessity of a publicly sanctioned authority: reinstatement of citizenship, public recognition of suffering, accountability, reparations, and perhaps others. It is the involvement of this public authority, combined with the political nature of the wound, that merits the name *political reconciliation* for the restoration envisioned here. But how is a public authority to accomplish political reconciliation? Should public authority be involved in all dimensions of reconciliation? Most importantly, are the procedures and practices of political reconciliation ones that the liberal tradition can endorse?

## How Does Reconciliation Proceed in Politics?

The practical form of political reconciliation will depend strongly on context. Some of the most explicit and innovative efforts to incorporate reconciliation into public institutions, for instance, are now occurring in the criminal justice system in the United States, where victims and offenders are encouraged to reconcile through mediation and restitution.[9] Here the context is transitional justice, the dilemma of addressing past injustices during a transition to democracy.

As described in the introductory chapter, political reconciliation is one of three alternative approaches to transitional justice, the other two being pragmatic compromise and punitive justice alone. Truth commissions have been the most prominent institutional context through which political orders have attempted reconciliation. The South African TRC, with its unique public hearings that brought together victim, offender, other parties affected by the crime, representatives of the state, and members of the public, with its public recognition of suffering and its language of repentance and forgiveness, was exemplary for seeking to manifest the six dimensions of political reconciliation. Other truth commissions have been impressive for the breadth of their investigations, as in Guatemala, and for their sophisticated character, as in East Timor, where a national truth commission was combined with trials and local reconciliation forums. Reconciliation in a political order may also occur within civil society, as it has, at least in partial degrees, in Northern Ireland, Bosnia, and elsewhere.

It is through five practices, I argue, that a truth commission or a related set of procedures in civil society instantiates the several dimensions of reconciliation in a political order.

## Truth Telling

Truth telling is the public discovery and revelation of past injustices. Crimes of a political nature are investigated by a truth commission, a constitutionally authoritative public body. Once it has completed gathering information about these crimes, it publicizes them with its official imprimatur and makes them known within an entire political order and beyond.[10] It is possible to conceive truth commissions as thinly pragmatic, merely informational. But several political philosophers have noted the value of truth telling in restoring persons and relationships. They compare how truth commissions manifest knowledge of the past from how criminal trials do so. In a trial, the point of knowledge is to establish guilt or innocence. Plaintiffs and defendants marshal it strategically, as adversaries, and often willfully, to a partial degree.[11] In a truth commission, truth is manifested precisely on the premise that ignorance of past injustices is itself a dimension of political victims' woundedness and thus itself an injustice. Its success depends not on the fairness of an adversarial proceeding but on the thoroughness, accuracy, and personal relevance of the knowledge about suffering attained.

Aside from the revelation of truth itself, truth telling accomplishes other dimensions of political reconciliation. It provides public recognition that the victim's rights as a human and as a citizen were violated and that the violation was heretofore suppressed. Public recognition is not only restorative in itself but also an important step in the full reinstatement of the victim's citizenship. Finally, truth telling recognizes the victim as a sufferer, not just as a violated citizen.

In South Africa, prior to the TRC, officials of the apartheid state by and large refused to admit to committing abductions, tortures, and killings. "For the victims," writes André du Toit, "this [refusal] is actually a redoubling of the basic violation: the literal violation consists of the actual pain, suffering and trauma visited on them; the political violation consists in the refusal (publicly) to acknowledge it. The latter amounts to a denial of the human and civic dignity of the victims."[12] When these officials then relinquish their denials, a special kind of truth obtains. Alex Boraine even proposes "healing and restorative truth" as a special form of truth, to be distinguished from "factual" truth.[13] Du Toit similarly makes the point by borrowing Thomas Nagel's distinction between "knowledge" of facts and "acknowledgment" of deeds, which involves stating their injustice publicly, admitting the suffering of the victims, confirming their membership in society, and thus restoring their dignity.[14]

Tina Rosenberg reports the story of Mzykisi Mdidimba, whose testimony to the TRC about being tortured by agents of the state "has taken it off my heart. . . . When I have told stories of my life before, afterward, I am crying, crying, crying, and felt it was not finished. This time, I know that what they've done to me will be among these people and all over the country. I still have some sort of crying, but also joy inside."[15] Mdidimba's phrase "among these people and all over the country" points to the crucial public dimension of his restoration. The presence of the commission, its public authority, the millions of witnessing citizens, and ultimately a permanent public record of the injustices committed all aid in this restoration.

Finally, truth commissions contribute to other dimensions of political reconciliation. In exposing the deeds of the offender through publicly told stories, they publicly shame him, a form of accountability. Though truth commissions may or may not be accompanied by trials, when they are, they help to disclose valuable information. Their exposure of deeds and accounts also amounts to the first step in repentance and forgiveness. Although South Africa's TRC did not procedurally mandate forgiveness and repentance, commission officials like Desmond Tutu openly urged parties to make this step a continuation of the truth telling of the hearings. In all of these respects, truth telling contributes to restoration in a political context.

## Accountability

In the family of practices that further reconciliation, that restore relationships, that usher a society toward *shalom*, accountability may not seem a natural member: Accountability amounts to punishment; the sort of justice it promotes is retributive; retribution, in turn, rests on the principle of desert. Analysts of transitional justice often pose accountability as an antithesis of, an alternative to, and a value to be balanced with reconciliation: retribution versus reconciliation, punishment versus restoration of relationships. How, then, can accountability be a component of, not a competitor with, reconciliation?

There are many versions of the retributive theory of justice, but most hold in common the simple requirement of proportionate punishment, justified by desert. One who has willfully and demonstrably wronged another deserves to be punished (roughly) proportionately simply because he did it. Punishment evens out the scales of justice, sets right the balance of good and evil in the world, and rightly brings the perpetrator down from the perch of superiority that he sought over his victim through his crime.[16]

But punishment need not be justified solely according to the logic of retribution. Theorists of restorative justice often speak of punishment as being restorative, justified as a mode of communicating the evil of his deeds to a perpetrator in the hope that he might come to a posture of remorse. Restorative punishment also regards the offender not just as a violator whose deeds need to be balanced but as one who has broken right relationship, with respect to both his victim and the moral order that surrounds him. Punishment further acknowledges the offender's dignity—that is, takes him seriously by treating him as a moral agent commensurately with the actions he has chosen. Rather than eliciting a mere abstract balancing of scales that inflicts an amount of pain on the offender roughly equal to that which he has caused the victim, accountability restores a condition where dignity is accorded victim and offender alike. Punishment can still be harsh in the restorative notion; perpetrators of the most egregious deeds may well require it.[17] It is even essential: without accountability, reconciliation would be cheap, its restorative achievement lacking an essential, costly, dimension. This is why accountability is one of the six dimensions of reconciliation.

Now, in the practical dynamic of transitional justice, trade-offs between reconciliation and accountability will still occur. But this arises, not because the concepts are intrinsically incompatible, but because some parties to reconciliation— outgoing generals and politicians—have the power to make some dimensions of reconciliation contingent upon abrogation of their accountability. Most commonly, they will secure general amnesty for their crimes in exchange for participation in a truth commission where they reveal their misdeeds.

But the trade-off is not necessary. When strict proportionate punishment is no longer required, possibilities open up for a variety of punitive options, tailored to the restoration of the offender and of the given set of broken relationships in a particular set of circumstances. Accountability can take many forms. Aside from imprisonment, it can take the form of a condemnation spoken by a public authority, shame imposed by a public, and reparations. Some forms of accountability will in fact promote the other practices of reconciliation more than others. The South African TRC, for instance, offered amnesty but made it conditional: the perpetrator was required to appear before an authority of the new regime as well as the entire public, recount the entirety of his crimes, face the cries of his victims, and endure the censure of the commission. Here, the restoration entailed in accountability also promoted the restoration of victim and community. The personalistic nature of the accountability—the requirement that the offender hear victims testify about their suffering, the presence of "sympathetic onlookers" who applaud the offender in his open acknowledgment of his deed—further encourage repentance and sometimes forgiveness. All of this mere proportionate punishment would not have accomplished. To some critics of the TRC, of course, accountability was inadequate and the other forms of restoration were too costly. Only proportionate punishment in the form of imprisonment could have satisfied the demands of justice. Others lauded the arrangement as being optimally restorative. These debates will continue. What is important here is that accountability can be designed flexibly to further the restoration of both the offender and his ambient broken relationships and to further the other practices of reconciliation. A strict trade-off between restoration and accountability is not inevitable.

## Reparation

This third practice of political reconciliation is simpler. It confers some type of material award upon the victim or group of victims in recognition of their wound. But it, too, is complex with respect to the parties and modes of relationship involved. It is a public authority that orders reparation. The authority may confer the reparation itself or order the offender to pay it. When the offender pays reparation, it also furthers accountability. In monetary form, reparation helps to alleviate the victim's brute suffering by enabling medical care and economic relief. This form and, even more so, reparation in the form of a public monument or memorial bestow the citizenry's recognition of the victim's suffering and denied citizenship. Reparation promotes several dimensions of reconciliation.

## Repentance

Repentance exceeds accountability or the acknowledgment of suffering involved in truth telling. Usually in the form of an apology, the offender openly expresses contrition and sorrow and assumes responsibility for his political violence. Since silence in these matters separates offender and victim, repentance is restorative.[18]

If the offender and victim are individuals, then neither a public authority nor the collective citizenry of a state can perform the speech act of repentance; only the offender can. Since sorrow and contrition are inwardly chosen, the state cannot mandate or institutionalize repentance into its procedures for reconciliation. Because, however, the act was one of political violence, committed in the name of a political community, a public authority may appropriately encourage offenders to repent and create a forum where repentance can be expressed. Such was precisely the strategy Bishop Tutu deployed in his leadership of the TRC in South Africa.

It could be the case, though, that the offender is a state, one who is apologizing to another state or some set of victims on behalf of the entire political community. President Bill Clinton's apology to Rwanda for failing to intervene to stop its genocide and President George H.W. Bush's apology to Japanese Americans interned in World War II are examples. Under what circumstances such collective apologies are appropriate is a large subject in itself. But here a public authority has an obvious role.

## Forgiveness

Forgiveness mirrors repentance, for it releases the offender from what he owes. Following the analysis of Nicholas Wolterstorff's essay, forgiveness is the enactment of a resolution to forego just claims against an offender. The claim could be one's right to exact retribution or to see him punished or one's right to be angry at him. Though forgiveness can be enacted inwardly and never expressed to the offender, to be an element of reconciliation it must be expressed. When it follows repentance, it completes the restoration that the apology has begun.

Forgiveness can be enacted by the victim but can also be performed by a spokesperson for the state, as Wolterstorff also argues. Political violence violates not only the human rights of the victim but the justice of the offender's own political order. In cases of transitional justice, his crime may not have been illegal under the regime at the time, or the regime may not have held him accountable for it, but now a new regime asserts his accountability. When this regime foregoes any or all of the punishment that it might justly inflict, it forgives. In itself, the state's forgiveness is restorative, for it restores the perpetrator as a citizen in good standing. But it best promotes reconciliation when it is fashioned so as to foster other restorative practices. Unconditional general amnesty, for instance, enacts forgiveness but foregoes all accountability, making reconciliation cheap. South Africa's conditional amnesty, by contrast, was a form of state forgiveness that also promoted accountability and truth telling. It is even possible for forgiveness to coexist with harsher, more typical, forms of punishment like imprisonment. The victims of a crime may choose to forgive its perpetrator, even though he remains in prison. Such a combination, though, would likely accomplish less restoration along all of its dimensions.

Any of these five practices could be, and have been, explored far more deeply. What is important here, though, is their common restorative purpose—together, they combine in a comprehensive vision of political reconciliation. Again, actual political transitions will manifest this vision only to a radically partial degree—this one will emphasize truth telling but not accountability, that one punishment and restitution but with little of the public acknowledgment of the victim that comes from truth telling; repentance and forgiveness between offender and victim in response to a public call will be rare. Only South Africa has combined elements of all five practices—and even here only imperfectly, and still with great controversy. The central question for political reconciliation, though, runs far deeper than its practicalities: Is it even an appropriate end for liberal politics?

## Liberal Objections to Reconciliation

On what grounds would liberals consider reconciliation inappropriate? Many of the liberals who have recently commented on reconciliation have in fact raised strong objections to it—even those who, on balance, support some of the five restorative practices just explained. Their objections run deep, raising fundamental questions about the compatibility of reconciliation and liberalism.

## The Argument from Punishment

One of liberalism's strongest objections to reconciliation arises from its alleged compromise of one of liberalism's oldest, most persistent themes—punishment for crimes. Although many versions of reconciliation, including the one articulated above, do not exclude accountability, several liberal political philosophers find inadequate those forms of accountability that fall short of proportionate punishment. Liberalism's oldest, most prominent justification for punishment, in turn, is the retributive principle—the perpetrator of a crime, political violence all the more, is subject to sanction mainly because he deserves it. Locke, Kant, and many contemporary theorists of liberalism all root punishment in retribution, as do the legal traditions of most constitutional liberal democracies.[19] Of course, liberals have also proffered other justifications for punishment—utilitarian, deterrence, public safety, rehabilitation, and moral education—whose merits and demerits have elicited great debate. Liberals across the board, though, hold punishment as a strong tenet.

Liberals have thus expressed skepticism that reconciliation warrants the curtailment of punishment in transitional justice. It may be argued that even retributive theorists envision a restorative purpose in punishment. John Finnis, for instance, holds that "[p]unishment . . . characteristically seeks *to restore* the distributively just balance of advantages between the criminal and the law-abiding."[20] But such a restoration is far less comprehensive than restoration along the several dimensions of woundedness that political violence has created—the offender's acknowledgment of the victim's suffering, the public's and the state's acknowledgment of the same, all of these parties' acknowledgment of the victim's violated citizenship, the reinstatement of this citizenship, repentance, forgiveness, and so on. Compromising punishment on behalf of this more comprehensive restoration—political reconciliation, progress toward *shalom*—can find little support in a tradition with such a central emphasis on punishment and with such a dearth of attention to any of these other dimensions of restoration as a concern of the political order.

So liberals are leery of amnesties, general and conditional. Amy Gutmann and Dennis Thompson assert the "moral burden of sacrificing criminal justice" by reminding us of the families of Steven Biko and Griffiths Mxenge, both murdered leaders of the movement against apartheid, who opposed the creation of the TRC because it would prevent retributive justice. They quote Mhleli Mxenge, Griffiths Mxenge's surviving brother: "[Some people] say that offering amnesty helps the truth come out. . . . But I don't believe that knowing alone makes you happy. Once you know who did it, you want the next thing—you want justice!"[21] In a broader statement about transitional justice, Aryeh Neier argues that accountability demands punishment.[22] The international legal scholar Diane Orentlicher asserts that the integrity of international standards of human rights and genocide makes a strong case for the prosecution of crimes.[23] Even liberals like Gutmann and Thompson and Kent Greenawalt, who ultimately concede a case for amnesty, describe the compromise of punishment as an injustice, one warranted only by a trade-off for greater justice in some other respect. For Gutmann and Thompson, this other kind of justice is deliberative democracy. For Greenawalt, it is revelation of the truth about the past and a few other social benefits. Both Gutmann and Thompson and Greenawalt explicitly reject reconciliation as a warrant for curtailing deserved punishment. Liberals, then, impose a strong burden of argument on any advocate of foregoing proportionate punishment.

## The Argument from the Public-Private Distinction

Just as liberals generally presume punishment as the proper public response to political violence, so they consider other dimensions of reconciliation like forgiveness, repentance, and the healing of the victims to be improper concerns of the state. Public versus private, the political versus the personal: the distinction is deeply rooted in the liberal tradition. Enlightenment philosophers like Locke and Kant conceived the chief purpose of government as the securing of safety and negative liberties; Mill's utilitarianism asserts individual liberty as the central avenue to happiness in the public realm; more recent liberals also give "equal liberties" pride of place in their thought.[24] These are negative liberties, demarcating spheres of activity in which the state is not to interfere, most notably choices about the pursuit of happiness, definitions of the good life, the constitution of the well-ordered soul, and assertions of "comprehensive conceptions of the good," provided that all such decisions are reasonably respectful of others. Liberals continue to disagree, of course, about the boundaries between public and private: that is, whether government should seek to shape the family structure, aid religious organizations, and the like; what the purpose of liberty is (to allow creative self-definition or ordered virtue?) and how liberty is to be balanced with distributive justice. But it is from the heart of the liberal tradition that a spate of recent commentators on reconciliation, particularly on South Africa, agree that the healing of victims through acknowledgment of their suffering, the transformation of offenders through repentance, and most of all forgiveness are not appropriate goals for states actively to promote. Among the dimensions of reconciliation outlined above, and among the range of goals that truth commissions promote, they support only those that reinstate the citizenship of victims, foster a stable, healthy, and just democracy, and contribute to accountability—all central and traditional liberal ends.

Questioning the priority that the TRC gave to reconciliation, Timothy Garton Ash indeed complains that "taken to the extreme, the reconciliation of all with all is a deeply illiberal idea," for it deprives people of the right to dissent from its vision. Similarly, Gutmann and Thompson argue that a "comprehensive" restorative justice, one that involves forgiveness, therapy, and reparations and seeks a psychological or spiritual social harmony, should not transcend or override the claims of punitive justice. They, too, regard this sort of reconciliation as illiberal, for it expects an entire society to subscribe to a single moral vision, as well as undemocratic, for it seeks to overcome the moral conflict that is the stuff of democratic politics. At most, societies ought to seek consensus on "some fundamental matters of political morality" such as civil liberties and nondiscrimination. The healing of a nation, they hold, is a utopian aim.[25] Similarly, Kent Greenawalt is willing to endorse truth commissions, even if they operate through amnesty, only if they prove better able than criminal trials to expose truth and promote accountability. He rejects restorative justice as an argument in their favor. If amnesty is to be allowed, this is only because it will help avoid civil war and help achieve a just, stable society.[26] Even du Toit, who argues so strongly for justice as public acknowledgment, believes that it is victims' "civic and human dignity," not the healing of their wounds, that is restored through acknowledgment.[27]

In arguing against the public promotion of reconciliation, liberals reserve their harshest criticism for the practice of forgiveness. Timothy Garton Ash relates the story with which this essay opens to illustrate the inappropriateness of governments asking victims to forgive. This is a decision that can be made only by an individual, freely.[28] Similarly, Bhargava holds that both repentance and forgiveness require a confrontation with one's soul and an inner transformation that state truth commissions are not equipped to provide. He does allow, though, that truth commissions might create the conditions for repentance and forgiveness.[29] Greenawalt argues against publicly encouraged repentance along the same lines: "[R]emorse is too difficult for outsiders to discern, and insincere expressions of remorse are worse than no expressions at all." He then says that "forgiveness cannot be demanded or expected from victims or survivors."[30] Most of these critics argue with the TRC in mind, which is puzzling. In neither its procedures nor its mandate did the TRC require victims to forgive: it left them free to practice it or abjure it, as they wished. It was only in a hortatory, justificatory sense that the state promoted forgiveness, largely through the chairman of the TRC, Desmond Tutu. But even this liberal critics object to, revealing their sensitivity to the transgression of the public and the personal.

It is not hard to see why liberals who insist on this distinction would indeed object to the concept of political reconciliation set forth above, for in it the public and the private, the political and the personal, are closely intertwined. The "personal" wound that political violence caused was inflicted in the name of the political order. Its meaning and its healing are bound up in that same order. The healing of the victim—the transformation of the "private" person—comes in part through the telling of the truth about his or her past and the acknowledgment of his or her suffering by the state, by the offender, and by fellow citizens, all in the context of a public forum. Reparations are granted by the state, but in part for the purpose of restoring the wounds of the victim. Repentance and forgiveness involve the transformation of both victim and offender but may well be encouraged by and flow out of the public proceedings. The accountability of transitional justice may well be designed to maximize the chances for the offender's transformation too. This was the case in the TRC, where victims' presence, their stories, and their family members, along with the deft combination of urging, cajoling, and encouragement of the commissioners, often led offenders beyond confession to an inwardly felt repentance. In all of these ways, political reconciliation mixes the public and the private, the personal and the political.

Now, there are a few liberals who share the broad liberal objection to the personal aspects of political reconciliation but nevertheless want to promote a version of reconciliation. They do so by distinguishing two sorts of reconciliation—"thin" and "thick." David Crocker, for instance, proposes "non-lethal coexistence" as the thinnest form of reconciliation, denoting a social condition in which the formerly estranged no longer commit political violence against one another. A thicker version of reconciliation is "democratic reciprocity," in which former enemies come to respect one another as fellow citizens with whom they now deliberate over the future of their country. He distinguishes both of these versions from Bishop Tutu's ideal of reconciliation, which, much like the political reconciliation set forth above, incorporates forgiveness, healing, and social solidarity. For reasons quite similar to those of other liberals, he rejects this vision as utopian. But he believes that thinner versions of reconciliation are more attainable.[31] Similarly, Bhargava distinguishes between the sort of reconciliation that elicits a cancellation of estrangement and a weaker sort that involves a culture of reciprocity, mutual respect, and minimal moral disagreement. He, however, rejects the pursuit of both forms of reconciliation, favoring the creation of a "minimally decent society" based on "pure, procedural justice" where deep disagreements are resolved through fair procedures.

Whether one is advocating or decrying it, the usefulness of a concept of "thin" reconciliation is doubtful. As a restoration of relationships in every sense of the concept of relationship, reconciliation, to be sure, demands a restoration of denied citizenship, the enjoyment of human rights, and the freedom to participate in democratic institutions. But if reconciliation means only this, then it is a redundant term. Why not simply speak of "nonlethal coexistence," "democratic reciprocity," "deliberative democracy," a "human rights culture," or the like? In what sense does the term *reconciliation* add to any of these concepts? Such a restrictive use of the term arbitrarily confines its traditional definitions. In its ancient Arabic, Greek, Hebrew, and Latin usages, it meant restoration of relationship at all levels, in every respect — *shalom*. Whether or not one thinks that reconciliation as *shalom* is a proper political end, it seems that little is accomplished in restricting what it has long meant. Far better would it be for liberal critics of political reconciliation to remain just that — critics of the concept, not advocates of a different version.

## The Argument from Public Reason

Similar in spirit is the argument from public reason. If the argument from the public-private distinction rejects government interference in decisions that are properly personal, the argument from public reason demands that laws, policies, and judicial procedures be articulated through discourse that is properly public. The most famous proponent of the "idea of public reason" is John Rawls, whose formulation has attained the assent of a wide company of liberal political philosophers, though not without some pleas for revision and wholesale dissent. Public reason, as he explains it, is public in three respects: first, it is the reason of citizens in their capacity as citizens; second, it is concerned with the public good and matters of fundamental justice; and third, in content, it draws from a society's conception of political justice.[32] "Nonpublic" reason, by contrast, proceeds from a "comprehensive conception" that demands assent to far more, and is shared by far fewer, than the shared political conception of justice, the basic liberal and democratic principles upon which the polity is grounded. Prominent among these nonpublic conceptions, Rawls tells us, are religious conceptions. It turns out to be religious conceptions, their pervasiveness in discourse, and precisely their nonpublic character to which liberals object so strongly in the case of South Africa's TRC.

To this liberal criticism, Archbishop Tutu would plead guilty as charged. So would some of the other commissioners who espoused and practiced a theological perspective through the hearings. One theologian who followed the TRC, Piet Meiring, tells the story of how some TRC officials, prior to the TRC's hearings in Johannesburg, tried to talk Tutu into toning down the religious content of the hearings. They argued that it would appear awkward in the presence of the media and the luminaries who were expected to attend the Johannesburg hearings in full force and that it was out of place in what were supposed to be judicial proceedings. Tutu initially acquiesced, agreeing to confine the religious to an initial opening moment of silence. The story does not end there, though:

> But Tutu was patently uncomfortable. He was unable to start with the proceedings. He shifted the papers on the table in front of him. He cleared his throat. When he spoke to the audience, he said, "No! This is not the way to do it. We cannot start without having prayed. Close your eyes!" In his inimitable way, the Archbishop placed the hearing of the day in the Lord's hands, asking that Jesus Christ, who himself is the Truth, guide us in our quest for truth, that the Holy Spirit of God grant us the wisdom and grace we need. After a resounding "Amen," he announced with a disarming smile: "So! Now we are ready to start the day's work. . . ." From that day onwards all TRC hearings were to start—and be closed—in a proper fashion.[33]

Religious language and ritual pervaded the proceedings. In publicly presenting the commission through speeches and writings, Tutu and other commissioners explained it in explicitly theological terms. Prayers and hymns opened and closed the hearings. More dramatically, at awkward moments in the hearings when victim or witness testified to a particularly harrowing experience of torture or death, moments when few present, including the commissioners themselves, could muster appropriate words or gestures, the people in the hearing room, participants and onlookers alike, would break out into hymn, thus acknowledging, ritualizing, marking, honoring, and strengthening wounded victims and witnesses. Victims made sense of their experience in theological terms too. Fr. Michael Lapsley, who was permanently injured by a letter bomb and has recently conducted a series of workshops on the "healing of memories," wrote: "For Christians, we need to remind ourselves that we belong to a remembering religion. 'Remember when you were slaves in Egypt' is a constant refrain of the Old Testament. . . . The words of Jesus—"Do this in memory of me"—are said at every Eucharist."[34] Offenders, too, reflected theologically. On the last day of his hearing before the TRC, the ex-minister of police Adrian Vlok told Meiring, "When the final question was asked and when the legal team of the South African Council of Churches indicated its satisfaction . . . my heart sang. I got a lump in my throat and I thanked God for his grace and mercy to me."[35] Some commentators attributed much of the TRC's success to its religious character. Meiring quotes Jorge Heine, the Chilean ambassador to South Africa:

> The powers and resources [of the South African TRC] are much more significant than those of the Chilean commission. . . . Yet, ironically for a body with such strong statutory powers, the South African Commission stands out for the relative absence of lawyers (except the amnesty committee) and an extraordinary religious component. Sitting at the hearings held at the Central Methodist Church in downtown Johannesburg some time ago, watching Archbishop Desmond Tutu say a prayer and Alex Boraine call on some of the witnesses, I could not help but reflect that this would have been unthinkable in many countries where the separation of church and state is taken seriously.
>
> Yet it seems to have worked in South Africa, where there is a great religious diversity but where the strongly Christian subtext of repentance and forgiveness that pervades the Commission's proceedings conveys both [sic] the right message as to what reconciliation is all about. It manages to put at ease humble, profoundly decent South Africans who have been offered, often for the first time, the opportunity to state their case.[36]

In the minds of observers like Heine, what is commendable about the TRC is precisely that its officials did not confine it to the boundaries of liberal public reason.

Liberal offense at the TRC's religious language accordingly revolves around a common criticism: such language entails, in the terms of Marius Schoon, one critic quoted by Ash, "the imposition of a Christian morality of forgiveness," or, in wider terms, a Christian morality of reconciliation.[37] The criticism, and the response of the commission's defenders, shaped the contours of debates among nongovernmental organizations, political groupings, and the public at large. Cosmas Desmond, a former Catholic priest, voiced one version of the criticism that concentrated on the clerical makeup of the commission:

> Such is that over-representation that the question arises as to whether the TRC is an arm of the state or the church. Most church leaders, including Archbishop Tutu, agreed that the new South Africa would be a secular state. Yet the first meeting of the Commission's Reparations Committee was opened not only with prayer but with an exclusive Christian one. And it appears to be assumed that all decisions of the Commission will be informed by Christian values. This would not be bad—though it would still be unacceptable to some—if the norms and values were indeed Christian. But the word "Christian" is all too often simply a synonym for "Western." This is clearly illustrated in the Commission's individualistic understanding of human rights and their violation, rather than a more African (and, I would contend more Christian) approach.[38]

Toward the close of this passage, Desmond softens: it turns out to be Western morality, not Christian morality, that is wrongly imposed. Not so for Gutmann and Thompson. "The difficulty," they argue, "is that many victims do not share Archbishop Tutu's Christian faith." Though others may share his faith, "many sincere and reasonable Christians" will not interpret it to mean forgiveness as he does, while "many other religious and secular moral understandings that also deserve respect" will not resonate with Tutu's at all.[39] Similarly, Greenawalt holds that "[s]ome societies may be so religious that an explicit religious justification of this sort could be sufficient to justify the treatment of political criminals; but the benefits to be gained from a transitional process need usually to be defensible in terms of a human morality that crosscuts particular religious outlooks and does not rely on explicit theological premises."[40]

Now the framework of "political reconciliation" articulated above is not described in heavily theological terms. Though its roots in Abrahamic religious traditions are identified, its concepts of violence, woundedness, and human rights are intelligible to those without religious commitments. Yet liberals will persist in asking whether, given the tensions between political reconciliation and components of liberal justice, theology will be required to account not only for reconciliation's intelligibility but also for its warrant—that is, the reasons why we should endorse it. It may turn out that only theological commitments can explain why restoration, not justice as desert or rights or entitlement, ought to be the conceptual lodestar of justice. It may also turn out that theologically inspired rituals are crucial for political reconciliation to function in a practical sense. If Piet Meiring is correct, this is indeed a lesson from Archbishop Tutu's leadership of the TRC.

## The Argument from Social Unity

The foregoing arguments against political reconciliation are ones that liberals draw from their deep political principles. They may well offer more practical objections to political reconciliation, too—not ones that are divorced from principle, but ones derived from liberals' desideratum for all political transitions: a stable liberal democracy, one where citizens enjoy human rights and free and fair elections. There are several reasons why liberals might regard political reconciliation as inimical to this goal. The public revelation and airing of political crimes may well open up old wounds and even create new ones for victims, alienating them rather than healing them. It may do the same for public onlookers who may otherwise have been prepared to forget about the past and embrace a new regime that promises a better future. If the public regards a truth commission as ineffective or unfair in depriving victims of their due, if it believes that only trials can render proper judgment on the old regime and its officials, then it will regard political reconciliation as a drain on the legitimacy of the new regimes. If the public is divided over the issue, or if a truth commission takes place amidst strong public opposition, then deeper social divisions may turn out to be the ironically dysfunctional result of a truth commission. Indeed, a 1998 poll showed that only half of South Africans regarded the TRC as fair and that only 17 percent thought that it promoted reconciliation.[41] Though one poll is not deep evidence of the TRC's long-term impact, it certainly creates doubt about its benefits for the legitimacy of the new regime.

If the argument from social unity is persuasive, then it seems to seal up the liberal case against political reconciliation. What could override liberalism's other objections to political reconciliation except a powerful set of practical arguments showing that despite its flaws in terms of justice it encourages stable, liberal democratic regimes to form? If it turns out that political reconciliation not only fails to exercise this positive power but has the opposite effect, then it is difficult to see how a liberal could endorse it. This does not mean that political reconciliation is impossible to endorse or intrinsically flawed. It simply means that its justification must lie outside liberalism.

## Assessing Liberal Arguments for Reconciliation

It turns out, though, that some liberals do not accept this negative verdict toward political reconciliation. They in fact argue for reconciliation, or at least for some aspect of it, such as political forgiveness. Though they may well endorse the traditional liberal principles behind the above objections, they do not regard them as defeaters of political reconciliation. What to make of these arguments? Do they temper liberalism's negative verdict? Or do they fail to make the case for political reconciliation? Such arguments come in two classes. One takes a pragmatic form, countering precisely the reasoning of the argument from social unity above. It holds that in situations where retribution or "normal justice" is not feasible, political reconciliation, or, again, at least elements of it like forgiveness, may be an effective "second best" mode of transition to a stable liberal democracy. Rather than sowing division and opening wounds, reconciliation can be healing and unifying. The second class argues for political reconciliation as a set of deeper principles, an alternative conception of justice to retribution. Though "restorative justice" may depart from the liberal tradition, it may nevertheless be placed on a liberal footing. In the end, though, neither sort of argument is persuasive in showing why reconciliation ought to appeal to liberals. The reasons will become apparent as each is examined.

### Liberal Pragmatic Arguments for Political Reconciliation

In a stable society where the rule of law is robust, justice involves "due" punishment for violators of human rights. But there are cases of extreme instability and lawlessness—the massive ethnic cleansing of Bosnia or Rwanda—where attempting "normal" justice is not feasible and might even prolong the suffering. Many of the recent episodes of transitional justice are just like this. In these instances, political reconciliation is a commendable alternative.[42]

This is the general form of the pragmatic argument for political reconciliation. Its claim that normal justice is infeasible in extreme situations comes in several variants. Some point to the impossibility of arithmetic justice. When eight hundred thousand have been killed through hand-to-hand combat with machetes in the course of a few months in Rwanda, or thousands have been violated over thirty years of apartheid, attempting to sort out who did what to whom in what degree is impossible. Gaining the information to conduct prosecutions, determining culpability in worlds where victims and perpetrators are often the same people, risking a perpetuation of the cycle of revenge— all appear to sink the prospects for the fair and equitable dispensation of just deserts. Others point to the limitations of judicial procedures. In a typical criminal trial, for instance, defendants have a strong incentive to adopt tactics that would block the discovery of facts about their crimes. The probability of the truth, of justice, about past crimes emerging, is small.[43] Still others point to the difficulty of conducting trials in the face of powerful opposition groups. In Argentina's political transition, for instance, powerful military generals ultimately foiled the efforts of the democratic government to prosecute military perpetrators of human rights violations. Similarly, in Chile, generals prevented trials altogether, at least at the time of the transition. Proponents of South Africa's TRC argued that trials of apartheid officials would risk civil war. In any of these cases, trials were unlikely to succeed and would have caused disproportionate chaos if they did. Far more auspicious would be a truth commission, the practice of forgiveness, and the pursuit of accountability in a form far milder than trial, imprisonment, and execution.

These critics rightly point out the difficulties facing retributive justice in political transitions. But they fail to make the case for political reconciliation as an alternative. It is not clear why, for instance, in arguing from the defects of retribution alone, blanket amnesty should not be adopted. Where retributive procedures are radically compromised, a society is arguably better off simply moving ahead with its political transition. A more appealing alternative for traditional liberals would be partial justice. In the wake of the wars in the former Yugoslavia, for instance, an international tribunal is now successfully putting to trial numerous commanders and soldiers who perpetrated ethnic cleansing. The fact that arithmetic justice is impossible, that every war criminal will not be apprehended and caught, does not point to the conclusion that it is unjust to try some of them. If anything, institutions ought to be strengthened and expanded so that justice may be more thorough. What the pragmatic argument objects to in retributive justice are problems that plague almost any set of judicial institutions—the impossibility of avoiding justice for some and not others, the limitations of the trial process, its subjection to power, and so on. But rarely do such problems alone lead to calls for the abandonment of the retributive principle and its replacement by alternative procedures based on an alternative conception of justice. It is not clear why any such abandonment ought to characterize political transitions either.

Stronger pragmatic arguments for political reconciliation will root it not merely in the defects of retributive justice but in its promise for achieving a separate good of great worth: a transition to a stable liberal democracy. Such arguments maintain a general consequentialist form, but one that runs contrary to the above argument from social unity. Far from being destabilizing, the practices of political reconciliation possess great advantages over trials in easing the transition to a robust, legitimate regime based on human rights. Attempting to prosecute and imprison leaders of the ancien régime, especially when its leaders continue to substantial popular support, it is argued, will only create social divisions, foster a permanent opposition to the new regime, and perhaps even bring civil war. Again, the pragmatic case of avoiding civil war was one strand of argument advanced by proponents of the TRC in South Africa.

This form of the pragmatic argument for political reconciliation is indeed stronger than a case based merely on the defects of retribution. But for it to succeed, it must present a consequentialist calculus showing that in fostering the transition to liberal democracy, political reconciliation's advantages outweigh its disadvantages. This will prove difficult. As the argument from social unity demonstrates, political reconciliation may reopen old wounds, disillusion victims who seek retributive justice, and alienate those who are unprepared to forgive. Other liberals have argued that trials of perpetrators of human rights violations are precisely what is needed to establish the legitimacy of a new regime on a foundation of justice. Or it may turn out that an approach of "pragmatic compromise"—essentially doing very little about the past—may, on balance, prove the best route of transition. Which consequences trump which? Will political reconciliation prove a more successful route to a stable, legitimate democracy than pragmatic compromise or retributive justice? It is highly unclear. Addressing the narrower issue of amnesty and punishment, Aryeh Neier writes:

> I do not claim that acknowledging and disclosing the truth about past abuses, or punishing those responsible for abuses, will necessarily deter future abuses. I doubt there is decisive evidence for this proposition. The same can be said of the contrary view, sometimes argued by proponents of amnesties, that an amnesty promotes reconciliation, while if a

government making a transition to a democracy attempts to punish those guilty of past abuses, it risks allowing those people to seize power again. Either outcome is possible. Whether the guilty are accorded amnesty or punished is only one among many factors that affect the pattern of events in any country.[44]

Such indeterminacy of consequences can be expanded to the entire question of what sort of transition best promotes a stable liberal democracy. The answers will vary widely from case to case and will be hotly disputed, by both scholars and participants, within single cases. Given this indeterminacy, any consequentialist case for political reconciliation will remain a weak one—not, perhaps, doomed altogether but always highly uncertain in its conclusions.

## Nonpragmatic Liberal Arguments for Political Reconciliation

There may be a stronger liberal case for political reconciliation, however, one that more decisively overcomes objections to it. This argument appeals not to the balance of consequences, but to deep principles of justice that political reconciliation itself instantiates. There are at least three such arguments, made respectively by Elizabeth Kiss, Martha Minow, and Amy Gutmann and Dennis Thompson. Each seeks to defend some version of political reconciliation in the South Africa context, particularly the TRC's sacrifice of strong retributive justice through its blanket amnesty and its favor of truth telling, repentance, forgiveness, and reparations. Though each echoes some of the pragmatic arguments for favoring truth commissions over trials, each also insists that the case for truth commissions goes far beyond their being a "second best" alternative to civil war. Rather, each advances other principles, deep and laudable ones.

As Kiss and Minow outline these principles, they correspond closely to political reconciliation's logic of restoration of people and relationships. Kiss, for instance, defends the TRC according to a principle of restorative justice that poses an alternative to retributive justice. Restorative justice entails restoring and affirming the dignity of those whose human rights have been violated, holding perpetrators accountable, and creating social conditions that promote respect for human rights. Truth telling is an essential practice in restorative justice, in part because of the therapeutic value of acknowledgment for victims of violence.[45] Minow espouses even more strongly the "healing," "therapeutic" value of truth commissions, which she says is a valuable goal in addition to accountability. The healing, the therapy that she describes is quite similar to the restoration involved in political reconciliation. For Gutmann and Thompson, the value that truth commissions promote is a different one: deliberative democracy. They too insist that truth commissions, especially ones that involve amnesty, must not be a second best alternative to strong retribution for human rights violators, which they are reluctant to forego. But they can be defended as an instantiation of the reciprocal, deliberative, democratic conversation between equals that, for them, is the heart of a just liberal democracy, the liberal democracy that they want to see realized in South Africa.

Can these stronger, more deeply principled arguments establish the case for political reconciliation? Each, to be sure, asserts and describes an appealing principle or set of principles in favor of which mere retribution is to be foregone and on behalf of which political reconciliation is to be adopted. The trouble with the arguments, though, is that they do little more than assert, describe, and demonstrate the intuitive attractiveness of these principles. What is not clear is why these arguments, though fortified with principles, not merely consequences, ought to trump liberal objections to reconciliation—the argument from retributive justice, the public-private distinction, and so on. In what sense does an assertion of the values of therapy, healing, and deliberation answer the concerns of the Biko and Mxenge families, Garton Ash's, and the like? Simply asserting these values, as appealing as they may be, does not explain why they should displace other liberal values that, after all, enjoy a far deeper pedigree and a far wider acceptance within the liberal tradition. To argue for such a displacement, one would need to provide a deep and thoroughgoing account of the person, the common good and social justice that both anchors and explains the superiority of the values that are offered as alternatives. To borrow John Rawls's phrase, a much more "comprehensive" doctrine of justice is required. But neither Kiss, Minow, nor Gutmann and Thompson offer such a conception. Each of them remains within a broadly liberal ethical framework. Their conception of justice revolves around the dignity of the rights-bearing, democratically deliberating citizen. Within these confines, they provide no strong set of warrants that can show why their values ought to replace more traditional liberal notions of justice. Kiss and Minow implicitly draw upon a conception of a person and a society that are restored by therapeutic healing, but neither develops a strong account of who this person and society are and how they compare with the conception of the person that underlies traditional liberal justice.

Without such an account, it is hard to see a deep principled reason why a liberal regime would forego just retribution or why it would involve itself in the restoration of souls. Analogously, imagine if a liberal political philosopher were to argue that within a stable domestic liberal democracy, ordinary criminal justice, say for a murderer or the chairman of the Enron Corporation, ought to be replaced with a truth-telling procedure that advances the alternative values of therapeutic healing or democratic deliberation. It is hard to imagine many liberals endorsing such a proposal. Surely, far fewer would endorse it than showed enthusiasm for South Africa's TRC. We may indeed wonder where Kiss, Minow, and Gutmann and Thompson would stand on it, for nowhere do they propose expanding their reasoning beyond the context of South Africa. Of course, they may reply that transitional justice as faced in South Africa and elsewhere involves special circumstances where there is a pressing need to establish a stable liberal democracy in the face of a terrible history of injustice and war. But this is to fall back on the pragmatic arguments, with all of their indeterminacy.

## Is There, Then, a Case for Political Reconciliation?

If the foregoing arguments are correct, it is difficult to make a liberal case for political reconciliation, at least a very strong one. The liberal tradition yields too many strong objections and does not provide strong warrants of its own for viewing justice as centrally concerned with the restoration of wounded individuals and relationships.

This conclusion does not deny the existence of warrants for political reconciliation, but only their ready availability within liberalism. Where might such warrants be found? Again, a comprehensive conception is needed, one that gives a deep and thorough account of the content of, and warrants for, the restoration of relationships and how this restoration is to be accomplished in the political order. Though there is no a priori reason why this account must be a theological one, it is in fact Christian theologians who have most explicitly, vigorously, and systematically argued for bringing reconciliation into politics: Donald Shriver, Desmond Tutu, Gregory Jones, Miroslav Volf, Walter Wink, Stanley Hauerwas, and others.[46] Muslims, Jews, and members of other faiths, although not as many, have also propounded the concept.[47] That the Abrahamic faiths would provide warrants for the concept is not surprising, and not simply because the word *reconciliation* is found in their texts. More importantly, each faith gives a central place to the mercy of God, by which God restores alienated humanity unto himself. In the Christian faith, this mercy is extended most fully though the Incarnation and the atonement of Jesus Christ; in Judaism, through God's restoration of his covenant with Israel; in Islam, through God's merciful beneficence. By contrast, the liberalism of the Enlightenment and later periods offers little role for divine restoration. To the degree that liberals consider God relevant for the political order, it is as the Creator of the natural law in which that order is rooted. How reconciliation as understood by the Abrahamic faiths manifests itself in politics requires far more development than provided here. The above description of the dimensions and practices of political reconciliation is the beginning of an approach. Again, it may not be necessary for a doctrine of reconciliation to have theological roots. If another kind of comprehensive doctrine puts forth properly deep arguments for reconciliation, then it may well prove to be a ground for it. But these grounds are likely to lie outside liberalism.

Some liberals, of course, may agree that reconciliation requires a comprehensive grounding but then conclude that this is precisely why it does not belong in politics. From the foregoing analysis, it seems indeed that an association between reconciliation and liberalism will be difficult to achieve. But it may not be entirely impossible. Not all versions of liberalism will take the form of those described above; a form of liberalism, drawn from the strands of actual liberal arguments, that is more receptive to a reconciliation grounded outside liberalism might conceivably be constructed. What would be its attributes? First, it would be open to warrants and rationales that lie outside liberalism. It would have to be open to language and concepts that are difficult to express through the language of rights, freedom, equality, utility, and other familiar liberal concepts. Second, it would be flexible in its view of retribution, open to forms of accountability that might fall short of proportionate punishment. Third, it would refrain from demanding any strong version of the public-private distinction, viewing the restoration of victims of political violence, in all of its dimensions, as a proper political end. Fourth, it would renounce any strong requirements for "public reason" and be open to importing into the political order concepts whose roots lay in theology or other comprehensive conceptions. Public explanations of reconciliation may not always have to be described and presented in the terms of this conception, but the public would widely understand its roots here. Finally, such a liberalism would allow the possibility that the effects of reconciliation for stability and legitimacy could be, on balance, positive. A liberalism with all of these features is hard to find these days. But it is not impossible to imagine. Each of the features alone has its proponents; there is no reason why all of them could not appear together in a composite form. Its open-ended character will be this form of liberalism's most central quality. If reconciliation is to be reconciled with liberalism, it will only be when liberalism is at its most liberal.

# Notes

1. Timothy Garton Ash, "True Confessions," *New York Review of Books* 44 (July 17, 1997): 36–37.

2. See Samuel P. Huntington, *The Third Wave: Democratization in the Late Twentieth Century* (Norman: University of Oklahoma Press, 1993).

3. For examples of approaches that are broadly pragmatic, see Kent Greenawalt, "Amnesty's Justice," in *Truth v. Justice: The Morality of Truth Commissions*, ed. Robert I. Rotberg and Dennis Thompson (Princeton: Princeton University Press, 2000); and P. E. Digeser, *Political Forgiveness* (Ithaca: Cornell University Press, 2001).

4. Amy Gutmann and Dennis Thompson, "The Moral Foundations of Truth Commissions," Elizabeth Kiss, "Moral Ambition with and beyond Political Constraints: Reflections on Restorative Justice," and Martha Minow, "The Hope for Healing: What Can Truth Commissions Do?" all in Rotberg and Thompson, *Truth v. Justice.*

5. Miroslav Volf, *Exclusion and Embrace: A Theological Exploration of Identity, Otherness, and Reconciliation* (Nashville, TN: Abingdon Press, 1996), and "Forgiveness, Reconciliation, and Justice: A Theological Contribution to a More Peaceful Social Environment," *Millenium* 29, no. 3 (2000): 861–77.

6. Of course, there are other forms of justice that will be relevant to transitional justice. One form of injustice that participants and commentators often highlight is the economic injustices of a previous regime. If their criticisms are legitimate, then a redistribution of wealth, or at least provision of economic and educational opportunities, will be an important part of any restoration of a political order.

7. Rajeev Bhargava, "Restoring Decency to Barbaric Societies," in Rotberg and Thompson, *Truth v. Justice,* 47.

8. Nicholas Tavuchis, *Mea Culpa: A Sociology of Apology and Reconciliation* (Stanford: Stanford University Press, 1991).

9. For a description of restorative justice in the domestic context of criminal justice, see Howard Zehr, "Restorative Justice: The Concept," *Corrections Today* 59, no. 7 (1997): 68–71.

10. For an explanation and description of truth commissions, see Priscilla Hayner, *Unspeakable Truths: Confronting State Terror and Atrocity* (New York: Routledge, 2001).

11. See André du Toit, "The Moral Foundations of the South African TRC: Truth as Acknowledgment and Justice as Recognition," in Rotberg and Thompson, *Truth v. Justice,* 135; Kiss, "Moral Ambition," 73–74.

12. Du Toit, "Moral Foundations," 133.

13. Alex Boraine, "Truth and Reconciliation in South Africa: The Third Way," in Rotberg and Thompson, *Truth v. Justice*, 151–53.

14. Du Toit, "Moral Foundations," 132.

15. Tina Rosenberg, "A Reporter at Large: Recovering from Apartheid," *New Yorker*, November 18, 1996, 92.

16. For a sophisticated account of retributive justice, see Jeffrie G. Murphy and Jean Hampton, *Forgiveness and Mercy*, Cambridge Studies in Philosophy and Law (New York: Cambridge University Press, 1988). See also Ted Hondereich, *Punishment: The Supposed Justifications* (Harmondsworth: Penguin, 1971).

17. On restorative punishment, see Christopher D. Marshall, *Beyond Retribution: A New Testament Vision for Justice, Crime and Punishment* (Grand Rapids, MI: Eerdmans, 2001), 131–40.

18. On apologies as restorative acts, see Tavuchis, *Mea Culpa*.

19. See A. John Simmons, Marshall Cohen, and Thomas Scanlon, *Punishment: A Philosophy and Public Affairs Reader* (Princeton: Princeton University Press, 1995).

20. John Finnis, *Natural Law and Natural Rights* (Oxford: Oxford University Press, 1980) 263, emphasis added.

21. Quoted in Gutmann and Thompson, "Moral Foundations," 26.

22. Aryeh Neier, "What Should Be Done about the Guilty?" in *Transitional Justice*, ed. Neil Kritz (Washington, DC: U.S. Institute of Peace Press, 1995).

23. Diane F. Orentlicher, "Settling Accounts: The Duty to Prosecute Human Rights Violations of a Prior Regime," *Yale Law Journal* 100, no. 8 (1991): 525–615.

24. See John Rawls, *A Theory of Justice* (Cambridge, MA: Harvard University Press, 1971).

25. Gutmann and Thompson, "Moral Foundations," 32–33.

26. Greenawalt, "Amnesty's Justice," 200–202.

27. Du Toit, "Moral Foundations," 134–35.

28. Garton Ash, "True Confessions," 36, 37.

29. Bhargava, "Restoring Decency," 61.

30. Greenawalt, "Amnesty's Justice," 199.

31. David A. Crocker, "Retribution and Reconciliation," *Philosophy and Public Policy* 20, no. 1 (2000): 6.

32. John Rawls, *Political Liberalism* (New York: Columbia University Press, 1993), 213.

33. Piet Meiring, "The *Baruti* versus the Lawyers: The Role of Religion in the TRC Process," in *Looking Back, Reaching Forward*, ed. Charles Villa-Vicencio and Wilhelm Verwoerd (Capetown: University of Capetown Press, 2000), 124.

34. H. Russel Botman and Robin Petersen, *To Remember and to Heal: Theological and Psychological Reflections on Truth and Reconciliation* (Capetown: Human and Rousseau, 1996), quoted in Villa-Vicencio and Verwoerd, *Looking Back*, 127.

35. Piet Meiring, *Chronicle of the Truth Commission* (Vanderbylpark, South Africa: Carpe Diem, 1999), 357, quoted in Meiring, "*Baruti*," 129.

36. Jorge Heine, *Sunday Independent*, August 2, 1998, quoted in Meiring, "*Baruti*," 131.

37. Garton Ash, "True Confessions," 36.

38. Cosmas Desmond, *Star,* February 29, 1996, quoted in Meiring, *"Baruti,"* 125.

39. Gutmann and Thompson, "Moral Foundations," 30.

40. Greenawalt, "Amnesty's Justice," 199.

41. "Only Half of People Feel TRC Is Fair and Unbiased: Survey," *Reports from the South African Press Association,* March 5, 1998, quoted in Kiss, "Moral Ambition," 88.

42. For a quite well-developed and argued account on these lines, see Digeser, *Political Forgiveness.*

43. See Minow, "Hope for Healing," and Kiss, "Moral Ambition."

44. Neier, "What Should Be Done," 182.

45. Kiss, "Moral Ambition," 71–83.

46. Donald W. Shriver, *An Ethic for Enemies: Forgiveness in Politics* (New York: Oxford University Press, 1995); Desmond Tutu, *No Future without Forgiveness* (New York: Doubleday, 1999); L. Gregory Jones, *Embodying Forgiveness* (Grand Rapids, MI: Eerdmans, 1993); Volf, "Forgiveness, Reconciliation" and *Exclusion and Embrace*; Walter Wink, *When the Powers Fall: Reconciliation in the Healing of Nations* (Minneapolis: Fortress Press, 1998); Stanley Hauerwas, *A Better Hope: Resources for a Church Confronting Capitalism, Democracy, and Postmodernity* (Grand Rapids, MI: Brazos Press, 2000).

47. See Marc Gopin, *Between Eden and Armageddon: The Future of World Religions, Violence, and Peacemaking* (New York: Oxford University Press, 2000); Mohammed Abu-Nimer, *Reconciliation, Justice, and Coexistence* (Lanham, MD: Lexington Books, 2001); and Michael L. Hadley, *The Spiritual Roots of Restorative Justice* (Albany: State University of New York Press, 2001).

# CHAPTER TWO

# The Theological Grounds for Advocating Forgiveness and Reconciliation in the Sociopolitical Realm

## ALAN J. TORRANCE

Twenty years ago, few political analysts would have had the courage to suggest that the marginalization and at times brutal oppression of the nonwhite peoples of South Africa by a small minority of the total population could end in anything other than bloodshed. There are, of course, many possible explanations as to why this did not happen. It would be hard to deny, however, that one ingredient in the remarkably peaceful transition from tyranny to democracy was the capacity of Archbishop Desmond Tutu to tap resources deep within the faith of the people and subliminal in their attitudes to their oppressor. Through his spiritual leadership of a people, most notably through the unique dynamics of the Truth and Reconciliation Commission, Desmond Tutu capitalized on those theological resources.[1] The man who embodied his insistence that "without forgiveness, there is no hope" may well be argued to have exemplified the capacity of forgiveness to realize hopes that transcend the expectations of the most optimistic political realist. It is the purpose of this essay to explore those theological resources and their significance. In doing so I shall seek to ask, not merely whether they have relevance for nations that are overtly Christian, but whether they can speak to those nations seeking, if this is possible, to operate from a religiously "neutral" base.

## Theological Prolegomena

When Christian theologians seek to interpret what it is to be human and the nature of human relationships, they are obliged to begin by considering Jesus Christ. The reasons for this include the following.

First, the Christian faith recognizes him as none other than the presence with humanity of the One through whom and for whom all things were made—the fullness of the Godhead dwelling bodily, as Paul puts it. But he is not merely God with us, he is with us as God's incarnate Word to us—the One who mediates God's purpose for humanity and for the world. To seek to interpret God's purposes for the contingent order from some other basis, some alternative ground—to begin from some other "word"—can only constitute a de facto rejection of God's Self-presentation to be known *in this way* and *from this center.* For the eternal Word's becoming incarnate must be understood as a divine endorsement of how God intends himself and his purposes to be known. This would suggest, therefore, that when we come to interpret God's purposes for humanity our thinking should be informed by this Word, not as an afterthought or as icing on a cake that has been prepared in advance but right from the outset.[7]

Second, beginning with the person of Christ takes cognizance of the fact that the Incarnation is revelatory as the Self-presentation not merely of God *as God* but of God *as human.* In God's Self-disclosure God presents us with all that it is to be truly human. Thus the Incarnation is an event that simultaneously and inseparably defines who God is and what it is to be human—indeed, the nature of the Incarnation is such that we do not recognize the One without simultaneously recognizing the other. We know who God is to the extent that we understand the humanity of Jesus, and we understand the humanity of Jesus in and through recognizing the Self-presentation in him of the Creator and his creative purpose for humanity. The incarnate Word constitutes the mediation not only of the one true God but also of the one true human. In him, therefore, we know what humanity is created to be and to become; we know humanity not in its supernatural but in its *natural* state—that is, as we are born to be.

This, however, brings us to a third issue. The recognition of God's purposes as they are present to us in the person of Jesus Christ is an irreducibly *ecclesial* event. God reveals Godself in a self-giving event of communion, integral to which is the creation of a community. The perception of God's being and purposes is thus given in, through, and with participation by the Spirit in the life of the Body of Christ. In short, what we term "revelation" is not simply the communication of ideas, ethical instructions, or information but God's Self-communication in an event of communion as this involves the creation of a creaturely context of noetic, epistemic, and semantic participation in the divine life. It commandeers our thinking, our knowing, and our speaking. It is an event in and through which our understanding and perception of God and humanity, our language and our categories of interpretation, are transformed ("metamorphosed," to use Paul's term) such that they are no longer "schematized" by the secular order.[3] In this way, God's Self-communication also must be understood as a *generative* event of communion. Through the presence of the Spirit, the *koinonia* or communion that God establishes with humanity engenders communion at the "horizontal" level not only among Christians but between Christians and non-Christians and hopefully, therefore, within the secular world itself. God was in Christ reconciling not some hermetically sealed church but the world. Intrinsic to revelation, therefore, is the reconciliation of our orientations and attitudes both toward God and toward others. "He who says he loves God and hates his brother is a liar."[4]

For our purposes in this chapter, the question that will occupy us most specifically is how precisely the relationship between the vertical and horizontal dimensions of this communion is to be conceived. The key to this is provided by the Judeo-Christian categories of covenant, *torah*, and righteousness. To appreciate what these do and do not mean, it is critical here to distinguish them from their translation in Western Christianity into the categories of contract, *lex* (Roman law), and justice respectively. This (mis)translation, I shall argue, has served to distort radically the categories definitive of the biblical tradition.

## Covenant versus Contract

The conception that lies at the heart of Judaism and that frames the whole exposition and indeed theological redaction of the Pentateuch/Hexateuch is that of covenant (Hebrew: *bᵉrît*).[5] The totality of God's relationship with the created order was interpreted retrospectively by its authors in the light of the category of covenant and the perception of God's covenant faithfulness (Hebrew: *hesed*) toward Israel. As J. B. Torrance has argued, integral to the grammar of *bᵉrît* are three key elements.

First, the divine covenant is unilaterally established by God with humanity. Here we must distinguish not only between a covenant and a contract but also between a unilateral covenant and a bilateral covenant. Whereas marriage denotes, of course, an unconditional commitment and, theologically speaking, must be conceived, therefore, as a *covenant* and not a *contract*, it is also the case that any marriage, to take place, requires the free consent and commitment of both parties—it is thus a bilateral covenant. At the heart of Judaism we also find a *covenant*, that is, between YHWH and Israel (and *not* a contract), but this covenant is not the result of a bilateral commitment, as in marriage—it was unilaterally established by YHWH. It was a one-sided commitment (made by one party, "the Lord") to be unconditionally faithful to Israel. It is thus a unilateral covenant.

Second, the divine covenant is both unconditional and unconditioned by considerations of human worth. YHWH's covenant with Israel (and the New Covenant of the New Testament) denotes a commitment to Israel that was in no way initiated or merited or obligated by Israel. It was thus free. Precisely the same applies, again, to God's commitment to humanity in Christ—the New Covenant.

Third, at the same time, this prior, unconditional, and unconditioned covenant commitment on the part of YHWH carries equally unconditional obligations—the apodictic obligations summarized in the "ten words" of the *torah*. That is, this unilateral covenant is "costly" in the obligations it places upon us. We are to be faithful and true both to God and to each other—and this is spelled out in that we are not to lie, to steal, to commit adultery, and so on. It should be clear, indeed, that to make the first two affirmations above is emphatically *not* to suggest that the unilateral covenant commitment plays down the importance of the human response. Precisely the reverse. YHWH's unconditional and unconditioned commitment to Israel placed Israel under an *unconditional* obligation to respond faithfully. Moreover, it called forth and indeed motivated such a response. The obligations were apodictic—there were no "ifs" or "buts"—but they could also be seen as the "natural" or "appropriate" response to perceiving the faithfulness of God.

What it is imperative to recognize here is that the *indicatives of grace* (the affirmations of God's unconditional, covenant commitment and faithfulness) precede and sustain the *imperatives of law* and not the other way round. "I am the Lord, your God, who has brought you out of the land of Egypt, out of the house of bondage. . . . *[T]herefore,* have no other Gods before me."

## Does a Contractual Interpretation Not Strengthen the Force of God's Law?

The universal tendency of human pride is to want to turn God's covenant of grace into a contract.[6] That is, we invariably want to make the imperatives of obligation prior to the indicatives of grace. This is due first to our desire for control—to control relationships on both the vertical and horizontal planes. The freeness of grace offends human pride. We desire to be able to earn God's rewards, to retain the initiative and control with respect to God's relationship toward us. Second, the fear of antinomianism leads us to seek to prop up God's laws by tacking on conditions. The tragedy of this is that nothing serves anti-nomianism more effectively than the fear of it. Adding conditions—and the legalism that results from this—invariably weakens the law. Precisely such tendencies were found in late Judaism (though they were only tendencies and this has been much overstressed in caricatures of Judaism), namely an inclination to reverse the indicative-imperative order. "*If* you keep the law, God will love you. *If* you keep the Sabbath, the kingdom of God will come." The imperatives were made prior to the indicatives, implying a conditionality and thereby turning a covenant into a contract. God's grace was made conditional upon humankind's obedience—we condition God into being gracious. It is precisely against this inversion of the order of grace that Paul protests in Galatians 3:17–22. If the law, which came 430 years after the covenant (to spell out the obligations of grace), introduced a single condition to God's covenant commitment, then the covenant would have been turned into a contract and, Paul argues, God's promises would have been broken.

In short, Paul categorically *refuses* to seek to bolster the force of the moral obligations upon humanity by suggesting that the law stipulates conditions of God's acceptance of humanity and faithfulness to it. But does the affirmation that God's covenant commitment to humanity is unchanging not serve to weaken the force of the moral law? Does the emphasis on the unconditional indicatives of grace not risk undermining the imperative that we do what is right—or, worse, may it not suggest that God in effect colludes in the wrong we do? That is, does it not threaten to undermine God's endorsement of what is right and upholding of what is just? For Paul, it is quite the reverse. When the promises cease to be unconditional the obligations lose their unconditional force and the whole *sense* of obligation is weakened. Covenants carry obligations in a profoundly different way from contracts. If you choose to enter into a contract and fail to deliver your side of the bargain, then, if no cost has been incurred by the other party, this may simply have the effect of returning the situation to a precontractual state.[7]

The situation with covenants is quite different. They introduce obligations ("I must . . . , "Thou shalt . . .") that are unconditional. A covenant changes things radically by creating apodictic obligations. It is precisely *for the sake of* the law and its force upon humanity, therefore, that the obligations of love must never be interpreted as the conditions of love. When Paul argued that Christ fulfilled all faithfulness and righteousness for us, in our place and on our behalf, he was accused of antinomianism. His response, however, was to emphasize that precisely the opposite was the case. When the Spirit gives humanity the eyes to see the full extent of what God accomplishes on its behalf and in its place by pure grace and convinces men and women of that reality, this inspires faithfulness (not its opposite) and liberates them for faithfulness. What this suggests is a divinely intended logic to the ethical dimension of Christian existence. God makes us ethical beings in and through reconciling our mixed intentionalities and motivations—that is, by transforming the whole character of our orientation toward God and thus toward humankind. This he does by generating a "filial" orientation as opposed to a "legal" one. Whereas one can obey laws driven by a whole raft of unsavory motives, one cannot love out of mixed intentions. Love denotes one's basal motive and intentionality—it stems from the center of one's being. It is the transformed orientation of our most profound commitments and motivation that God desires. This is what is denoted by the term *righteousness.*

In short, God's will is not that we simply mimic prescribed actions, enact legal norms, but that we desire to live in the manner articulated in the *torah* and the Gospel, and his engagement with humanity is concerned to generate precisely such a free desiring. The form of life that he prescribes and seeks to engender is an intentionality that, by its very nature, we *cannot* achieve through the introverted actions of oneself upon oneself.[8] It is neither subjectively manufactured nor self-determined but *generated* in and through an event wherein the Spirit directs us to perceive the unanticipatable, historical Self-giving of God to which the Incarnation testifies and that the self-same presence of the Spirit embodies.[9]

This was the insight behind Luther's dicta, first, that we do not *do* God's will until we delight to do God's will, and, second, that that delighting is characterized by our being turned away from ourselves such that we are brought to think from a center outside us. When this takes place one is brought to live *excurvatus ex se.* Such an attitude does not and cannot result from an introverted act of oneself upon oneself—that is, an *incurvatus in se* act.

What does all this mean? It means that the *torah* that concerns not just our actions but our whole intentionality is realized in us (its function is fulfilled) in and through the discovery of the extent of God's unconditional commitment toward humanity.[10] Precisely in and through discovering that reality, the unconditional grace of God, we are brought to live out of it: the mode of existence described in the *torah* is generated within us. The Christian ethic can be described, therefore, as an "evangelical" ethic—an ethic lived in response to the perception of Good News. It is an ethic that "gives light to the eyes," to use Oliver O'Donovan's phrase.[11] Such an orientation can fulfill the *torah* precisely because it refuses to be translated into a "legal" ethic—where the object of focus is not the Good News but the brute force of *lex*. God's primary purposes for humanity are therefore to be described not as "legal" but rather as "filial," to quote John McLeod Campbell.[12] The law is fulfilled in and through our loving God and our neighbor—a love that can take place only because God *first* loves us, then gives us the eyes to see the full extent of this and, by the Spirit, brings us to live in the light of that all-encompassing reality.

An analogy of the inner logic of this is easily illustrated with reference to marriage. When a woman makes it clear to her husband that she will continue to love him and be faithful to him even if he is unfaithful, this inspires faithfulness. By contrast, the opposite scenario—where she says her love is contingent or conditional upon his behaving himself (and thus implies that it is contractual)—is likely to discourage faithfulness. Why? Because conditional commitments suggest that the partner is not really loved. That is because love is by nature unconditional. To recognize that a spouse's "love" is conditional is to find oneself doubting whether one's spouse loves one at all. As this is doubted, the sense of obligation is undermined. The relationship becomes depersonalized, appearing "nominal" or merely "legal"—contractual indeed. In short, it reposes on verbal vows torn from the personal presence that undergirds them. To the extent that one's spouse no longer loves one "for better or worse," it constitutes an obligation to keep vows grounded in a bilateral covenant that has ceased to be "bilateral." The thrust of what we are suggesting is that unconditional faithfulness both begets and sustains faithfulness.

It may seem that we are in danger of reducing theology to psychology and assuming too idealistic an account of human life—one, indeed, that lacks the sharp edge necessary to sustain ethically responsible existence. By contrast, however, I should like to argue that this takes us to the heart of a relational logic that flows from the Judeo-Christian tradition and constitutes the grammar of the love that defines (1) the being of God and the relationship of the Father and the Son in the Spirit constitutive of the divine life; (2) God's relationship to human creatures conceived as an overflowing of the divine *koinonia* in the Spirit; (3) the nature of our response—that is, our participation in that same *koinonia;* (4) the nature and character of the church's outgoing orientation *(ekstasis)* toward the world; and, finally, (5) the grammar of that healing and reconciling sociality sustained through the generative presence of the Spirit.

In sum, central to both Judaism and the Christian faith is the recognition that God's primary purposes for humanity are not legal but filial, not contractual but covenantal, not juridical but koinonial. The Christian understanding of atonement (lit. at-one-ment) is to be understood not as a condition of God's forgiveness of humanity but as the consequence of an unconditionally forgiving covenant love that stems from the heart of God and in which humanity is given to participate by the Spirit.

## Liberating Western Christianity

Unfortunately, Christianity in the West (both Catholic and Protestant) has too often failed to appreciate this logic at the heart of Christianity, with the result that its sociopolitical relevance has been severely skewed. This failure is due in no small measure to a problem of translation. Hebrew concepts have been translated into Latin concepts, leading to the subliminal imposition on the Judeo-Christian frame of reference of a profoundly foreign conceptuality. The translation of the controlling terms from Hebrew to Greek to Latin to English has taken the following form:

*berith,* covenant (Heb) → *diatheke* (Gk) → *foedus* (Lat) → contract

*torah,* covenantal law (Heb) → *nomos* (Gk) → *lex* (Lat) → Roman/stoic/juridical law

*tsedaqah,* righteousness (Heb) → *dikaiosune* (Gk) → *iustitia* (Lat) → justice

The effect of this has meant that God's filial purpose (unconditional, unilateral) comes to be conceived as denoting a somewhat impersonal legal purpose—too often conceived in bilateral and indeed conditional terms. The relational or filial categories of God's covenant love, unconditional faithfulness and righteousness, are translated into the individualistic categories of contract, conditional acceptance and a forgiveness conditional upon the satisfaction of legal requirements. *Torah,* conceived as denoting the unconditional obligations (in relation to God and humanity) that stem from God's unconditioned and unconditional covenant commitment, is translated into the categories of *lex*— Roman or Stoic concepts of law. The "righteousness" of YHWH, as this referred primarily to God's sustained faithfulness to his creatures despite their continual waywardness, is reduced to impersonal and ultimately juridical conceptions of justice and the divine "will."

These manifold consequences undermine the integral relationship between the vertical and the horizontal and thus between worship and ethics—what is more appropriately termed *worthship*. (As the etymology of *worship* rightly suggests, there is, properly speaking, no dichotomy between these two definitive dimensions of the Christian life—participation "in Christ" concerns an orientation for which worship and worthship are two sides of the same coin. They denote one, not two, forms of behavior/orientation.) These same consequences also undermine the integral relationship between spirituality (which is consequently privatized) and ethics (which essentially comes to concern public acts)—dichotomies that were unthinkable in Judaism. The resulting misconception of the divine life and purpose conceived in terms of contract, *lex*, *iustitia*, and a juridical relationship between God and humanity has compounded our tendency to interpret social relations between human beings in contractual terms—as a "social contract." As our view of God is, so is our view of the human—and vice versa.

The purpose of the above is emphatically *not* to suggest that God is uninterested in what we mean when we use the English term *justice*. Rather, it is simply to suggest that what God desires and intends not only transcends but is in tension with the limited compass of that term—especially if it is interpreted in contractual terms or when it implies that the ultimate reality that we must obey and that must govern human and social relations is the formulated demand of some remote, impersonal, legal will. Put simply, the English term *justice* must be commandeered by the historical content of God's self-disclosure and not the other way round.

### Social Transformation and the Distinction between "Legal" and "Evangelical" *Metanoia*

Human and social transformation are intrinsic to the raison d'être of God's mission to this world, and this is expressed, in the New Testament, by way of the language of *metanoia*. Traditionally translated as either "repentance" or "conversion," it denotes the transformation of the orientation of our minds— *noia* comes from the Greek *noein*, meaning "to think." This is not a transformation that we can bring about within ourselves. It is neither a perspectival change nor merely a Gestalt switch (which implies that both ways of understanding are valid). As Murray Rae argues, it is closer to a "paradigm shift" that delivers us from an erroneous, alienated processing of reality to which there is no option to return.[13] Again, clearly erroneous paradigms cannot in and of themselves deliver new paradigms. This paradigm shift is initiated not internally but in and through the dynamic of divine Self-disclosure (it is "from above") and involves the transformation of our identities (lit. their regeneration) in and through our being given "eyes to see" or "ears to hear" what we could not otherwise see, namely God, ourselves, and not only our loved ones but also our enemies in the radically new light of God's love. Contrary to the lie of "naturalism," this is to discern "in truth."

My argument will be that the nature of the transformation of our orientation toward God, others, and the world (namely *metanoia*—a word whose significance is all too easily misconstrued when translated as "repentance") should be conceived as "evangelical" rather than "legal." This was a distinction to which Calvin referred (but that, frustratingly, he did not develop as extensively as he might have done). It was later taken up by Thomas Boston and the "Marrowmen"[14] and then again by F. D. Maurice in the 19th century.

"Legal repentance" suggests that the inducement of "repentance"—that is, this transformation of our orientation—stems from our being confronted with the law. Such a view does not necessarily imply contractual categories—it could be that the law does, indeed, have a self-authenticating and convicting "use" or capacity that transforms in and of itself. However, legal repentance has tended to play right into the church's utilization of the "carrot and stick" approach. And the motivation here has, of course, been "control"—a concern to *bolster* the "transformative" effect of its message. When this takes place, the force of the law is conceived contractually. "*If* you want God to be merciful toward you, *then* do the following: Repent! Obey the law!" Sadly, however, the consequences of this are considerably less positive than is assumed, not least with recourse to the force of the law. First, the implication is that God does not love or value humanity as it is. Rather, God *may* love and forgive one if and only if one manages to deliver what is required. What it is imperative that we appreciate here is that such an approach does not and cannot deliver love of God (any more than such a contractual imperative would bring children to love, let alone admire or respect, their parents). Second, it neither does nor can achieve love and respect of other persons or their human dignity. One's orientation toward other human persons comes to be perceived as a means to egocentric ends, namely receiving the divine carrot and avoiding the divine stick. It tends to deliver a self-interested, egocentric orientation—and thus tends to compound sin. Third, it generates and utilizes existential *fear* as the driving force in our orientation to the world.

The transformative dynamic that stems by contrast from "evangelical repentance" is radically and profoundly different. Evangelical *metanoia* denotes the transformation of our orientation or apperception that emerges in response to our unconditional acceptance and forgiveness *as alienated, sinful, oppressive human beings.* The specific form of this Gospel is that God provides in our place the response, the "amen" to his covenant faithfulness that is required of us and that is articulated in the law. The *torah* is thus "fulfilled" on our behalf in the One who provides the all-embracing response to the Father that is obliged and required of us by virtue of his unconditionally forgiving, loving-faithfulness toward his people. Consequently, the Spirit brings humanity to repose in the peace, the *shalom,* of participating in this response, of participating "in Christ" *(en Christo)*—an expression that Paul uses more than 150 times.

The transformation that this generates is emphatically *not* grounded either in fear or in self-interest,[15] or, indeed, in introverted attempts to make ourselves morally acceptable before God.[16] In short, whereas the transformative dynamic at the heart of legal repentance turns people back upon themselves (focusing their gaze on their sin and their need both to repent and to transform their own state of mind), the transformative dynamic at the heart of evangelical repentance liberates people to look away from themselves through referring them to God's unconditional affirmation of their dignity as this is grounded in their unconditional acceptance and forgiveness in Christ. As they are given the eyes to see the length, breadth, height, and depth of God's love for them and for the world, *metanoia* begins to take place subjectively within. In short, what we have traditionally termed *repentance* should be interpreted as taking place not before forgiveness but after it—as stemming from the discovery of our prior unconditional forgiveness in the love of God. In radical contrast to this, legal repentance suggests we should repent in the hope that we might thereby generate forgiveness in God. That is, it constitutes an attempt to condition God's forgiveness of us and thereby our acceptance in the heart of God.

As John Wesley saw so clearly, the New Covenant *(kaine diatheke)* held forth in the Eucharist or Mass constitutes a "converting ordnance." Jesus' presentation to the sinner of his life lived and completed in the place of the recipient and presented to him or her as a gift *transforms* the recipient, generates *metanoia,* and bestows insight into the real nature of his or her sins as sins against the One who continues to forgive them unconditionally. In and through this recognition, repentance/*metanoia* of a far more profound and radical kind is generated in the subject than is conceivable in advance of this perception.

The story of Zacchaeus exemplifies this evangelical *metanoia*.[17] Zacchaeus is presented as an exploitative white-collar criminal whose desire to see Jesus is motivated by nothing more than idle curiosity; this is emphasized to obviate any suggestion of his being driven by a preparatory sense of guilt or an incipient desire to repent. In the midst of those who have suffered as a result of Zacchaeus's exploitation and who despise him, Jesus offers an unambiguous, public endorsement of his dignity by expressing the desire to have dinner with him at his home. In the light of this act of unconditioned and unconditional acceptance, Zacchaeus sees himself for what he is, a loved and accepted sinner. That perception expresses a *metanoia* in his whole orientation, not least toward others—a spontaneous desire to recognize and affirm the dignity of those whom he has used and abused. The result is a self-giving desire to make amends of a kind that legal repentance cannot conceive—it is profoundly different from any desire to satisfy legal conditions for contractually conceived ends.

The continual misconstrual of the so-called parable of the "prodigal son" as a parable of repentance illustrates the widespread Western misconceptions to which we have referred. Too often, it is misinterpreted as a story about a son who takes his father's money and squanders it in sinful living but then "comes to his senses," repents, and *because he repents* is forgiven by his father and accepted back into his father's home. But the thrust of the story is quite the opposite. A wealthy father loves his rogue son unconditionally and vulnerably—allowing himself to be humiliated by his son before his own household. Throughout the story, the son remains determined to use his father for his own ends. Having insulted his father (as Kenneth Bailey shows)[18] and wasted his funds, he finds himself in abject poverty. Comparing the quality of food enjoyed by his father's servants with the pig food he may have to start eating, he "comes to his senses" and decides that the rational thing to do is to go home and seek his father's pity—in an attempt to redress the unhappy consequences of his cash flow problem. In short, it is left open whether he may not be using his father still further, possibly even more cynically than before by spinning a yarn suggestive of contrition. Far from describing any *metanoia* on the part of the son, the story is quite candid in its description of the son's motives in returning home. The reason for this is that the function of the parable is to illustrate quite specifically that God's love is unconditional and unconditioned by any repentance or transformed motivation on our part. The father does not look for any newfound respect for him on the part of his son—nor, indeed, is he influenced in any way by the desire for respect in the eyes of others. (Bailey comments on the implications of the reference to the father's running to meet his son. "An Oriental nobleman with flowing robes never runs anywhere."[19] It requires him to lift his long robes above his knees before a household who sees a foolish old man throwing away money and pride out of unrestrained love for a wanton son.) Although the story recounts no *metanoia* on the part of the prodigal, one is inclined to think that if there were any such transformation, it would have taken place in the arms of the father, who neither asked his son for an explanation nor waited for words of explanation, confession, or contrition but instead loved and forgave and accepted him unconditionally. The father's embrace, like the Eucharist, constitutes a converting ordnance. The story then goes on to relate the love of the father for another son who is also using him, precisely in and through playing by the rules (laws)—thereby, of course, turning the *torah* on its head.

If the transformative dynamic at the heart of the Gospel were characterized by "legal repentance" and thus an acceptance and forgiveness that were conditional, the story of Zacchaeus and the parable of the love of the father for his sons would be unrecognizably different. Jesus would have weighed up evidences of true repentance or penitence or contrition (which both the medieval church and the Puritans considered to be a condition of forgiveness), and *only then* would he have forgiven and accepted them—or not, as the case might be. In the parable, the details of this would have been recounted in the father's handling of the son—the logic, of course, would have been that the attitude of the elder son deserved commendation. In the case of Zacchaeus, prior satisfaction of the demands of justice would have been required for forgiveness to be contemplated. Similar accounts would have been recorded with respect to the woman at the well and the woman caught in adultery.

A great deal more needs to be said. For our purposes here, however, I suggest that at the heart of the Christian faith stand the unconditional love and forgiveness of God toward a confused and alienated humanity. The ramifications of this at the horizontal (social) levels are spelled out as the fulfillment not of a supererogatory ethic but of the only law it recognizes as God's—namely the law that articulates our righteous response to God's righteousness.

In sum, God's transformation of humanity operates in and through the fullest conceivable presentation of the unconditional nature of his love and forgiveness. In faithfulness to this, the Christian faith bears testimony to a metamorphosing dynamic that we must refuse to "reschematize" with reference to the contractual, self-oriented categories of means and ends characteristic of the secular world and the prodigal son.[20]

## Summary

To operate from a Christian epistemic base (and to be a Christian is to do precisely that) is to interpret proper human function in the light of that one Word to humanity that defines what it is to be human. To be human in truth *is* thus to love not only one's friends but one's enemies—and to do so unconditionally. Moreover, to love unconditionally *is* to forgive unconditionally. To refuse to do so, or indeed to make conditional this orientation toward others, is to dehumanize both others and ourselves.[21] We are to forgive seventy times seven, as the one true human, the *eschatos Adam,* forgives seventy times seven. To the extent that Jesus forgives seventy times seven, God forgives seventy times seven. Just as the atonement did not condition God into forgiving humanity but stemmed from God's unconditionally forgiving love for humanity,[22] so the Christian faith does not conceive of "reconciliation" or "atonement" as making forgiveness contingent upon the satisfaction of conditions. The unconditional forgiveness of one's enemies is the *only* orientation toward them that is in accord with the only will of God we know—namely that mediated not merely in but *as* God's once-and-for-all Self-presentation to humankind as the incarnate Word. If we are not to endorse some kind of "methodological naturalism"[23] in politics, then we are required to think out of this center and from these grounds.

## Reconciliation and Forgiveness in the Political Context

The last decade has witnessed a period of immense transition worldwide. The end of apartheid, the breakup of the Soviet Union, and the strife-ridden emergence of new nation-states has meant that the language of reconciliation has acquired an unprecedented international currency in the political arena. There have also been transitions from oppressive regimes in Latin America and the resolution of bitter wars in Africa, most notably in Angola, all of which have seen a number of young democracies struggling to settle violent conflicts. Over twenty countries have created "truth commissions" to address the injustices of past regimes. Most famously, there has been the Truth and Reconciliation Commission in South Africa, inspired in large measure by the Christian leadership of Desmond Tutu. On February 28, 1998, cross-party support was announced in Northern Ireland (in the aftermath of the Good Friday peace accord) for the creation of a truth and reconciliation commission there. Similar proposals have been considered as a means of resolving multilateral tensions in the Balkans.

In contexts such as Rwanda and Bosnia (let alone in the aftermath of the Holocaust), however, one cannot help but ask about the propriety of the word *reconciliation*, let alone the language of "forgiveness" in the political realm. Given the unthinkable atrocities, the scenes of mass murder, rape, and gratuitous violence, and the sustained pillaging and burning of homes, one must ask whether talk of forgiveness and reconciliation does not border on the grotesque where survivors are stalked by events that are unthinkable for us, unforgettable for them.

The universal and indeed natural reaction is to view forgiveness as inappropriate before the demands of justice have been met—which means, in the political context, until the international war crimes tribunals have completed their work. After justice has been done, forgiveness *may* be interpreted as an admirable act of extreme supererogation by individual victims. Before this, however, it is counterintuitive to see it as an appropriate act by individual victims, let alone a concept with any kind of sociopolitical relevance. Even God—or perhaps especially God—does not forgive before the demands of justice have been satisfied. St Anselm articulates the issue concisely in *Cur Deus Homo*: "[I]f it [sin] be not punished, it is unjustly forgiven." Consequently "it beseemeth not God to forgive anything in His realm illegally."[24]

## The Right Time: The *Kairos* of Forgiveness

The universal assumption is that, if the language of forgiveness is to have any meaning whatsoever in the political context, this can be the case only once the requirements of justice have been fulfilled and the injustice has lost its sting. But when precisely is the time "right," or should one say "just"? Is it when the injustice has played itself out, as it were, when the acts of the oppressor—transmuted into the life-sapping affliction of memories—cease to oppress? And when is that? Once memories have dimmed and the associated hurt has faded? Or is the time "right" politically when the economic benefits to the victims of cooperation outweigh their residual memories? If this is the case, then any application of the language of reconciliation to the sociopolitical context refers to little more than the passage of time and the healing impact of the global market. The effect of this is to make "reconciliation" become the retrospective description of a "resolution" conceived naturalistically and pragmatically—the primary cleansing agents are the rivers of forgetfulness and economic pragmatism. That is, the *retrospective* dimension of "atonement" becomes the passage of time and the *prospective* ingredient the contemplation of financial benefit.[25] Christians have been all too quick to go along with this. The tendency has been to suggest that the essential sociopolitical contribution of Christianity is to be conceived not in terms of reconciliation and forgiveness but in terms of justice and liberation—concepts whose advocacy is considerably less problematic and that most can appreciate, endorse, and admire. Reconciliation is left to natural processes, and forgiveness translates to forgetfulness.

One consequence has been the displacement of reconciliation and forgiveness from the sociopolitical arena into an individualized realm of private morality. The question that this poses is whether the Gospel of reconciliation and forgiveness has anything whatsoever to offer the political arena: that is, how we approach situations of political enmity and alienation.

No one has done more to focus attention on the theological issues here in recent years than Miroslav Volf. In the third chapter of *Exclusion and Embrace,* the political relevance of his own theological approach begins to emerge. There he shows that forgiveness *serves* justice, that it is intrinsic to the creation of the just society—and that far from weakening or constituting a threat to justice and the universal rule of law, as is so often assumed, forgiveness serves and preserves justice.

In explaining how this is the case, Volf describes the two basic predicaments that characterize contexts of alienation and hostility. The first is the "predicament of partiality"—the problem of the diversity of perceptions that characterizes alienated parties, which he terms the "lack of sync between the perspectives of social actors."[26] One party will interpret its own actions as simply seeking justice or even settling for less than justice, whereas the other party may perceive those same actions as perpetrating injustice or even taking revenge.[27] Parties at enmity with each other invariably see and interpret things from different perspectives. To put it another way, a hermeneutical problem arises leading to discrepancies in the calculi that two hostile parties bring to bear on the assessment of the propriety of actions. As the *intended justice* of one party is translated by the other party into *actual injustice,* "a 'just' revenge leads to a 'just' counter-revenge." The result is a "spiral of vengeance" deriving from "the inability of the parties locked in conflict to agree on the moral significance of their actions."[28]

Undergirding all this is what Hannah Arendt calls the "predicament of irreversibility." By nature we find it difficult to countenance the hard fact that evil acts cannot be undone. No one can undo what they have done. If they could, of course, then revenge simply would not be necessary.[29] It is this predicament of irreversibility and its offense to the natural human psyche that drives people to seek revenge in the ill-conceived belief that revenge can serve to cancel a debt. Revenge, in which the victim gauges the penalty, becomes a substitute for reversibility. As Volf points out, this kind of restorative justice can never be satisfied and justice can never be its outcome because partiality means that revenge will never be mutually perceived to be right and appropriate and also because the evil act simply *cannot* be reversed. He concludes, "If the predicament of partiality puts the lid on the coffin of such justice, the predicament of irreversibility screws the lid tightly down."[30]

But why should this dilemma lead us to opt for forgiveness as opposed to a *genuine* justice—that is, a *measured,* just retribution? Clearly, a great deal must be said here. Space, however, allows me to make only a couple of comments.

One practical reason concerns the failure of "justice" to deliver what it promises—to make things *iustus,* "right." Indeed, the demands of retributive justice are no less difficult to satisfy than those of revenge. How much retribution and what kind of retribution could ever be supposed to redress the injustice of an event such as the Holocaust, for example? How could the demands of retributive justice ever be "satisfied" in the context of the murder of a child? What could it possibly mean to speak of satisfying society's, let alone the parents', desire for justice? Justice requires that the child be allowed to live his or her life fully and in peace. When that has been irretrievably denied, even the ultimate retributive act, namely the death penalty, cannot make the situation *iustus*—that is, "right." Indeed, it arguably does little more than give the last word to the social, familial, neurological, biological, and other evils that serve to create murderers.

## The Myth of the Scales

So wherein lies the universal, intuitive appeal of retributive justice? In large measure, it reposes on what I shall refer to as the "myth of the scales"—a myth sustained by a metaphor that feeds on the problem of irreversibility. A factor that all too easily leads the predicament of irreversibility to generate revenge is the tyranny of a metaphor deep within the natural psyche of human beings— the symbol of which can be seen above the High Court in London. The supreme metaphor of retributive justice, namely a set of scales, towers over it as the lord of its proceedings. Whereas the scales may be argued to denote the weighing of evidence, they are normally taken to imply that justice calculates (adds up) crimes on the one hand and balances them out by meting out just punishment on the other.[31]

To critique such a metaphor is not to deny that sometimes the damaging effects of an evil can indeed be undone at least to some degree—compensation can counterbalance the effects of very specific forms of culpable action, stolen items can be returned. But it is appropriate only in very specific kinds of contexts or where we are concerned with straightforwardly quantifiable kinds of evil and where fair, equitable, and restorative means of compensation are available—by the delivery of appropriate, quantifiable "benefits." The metaphor loses its propriety in attempts to balance out "injustice" by negative means following acts of brutality or oppression or the irreversible effects of fraud. In such contexts the metaphor can become tyrannical or, from a theological perspective, idolatrous when it prescribes counterbalancing evils—what too often amounts to revenge. In such situations the glaring problems with this metaphor come to the fore. First, it compounds the supposition that there is an objective "scale of justice" in nature that calls for evils to be balanced out by other evils, thereby implying that the second set of evils is a good. This takes the form of suggesting that if a person commits act "x," then the situation is made just by his or her receiving punishment "y." The suggestion is that there is now a debt that means an appropriate payment is "due." Evil actions become a positive currency. Indeed, they become a good. But such an approach thinly veils a mythical (Neo-Platonist) supposition of an intrinsic harmony or balance in nature that we have a duty to preserve—a supposition that the biblical concept of righteousness, however, seems to deconstruct. Can one argue that the worship of the God and Father of our Lord Jesus Christ allows (let alone requires) us to bend the knee before any such abstract set of scales—let alone identify them with the Father's righteousness? What warrant could there possibly be to suggest that there is divine ratification for the business of counting up wrongs, calculating what is due, and seeking to balance out one set of evils with another?

The second problem with this approach is the implication that evils and wrongs are reasonably tightly quantifiable—that we are in a position, therefore, to balance out a *wrong* of a certain kind with a counterbalancing evil or due payment of a quantitatively equivalent kind. But even if we are to suppose that "natural justice" dictates an eye for an eye and a tooth for a tooth,[32] what does it dictate for an act of ethnic cleansing, or a Holocaust, or mass rape? Or, much less dramatically, what could it mean in the case of the public slander and humiliation of a woman who dies utterly distraught from a resulting stress-related illness? What imaginable kind of activity could ever "restore balance" or pay what is "due" in these kinds of cases? And what kind of restoration of balance might then be interpreted as the will of God? And on what grounds? In sum, our ability to enact justice by restoring balance through the payment of retributive dues, let alone our warrant for claiming *divine endorsement* for the relevant calculi, not to mention their application, is at best limited in scope and at worst a grotesque contravention of God's righteous purposes.

In short, the metaphor of restored balance breaks down before the surdlike reality of irreversible evil. If this simply serves to point out that pragmatic arguments will be difficult to proffer, the really significant issues are not pragmatic but theological. From a theological perspective, the appeal to balance in such situations is generally sacrilegious — and its consequences are too often hideous.[33] Theologically speaking, applying the death penalty to a murderer can never make such a situation *iustus* — that is, "righteous." The simple reality is that no crimes are actually reversible and few approximate to this state. For Arendt, forgiveness alone takes seriously the realities of this brute fact.

It is important to guard against misunderstanding at this point. My argument is *not* that we should advocate reconciliation and forgiveness in place of retribution simply on account of the pragmatic problems associated with the application of retributive justice or, indeed, with perspectival discrepancies. What I am suggesting is, rather, that there are fundamental errors and dangers inherent in appeals to retributive justice. And I am also asking whether Christian thought really is compatible with the controlling metaphor lying at the heart of retributive justice — and whether its resources do not suggest the need for a radical reconstruction of the assumptions associated with retributive justice and the grammar of our penal system.

## Forgiveness and Punishment

The implication of my interpretation of the Christian faith is that it recognizes no orientation toward anyone, and this includes enemies and wrongdoers, that does not reflect unconditional forgiveness. This, however, begs an obvious question. Is there no place for punishment in a legal system interpreted from a Christian "epistemic base" or within a Christian frame of reference? What I have suggested may well be perceived as calling into question not merely excessive punishment, cycles of revenge, and the death penalty but the very institution of punishment itself. What grounds could possibly justify punishment — that is, make it "righteous"? Is there any place at all for punishment on the approach that I am advocating, and, if so, how might it look? These are questions I am addressing more fully elsewhere. For our purposes here, however, let me simply outline some basic comments.

1. Absolutely no facet of punishment can or should be a reflection or expression of hatred of the guilty. This cannot be reconciled with a Christian epistemic base as I have sought to articulate it.
2. Not only must punishment not be at odds with the unconditional affirmation of the dignity of the *guilty*—the recognition that they are forgiven "in Christ"—but it must in and of itself *affirm* that dignity. From a Christian perspective, it must speak that reality in some way.
3. A penal system must simultaneously and publicly affirm the dignity of the *victim* by exercising measures that uphold and protect both actual (present) and potential (future) *victims*. It cannot, therefore, serve to condone or, indeed, collude in the dehumanization of victims. The system must speak clearly on both counts.
4. It must affirm the dignity of *potential perpetrators* of crimes by actively discouraging them from acting in either socially destructive or dehumanizing ways. It must protect the institution of the law to the extent that it serves to uphold the dignity of all those loved by God. This is in no respect incompatible with the all-inclusive love that sustains an orientation of all-inclusive and unilateral forgiveness. Quite the contrary. It is an expression of it.
5. Finally, the state must refuse to endorse practices that, by way of their *failure* to uphold the dignity of the criminal, serve to denigrate society and dehumanize its members. When the state endorses dehumanizing modes of punishment, it dehumanizes all those to whom its practices speak. To dehumanize another is to dehumanize oneself. To the extent that a judicial system is in place positively to serve and sustain the dignity of all people, it must fulfill that task in unambiguously transparent ways in and through refusing to condone forms of punishment that are an expression of hatred of the guilty. This is integral to the state's proper function of upholding and affirming the dignity of *all* the members of society. In sum, systems of punishment must be restorative not only of the criminal but also of those dehumanized by the desire for revenge.

But is there not a conflict between these different aims—a tension that means one is undermined by attempts to meet another? How do we avoid the dangers of consequentialism where the suffering of either criminal or victim is justified by perceived benefits for the other or for potential criminals or for society as a whole? The simple answer is that to the extent that (1) a Christian epistemic base unambiguously affirms the dignity of all and (2) the dignity of all cannot be affirmed without affirming the dignity of each, all actions affirmative of the dignity of each group have positive ramifications in all directions. Consequently, this problem should not arise. In short, the problem arises only when we affirm a trade-off between the demands of the "scales of justice" and a restorative agenda. The thrust of our argument above is that there are no such scales that demand retributive evils. Consequently, there is no such trade-off.

What does this suggest about judicial practice? Clearly, custodial and similar sentences are warranted on various, interrelated grounds. First, they constitute impartial, public statements as to the intolerability of criminal acts. As should be clear from what has been argued, such statements, by the very nature of the case, do not simply *uphold* the dignity of the victim, they are integral to the positive *affirmation* of the dignity of the criminal.[34] Second, they serve the protection of innocent victims. In endorsing that, they uphold the dignity of criminals. The dignity of criminals, like that of all citizens, is affirmed in and through protecting potential victims from violence. Third, they serve the need to treat those whose social actions are destructively dysfunctional.

What becomes clear is that such systems, justified along these lines, allow for a wide range of forms of punishment/treatment and that their rationales do not need to be interpreted in terms of the principle that punishments "fit the crime" with respect to either their character[35] or their duration.[36]

## Approaching Politics from a Christian Epistemic Base: A Brief Excursus to Consider a Possible Objection

The argument so far has been to approach issues of reconciliation, forgiveness, and punishment in the sociopolitical context from a perspective shaped by Christian theological convictions. Before proceeding further, it is necessary to address, albeit briefly, a widespread objection to this kind of approach. Is it really appropriate, it may be asked, for Christians to approach issues of public policy from the particular perspective of their religious faith? Does this not involve the imposition on others of one's own particular religious views—in a world that is now multifaith, multicultural, and, in many contexts, post-Christian and secular? Worse still, does this kind of approach not open the door to endorse political sectarianism? Is it not in radical tension with the whole ideological basis of modern, liberal, and indeed liberated democracies?

Clearly, this kind of objection raises a series of issues that demands more space than we can devote to the matter here. One observation, however, is pertinent. We all determine what is or is not the case, and what should or should not happen, in the light of our beliefs and convictions. Not only is it irrational not to do so, it is not possible to avoid doing so. All of us continually and in every sphere of our lives make judgments and decisions and then act on these in a manner informed and driven by the beliefs, convictions, and values that constitute our epistemic bases. It is in the light of one's epistemic base that one assesses probabilities, likelihoods, possibilities, and the like. We have no option but to operate from these beliefs. Doing this is no more peculiar to Christians than to agnostics, atheists, humanists, and pluralists. The briefest consideration of "so-called" pluralists illustrates the point. To be a pluralist is to hold to a series of claims about what is and is not true and to what extent we can and cannot have access to the truth. To be a "pluralist" of the kind that believes not only that the world is populated by plural and diverse sets of claims but that no one has significantly more or less access to the truth than anyone else is itself to hold a position characterized by a series of (rather unusual) claims. As Gavin D'Costa has shown so convincingly, all so-called "pluralists" and "inclusivists" are, as a matter of fact, "exclusivists" to the extent that they hold a position that is logically exclusive of all contrary claims.[37] All claims are logically exclusive of contrary claims. In short, every politician, no matter how "apparently" pluralist, inclusivist, or liberal, operates—and can only operate from—an epistemic base that, if articulated, would take the form of a whole series of logically exclusive truth claims. There is no third option. It is a confused—and now largely discredited—Enlightenment myth to assume that there is some Archimedean point (or, indeed, city) that the objective, rational political philosopher or politician can inhabit whereby his or her convictions are informed and driven by purely rational and faith-free considerations. Every political and religious claim reposes on a background series of values, convictions, and beliefs. There is no neutral, belief-free position from which one can adjudicate between, for example, the ethical principles (and epistemic bases) driving the approaches of John Rawls, Robert Nozick, or Peter Singer.

In sum, the objection to people operating from a Christian epistemic base is too often driven by a confused assumption of possible "neutrality" or "detached objectivity" or the possibility of adopting a genuinely inclusivist or pluralist position. To be a Christian is to believe that God exists and has purposefully created the contingent order and those who populate it *with a purpose.*

For Christians not to allow that conviction to inform their whole sociopolitical and ethical worldview would be the height of irrationality. It would be for them to lay aside the most significant interpretative tool they have.

But does this not open the door to the implication that all epistemic bases are equally true or acceptable? Emphatically not. To say that there is no Archimedean point and that it is irrational for people not to make recourse to their epistemic bases when making judgments is not in any way to suggest that their beliefs are true or true to the same degree as those of others. It is also not to assume that their beliefs and epistemic bases might not change.

If one is a Christian and actually believes that God not only exists but affirms and upholds the dignity and value of all persons, be they young or old, women or men, Christian or Muslim, poor or rich, not only is it impossible not to allow one's whole value system to be informed by that, but it is confused folly to think one should not allow those convictions to inform one's approach to the world.

Finally, it is relevant to note that a Christian epistemic base informed by the all-inclusive love of God involves the unambiguous endorsement of the dignity of all persons. Intrinsic to it is the categorical imperative that we value and affirm the dignity of all people, whatever their epistemic base or religious views. This means there is unambiguous warrant for respecting them, for listening to them, and for not marginalizing them by ignoring their convictions and concerns. In short, Christian claims, precisely by virtue of their being logically exclusive truth claims, articulate a radically *inclusive* approach to persons of all faiths and backgrounds. And if we cease to believe in God and God's unconditional covenant love for all persons, it is less than clear that the obligation to respect all persons retains its warrant.

So how does a politician whose approach is informed by a Christian epistemic base actually operate in the secular political context? Clearly, one functions by using arguments. These arguments may be chosen to appeal to foreign epistemic bases in such a way that one presupposes some kind of intersection of different approaches on significant practical matters. One will operate in pragmatic ways using arguments that may be less convincing from one's perspective but will be more convincing to others. At the same time, there will also be occasions when one simply paints things as one sees them in the hope that, by God's creative presence, others may be given the eyes to see the truth that one is affirming. One may argue for forgiveness, as Tutu did, in the conviction that opponents will glimpse the light and healing that attends it and the humanity of those who have the courage and magnanimity to live it.

## Is Forgiveness Ethical? Revenge, Retribution, and the Problem of Honor

It is now appropriate to turn to consider a different kind of objection to the political endorsement of forgiveness from a Christian epistemic base. My earlier arguments about the form of God's involvement in the world and our participation in this sought to suggest that any controlling recourse to the "myth of the scales" (as this has served to underwrite a retributive approach to justice in the public realm) stands in radical tension with the nature and character of God's Self-disclosure.

An implication of my underlying argument is that there is a thin (if not indistinguishable) line between "just" retribution (conceived as an attempt to satisfy the insatiable hunger for reversibility in contexts of injustice) and revenge. However, it might be objected that the rhetorical drawing of parallels between retributive justice and revenge can cut two ways. Rather than suggesting that we should reject the principle undergirding models of retributive justice, it may serve to suggest that we should acknowledge factors inherent in the ethics of revenge. And it is to this issue that I now turn. In his book written in response to the Balkan crisis, *The Warrior's Honor: Ethnic War and the Modern Conscience*, Michael Ignatieff argues that a highly significant virtue underlies and motivates revenge, namely "keeping faith with the dead." He writes:

> The chief moral obstacle in the path of reconciliation is the desire for revenge. Now, revenge is commonly regarded as a low and unworthy emotion, and because it is regarded as such, its deep moral hold on people is rarely understood. But revenge—morally considered—is a desire to keep faith with the dead, to honor their memory by taking up their cause where they left off. Revenge keeps faith between generations; the violence it engenders is a ritual form of respect for the community's dead—therein lies its legitimacy. Reconciliation is difficult precisely because it must compete with the powerful alternative morality of violence. Political terror is tenacious because it is an ethical practice. It is a cult of the dead, a dire and absolute expression of respect.[38]

What this suggests is that if we are to address appropriately the concern for justice that drives the culture of retaliation and counter-retaliation, two issues must be confronted. The first concerns respect for the dead—the desire that those who have given their lives and all the future opportunities and loves and joys that lay before them for a cause should not have done so in vain. The second (which space does not allow us to consider here but which has been discussed extensively by Miroslav Volf and Gregory Jones) concerns the healing of memory. Suffice it to say, these issues go hand in hand. To seek reconciliation is to seek at-one-ment, and there can be no atonement if one party sees itself as having betrayed the sacrifices of its kith and kin, as having sold out on the costly sacrifice of friends and relatives. Nor can there be atonement without the healing of memory—a healing that must transcend the simple fading of memory—forgetfulness—or the annihilation of memories through death.

The question of respect for those who have suffered, most notably those who are now dead and are no longer in a position to initiate forgiveness, is perhaps the dilemma that, more than any other, constitutes the stumbling block to the prioritization of forgiveness in the sociopolitical arena. The nub of the problem concerns who has the right to forgive whom. Are we in a position to forgive evils perpetrated against others? If we were to speak of forgiving Serbs for atrocities they have committed, what conceivable right could we have (as Scots or Irish or Americans) to forgive Serbs for atrocities committed against Bosnians? Is it not Bosnians alone who can forgive? Moreover, if only Bosnians have a right to forgive, do the living have the right to forgive the perpetrators of those atrocities, or is it not those against whom the atrocities were committed who alone have the exclusive right to forgive? If the living forgive atrocities perpetrated against the dead, is that not a betrayal of respect for the dead? Dostoyevsky articulates precisely this issue when Ivan Karamazov argues, "I do not want a mother to embrace the torturer who had her child torn to pieces by his dogs. She has no right to forgive him."[39]

To repeat, by way of summary, is forgiveness issued by anyone other than the victim not an illegitimate appropriation of what is the victim's and the victim's alone to offer? Does this not constitute, indeed, the supreme form of dishonor, namely to offer on behalf of those who have been brutalized and are now dead something that is theirs to offer and that they themselves may not have wished to be offered?[40] If there is no resolution to what is clearly an ethical dilemma, then any reference to forgiveness whatsoever in the aftermath of war and conflict is going to be vacuous at best, and at worst the instigation of a further evil against the dignity of the voiceless dead.

No one has articulated this question more poignantly or more tellingly than Simon Wiesenthal in his profoundly moving book *The Sunflower: On the Possibilities and Limits of Forgiveness*. The book opens by reminding us, albeit briefly, of some of the unthinkable horrors that Simon Wiesenthal witnessed in a Nazi concentration camp—the endless sadistic games of the SS men who would swoop down on helpless prisoners and bully them for their amusement. He refers to "the pipe"—a long, caged corridor into which prisoners were herded when they were too weak or ill to work. There they would be left by the SS until there were sufficient numbers to make it worth their while to take them away and shoot them. Wiesenthal's friend Adam sprained his ankle at work, was spotted limping, and was forced to wait in the pipe for two days before he and the rest of the group were finally taken away and executed.[41] The focus of the book, however, concerns the events surrounding a particular work detail. Wiesenthal and his group were marched out of the camp to help dispose of the waste in a local hospital. The route took them past a cemetery for German soldiers who had died in action. Not only did the graves have gravestones denoting who the relevant soldiers were, but on each was planted a sunflower. These held Wiesenthal spellbound. "The flower heads seemed to absorb the sun's rays like mirrors and draw them down into the darkness of the ground. . . . [B]utterflies fluttered from flower to flower. . . . Suddenly I envied the dead soldiers. Each had a sunflower to connect him with the living world, and butterflies to visit his grave. For me there would be no sunflower. I would be buried in a mass grave, where corpses would be piled on top of me. No sunflower would ever bring light into my darkness, and no butterflies would dance above my dreadful tomb."[42]

When the young Wiesenthal arrived at the hospital, a nurse approached him and asked him to confirm that he was a Jew. She then led him through the hospital and into a private room where there lay a man dying of wounds he had sustained in battle. He had been blinded and his head was completely concealed by bandages. The nurse left Wiesenthal and shut the door. The patient, it turned out, was an SS soldier who had been involved in an appalling atrocity. On his deathbed, he found himself overwhelmed with guilt and wanted a Jew to offer him forgiveness so he could die in peace. Over the following hours, the twenty-one-year-old SS man detailed the events in which he had been involved. In the city of Dnepropetrovsk, in what is now the Ukraine, the SS had herded nearly two hundred Jews, many of whom were children, into a building in which they had placed drums of gasoline. The doors were then locked and the SS men ordered to circle the building, throw hand grenades through the windows and then stand with rifles at the ready to shoot anyone who tried to escape. As flames licked the building and cries were heard from within, the young soldier noticed a man with a small child in his arms standing behind the windows of the second floor. His clothes were alight. By his side stood a woman, doubtless the mother of the child. With his free hand the man covered the child's eyes as if to hide the scene from his child. He then jumped into the street, followed seconds later by her, only to be shot by the SS.[43]

The man insisted on describing every detail, hiding nothing, in the desperate hope that he might receive forgiveness for all these acts and thereby find the peace he craved. Wiesenthal sat silently and feeling helpless. Between the SS man's folded hands there seemed to rest a sunflower. Finally he made his decision and left the room without uttering a word.[44] The next day the SS man died. Wiesenthal returned to the camp haunted by the episode and by the question as to whether he should have uttered a word of forgiveness. Indeed, the question has remained with Wiesenthal ever since, and the book was written with the intention of asking whether he was right and whether such a situation does denote the boundary or limit of forgiveness. The fundamental question posed concerns quite simply whether Wiesenthal had the *right* to forgive the SS man. He was in a position to forgive SS men for the daily suffering they were causing him—but could he forgive on behalf of those victims who were now dead—anonymous bodies who did not even receive the acknowledgment and dignity of a grave, let alone a sunflower? His final decision was that it was not his place to offer forgiveness on their behalf.

How do we respond? If Wiesenthal is right, then there can be no forgiveness or advocacy of forgiveness of the most tragic and divisive events in the histories of those contexts that most require it—the Balkans, Rwanda, Northern Ireland, and so on. And if there can be no *forgiveness* without selling out the dead, how can there ever be genuine *reconciliation* without selling out the dead? How can there be a reconciliation that heals the memory of atrocities and injustices perpetrated against those no longer here to forgive on their own behalf? The connection between Wiesenthal's dilemma and Michael Ignatieff's analysis of the spiral of vengeance should be clear—both concern a fundamentally ethical dilemma, namely how we honor victims, most notably those no longer with us.

Precisely this issue was a source of concern to Plato, as we discover in the *Phaedo*. Toward the end of the book he discusses the myth of the four rivers of the underworld. If someone has murdered another in a fit of passion "and yet [has] lived thereafter a life of repentance" he and those like him will be cast into Tartarus. After a year, they will find themselves swept along to a point near the Acherusian Lake, where "they call to those whom they have slain or despitefully used, begging and beseeching them that they would suffer them to come forth into the lake and give them a hearing. If they can prevail, they do come forth, and find an end to their trouble; but if not, they are swept back into Tartarus, and thence into the rivers again; nor can they ever have respite from their woes until they prevail upon those whom they have injured; for such is the penalty appointed by their judges."[45] For Plato, in other words, justice requires that forgiveness be the exclusive prerogative of the victim, and remain so for all eternity.

The question I wish to raise here is whether Christian theology has any distinctive resources that address this dilemma—a dilemma that not only restricts the right to forgive to the one against whom the offense has been committed but, at least as significantly, makes it exclusive to that *element* of the offense that relates to the particular victim. Most crimes, of course, affect not only the primary victim but a host of secondary victims, not least those by whom the primary victim is loved. This means, for example, that the victim of a rape could forgive the rapist for the act perpetrated against her but would not be in a position to forgive the rapist for the suffering that that same crime had caused her family. Similarly, her family would clearly not be in a position to forgive him for the crime he had committed against her. The family could only ever forgive him for the suffering that he had caused them. For either the rape victim's family or the rape victim herself to forgive beyond what it was their particular right to forgive would be to perpetrate a further evil. It would be to offend further the rights of the respective victim(s) by appropriating what was theirs and theirs alone to forgive. But the ethics of the situation becomes still more complex. If the family members of a rape victim were to forgive the dimension of the offense that was an offense against them, could they do so independently of their daughter's or sister's forgiveness of the perpetrator? If they did, would that not be to deny that what remained an offense against the victim continued to be an offense against them until the former offense was forgiven? Would there not be, in effect, a principle of solidarity that would have to be acknowledged whereby the forgiveness of every victim would have to be contingent upon the forgiveness of the perpetrator by every other victim?

These problems pose the question as to whether any act of forgiveness can ever avoid ethical compromise. More significantly for this essay, however, they concern whether forgiveness can have any kind of ethical legitimacy in the sociopolitical context. The implication would be that no one can ever be in a position to forgive the Nazi perpetrators of the Holocaust, or those associated with the Rwandan atrocities, or the Serbian *cetniks,* or Islamic extremist terrorists, or Loyalist or Republican terrorists in Northern Ireland. They simply do not have the right to do so. This is not because they have never been victims and cannot identify with their plight. Rather, it is because they are not *those particu-*

*lar* victims and did not suffer *those particular* crimes. Clearly, those who endured Nazi concentration camps would be in no more of a position to forgive those who suffered at the hands of the Hutus or the Serbian *cetniks* than the rest of us. If, of course, there is and can be no forgiveness, then to put past injustices to rest constitutes ethical apathy or callousness—features that erode the moral standing of a state or community.

The issue here, moreover, raises substantial theological questions—questions that concern the fundamental legitimacy of the doctrine of the atonement and penetrate to the heart of the scope or compass of divine forgiveness. When forgiveness from sin is pronounced, does this apply simply to the dimension of sin against others that constitutes an offense against God? Or does it suggest that we are forgiven by God for sins committed against other human beings? If so, on what grounds can we assume that it makes ethical sense for God to be construed as forgiving sins that are sins against other human beings? Does this not involve a violation on God's part of a prerogative that belongs exclusively to the relevant human victims? If this is the case with forgiveness, does it not raise further questions as to whether reconciliation can ultimately be even *God's* to offer? To raise this question is to ask whether divine reconciliation can have any relevance whatsoever at the horizontal level. Is there reconciliation in the Kingdom of God, or is this conditional upon the forgiveness by every victim of every perpetrator of injustice, as Plato suggests? In sum, the question of the potential of forgiveness, to have sociopolitical significance, is irreducibly bound up with the question as to whether the atonement can ever (even in eternity) liberate us from the horizontal dimension of sin. Can it ever have any relevance for sins against other human beings?

## Forgiveness as Participation? A Proposal for a Christian Solution to This Dilemma

The question I wish to pose concerns whether the Incarnation may serve to address this problem—and do so in a way that provides theological warrant for advocating forgiveness in the political realm. My thesis will be that the doctrine of Christ's vicarious humanity, together with the pneumatological element intrinsic to it, constitutes precisely such grounds. Moreover, I shall suggest that this testifies to a profound and radical distinction between approaches to the most difficult political and diplomatic issues of our day that are grounded in a Christian epistemic base and those that are not. Whereas a Christian epistemic base can endorse acts of forgiveness that possess profound significance both internationally and intranationally, operating from a non-Christian epistemic base will leave politics seeking to address an irresolvable dilemma—how to serve peace without being inexcusably ethically compromised.

The faith of the church worldwide affirms that God became incarnate as a marginalized Jew and that he vicariously took to himself the suffering of the sinned against—the brutality, the physical and psychological (even sexual)[46] abuse, the sadism, torture, mockery, and inconceivably painful death associated with crucifixion. As the One on behalf of the many and the One in whom the many participate, the eternal Son becomes one with human victims as *Immanuel* (God-with-us), identifying with them to such an extent that he can say, "In as much as you have done it unto the least of these, you have done it unto me." The implication is that sin against a fellow human is not simply sin against human beings (horizontal sin) and then, additionally and in parallel, sin against God (vertical sin)—suggesting two different and distinct objects and two different and distinct kinds of sin. Rather, the sin against the human victim must be seen as sin against God conceived as one and the same object as the victim. And it also must be seen as the same sin against both. In short, the sin against the victim, christologically and pneumatologically conceived, is identical—both as the particular act that it is and with respect to its particular human object—with sin against God. The vicarious humanity of Christ effects an appropriate and valid forgiveness on both the horizontal and the vertical plane.

At the heart of the Christian faith, therefore, stands not simply an "ethic of forgiveness" generating exhortations to forgive. (As we have seen, this could only involve an advocacy of forgiveness that, in order to be ethical, would necessarily have extremely limited and somewhat egocentric reference and compass.) Rather, what is presented is an ontology of forgiveness. In the crucified God we have the One who alone is entitled to forgive on behalf of the victim (both the primary and the secondary victim) because the victim is "in him" and he "in the victim." But not only does he, in forgiving, do what he is entitled to do, he does it as the one who does not dishonor the victim in this act but upholds the eternal dignity of the victim—not least that of victims now dead. Indeed, for reasons that should be clear, God's forgiveness can be seen to be intrinsic to upholding and affirming the dignity of the victim, since only God's unconditional love and forgiveness can ultimately expose, affirm, and address the full evil of the offense for what it is, namely an eternal offense, as Nietzsche so pertinently insists.[47] What we are suggesting is that only God is in a position to forgive in a manner that upholds the dignity of the victim and only the incarnate God can forgive justly.

Does this, however, not risk universalizing Christ's humanity in a way that fails to take seriously the particularity of suffering and thus the particularity of forgiveness? Does it not serve to trivialize the pain of the victim and the specific obligations laid on the victimizer? Does it not lead to a cheapening of grace and forgiveness? Two brief comments: first, the Christian understanding of Christ's vicarious humanity does *not* suggest that Christ represents either humanity in general or some universal form of humanity in which we participate.[48] Rather, the Pauline concept of participation (that is, of *metechein* and *koinonein*) suggests that the victim means more to the incarnate Son than the victim means to him- or herself[49] and that, in and through the Spirit (the *ens concretissimum*),[50] the incarnate Son identifies concretely with the particular pain and suffering of the particular victim. The divine *agape* attaches ultimate significance to the particularity of persons, and the significance of Christ's vicarious humanity lies precisely in the fact that it confirms the full significance of this.

If, by contrast, there were no resources intrinsic to the faith that served to address this issue, then we would be obliged to affirm that God could forgive only, as God, sins against the divine will and those elements of sin that constitute sin against God, or, as the particular human Jesus, sins perpetrated exclusively against that particular historical individual. Were that the case, the doctrines of the atonement and reconciliation would be evacuated of all horizontal significance whatsoever. Only by virtue of Christ's vicarious humanity—the doctrine of the One standing in on behalf of the many and the One in whom the many victims subsist—do we discover the two forms of liberation that are intrinsic to atonement: first, liberation as victimizers for our sin of victimization; and second, liberation as victims from the bitterness and hatred that attend the sense of irreversible injustice, the hurt of damaged lives, irretrievably lost opportunities, and all the other evils that result from sin. There is liberation here because precisely at the point where we cannot forgive our enemies the Gospel suggests that our sole representative, the sole priest of our confession, does what we cannot do—stands in and forgives our victimizers for us and in our place as the One on behalf of the many—and then invites us to participate in that forgiveness that he has realized vicariously on our behalf.

On these grounds we are not only permitted to forgive but obliged and indeed commanded to forgive others—and that means all others. Where *we* are not entitled to forgive, the crucified Rabbi is. And where we are unable to forgive, we are given to participate in his once-and-for-all forgiveness and to live our lives in that light and from that center—not least in the political realm.

J. B. Torrance has defined worship as "the gift of participating by the Spirit in the Son's communion with the Father." Any ethics that warrants the title *Christian* must be conceived in parallel terms, namely as the gift of participating by the Spirit in the incarnate Son's communion with the Father. I am arguing here that forgiveness is the gift of participating in a triune event of forgiveness. In an act of forgiveness, the Father sends the Son, who, by the Spirit, forgives as God but also, by the Spirit, as the *eschatos Adam* on behalf of humanity. The mandate to forgive must be understood in this light.

This means that the Christian learner (Gk. *mathetes*—usually translated as "disciple") is brought to recognize no sociopolitical ethic that does not ultimately need to be construed as the gift of participation in the divine life and that is not, therefore, an ethic of unconditional, unilateral faithfulness and forgiveness. As such, forgiveness does not concern an abstruse, amorphous ethical principle or ideal with practical psychological or political relevance. Rather, it denotes concrete participation by grace in God's unconditional forgiveness of enemies that, to the extent that they are ours, are also his but whom he also loves and forgives.[51] It is in this light that the profound difference emerges between approaching the problems of political alienation and social guilt from a Christian epistemic base and approaching them from a non-Christian one.

## The Diachronic Perpetuation of Evil—Waskow and Tutu

One obvious area where a Christian approach may have particular relevance concerns the ongoing, diachronic dimension of human evil. In support of Wiesenthal's decision not to offer a word of forgiveness, Arthur Waskow considers what he would say if he were to meet the young SS man today. He would say, "There is no way for you to repair the rips and tears in relationship that have left the Jewish people still struggling to be able to trust, connect, make peace, to govern itself responsibly with its new-found power in the world. And, in terms of Spirit, there is no way for you to repair our sense of God in hiding. I may be able to make these repairs for myself (at least the ones in Relationship and Spirit); we Jews may be able together to do these for ourselves; but not with you. You can take no part in these . . . repairs. So I cannot 'forgive' you."[52]

Waskow's exclusive stance is a powerful and impressively honest articulation of the fact that evil acts extend across the decades and continue to oppress their victims. This takes us to the heart of the challenge. Three elements in Waskow's response warrant comment. First, may it not be that the responsible use of power (responsible government) is a consequence of the ability to forgive, the supreme gift to the one who is inconceivably and inexplicably liberated to forgive? Second, is it not through forgiveness alone that the internal repairs of which he speaks begin to take place—both at the social level, as evidenced so remarkably in South Africa, and at the personal level?[53] And, third, are these questions not perhaps tragically bound up with the loss of the sense of God's concrete presence of which he speaks so honestly—the perception that "God is in hiding," as he puts it? To this one asks, what would be the significance of the rabbi's perception of Immanuel alongside the hanging boy, as recounted so movingly by Eli Wiesel in *Night*? What would such a recognition mean for the question whether the Lord *is* in hiding? And what would that response mean for Israel's identification as uniquely chosen to be the suffering servant of YHWH—elected, moreover, as Deutero-Isaiah has it, to witness to the Gentiles that God's covenant faithfulness *(hesed)* includes them? It is not for a Gentile, however, to provide an answer. The question is whether anyone other than the crucified Rabbi can ultimately speak into this situation. It is neither to judge nor to condemn Waskow to observe that the inevitable and poignant consequence of his rejecting the language of forgiveness can only ultimately lead us to cling to "myths" of retributive justice, to exclusive withdrawal, and to a psychotherapeutic approach to healing.

Desmond Tutu's response to Wiesenthal's question stands in stark contrast to Waskow's. As chair of the Truth and Reconciliation Commission, he heard sustained testimony to appalling brutality and injustice. Replying to Wiesenthal's "What would you have done?" he refuses to answer for himself, choosing rather to refer humbly to another.

Our President, Nelson Mandela, was incarcerated for twenty-seven years and not mollycoddled. His eyesight has been ruined because he had to work in the glare of a quarry; his family was harassed by the state security police. He should by rights be consumed by bitterness and a lust for revenge. The world watched with awe when he so magnanimously invited his white jailer to his inauguration as South Africa's first democratically elected president. I could tell of others, both black and white and less well known, who if asked, "What would you have done?" would have done the same—they have forgiven amazingly, unbelievably. Many claim to be Christians. They say they follow the Jewish rabbi who, when he was crucified, said, "Father, forgive them for they know not what they do." I sit and marvel at it all as I preside over the process of seeking to bring healing and reconciliation to a deeply divided, wounded and traumatized nation.

He concludes: "It is clear that if we look only to retributive justice, then we could just as well close up shop. Forgiveness is not some nebulous thing. It is practical politics. Without forgiveness, there is no future."[54]

What led Tutu to make this affirmation was the fact that he grasped with profound clarity the difference between evangelical and legal repentance. Nowhere does this become more plain than in Antjie Krog's remarkable documentation of the Truth and Reconciliation Commission, the inner logic of its approach and of Tutu's contribution to its success.[55]

Krog bears witness to the logic of what we are terming evangelical repentance at different levels. Let me mention two examples. The first is the remarkable account of the way Tutu handled Winnie Mandela. Despite the extensive testimony presented against Winnie Mandela that documented various atrocious acts, she categorically refused to admit to having done anything wrong. Repentance was nowhere on the horizon. Precisely at the point where the entire credibility of the commission seemed to be being placed in question, Tutu rose to his feet and, offering genuine and unqualified public affirmation of her dignity and honor, walked over toward her, holding his arms as if to embrace her, with the words "I speak to you as someone who loves you very deeply" and then pled with her to admit that "things had indeed gone wrong." She responded by confessing, finally, that "things went horribly wrong" and continued, "For that I am deeply sorry."[56] In unconditional affirmation of her, Tutu had created a space[57] for repentance—a *metanoia* that was a response to the loving and forgiving endorsement of her dignity despite all that she had done. What this evoked was a moment of truthfulness and confession that the presentation of law, judgment, and condemnation could never have achieved. Precisely this same logic of repentance is affirmed negatively in Krog's penetrating observation that "whites prefer to think that they are being hated; then they don't need to change."[58]

The second example in the book is the effect that the expansive attitude of forgiveness and reconciliation of Tutu and the Truth and Reconciliation Commission (in Xhosa, "The Truth and Forgiveness Commission")[59] had on the author herself. Concluding with some personal reflections, Krog, a white Afrikaner, testifies to the sense of liberation and extreme pride it enabled her to take in the new South Africa. Most significantly, it took the form of an all-embracing desire to seek forgiveness and to be with those whom her people had oppressed. This liberating pride and delight stemmed from her having met in them such profound depths of forgiveness.[60]

In sum, the Truth and Reconciliation Commission witnessed to the redemptive, creative, and transformative effect of forgiveness. This is a forgiveness that heals while simultaneously honoring past victims precisely by bringing their history into a redemptive and creative movement toward what the Christian faith calls *koinonia*—a communion that transcends the categories of "justice" by elevating a righteousness that the conceptions of neither *lex* nor contract *(foedus)* could generate or anticipate.

## Conclusion

When, with Tutu, we have the courage to interpret God's koinonial purposes for humanity and thus the place of forgiveness in these purposes in the light of God's Self-disclosure as Jesus Christ, we glimpse something of the transformative dynamic of which the Gospel speaks—a dynamic that, as grounded in the divine life, the Spirit sustains and honors in the sociopolitical sphere. What this requires of Western religion, however, is that it break with the contract God, the nature-grace model, and the justice-justification approach together with all the associated conditionalities. Only then can we begin to grasp the social and anthropological logic and relevance of grace—that it transforms, heals, and redeems contexts of sociopolitical hostility and, in and through this, strengthens the law. In short, justice is served precisely where forgiveness is no longer seen as needing to be conditioned by its object and is liberated to become unconditional with respect to its object.

By contrast, the traditional tendency has been to stress the priority of justice over forgiveness in the fear that otherwise the ends of justice will be short-circuited. The irony is that the controlling fear here all too easily means that neither is served. The concern for justice begets violence, the desire for retribution begets revenge, and evil increases exponentially. As Volf and Welker argue, forgiveness enthrones justice; it draws attention to its violation precisely by offering to forego its claims.[61] But not only that, it exposes injustice for what it is. Whereas legal repentance diminishes the nature of their offenses in the eyes of the perpetrators, undermines the sense of sin, and thus demeans the law, evangelical repentance upholds it—just as YHWH's forgiving faithfulness sustains the *torah* and its obligations and thus exposes the form of life from which we need to be delivered, of which we need to repent, and with respect to which *metanoia* is God's ongoing, reconciling work. In sum, God redeems by way of the righteousness that sustains evangelical repentance—and God does so in the sociopolitical context too.

In sum, the church is never more sociopolitically relevant than when it has the courage to be itself, to think out of its own center, to act from what it knows. When it does that, it has something relevant to say in contexts of alienation, oppression, racism, sexism, and the national and ethnic polarization that have so haunted the last decade. Simultaneously, it is never more obviously irrelevant than when it seeks to endorse common ground (that is, what everyone "knows") and seeks to justify its own existence by defining its own mission with recourse to what it does not need to contribute to public knowledge.

During a year that I spent at the University of Notre Dame, the route to and from my office took me past a car with a bumper sticker that read "If you want peace, strive for justice." Every day this prompted questions in my mind. At one level it is profoundly true—it can be both distortive and destructive to advocate peace in contexts of oppression, exploitation, or racism. Love without a concern for "justice" is mere sentimentality. At the same time, appeals to justice too easily forget that perspectives can be "out of sync": they can speak of condemnation and even self-righteously use the law to condemn, so that the law becomes the strength of sin. That to which the Christian faith points penetrates so much deeper than impersonal appeals to *"iustitia."* The justice that the Gospel knows is a righteousness that transcends universalizable legislation, just as the peace to which it testifies transcends the absence of strife. The sticker might have read, "If you want peace, strive for righteousness." The righteousness that is participation in the righteousness of YHWH affirms the dignity of the oppressed as well as that of the oppressor, it honors the dishonored as well as the guilty, and in all of this it strives for forgiveness—a forgiveness that transforms the oppressor's perception of the oppressed and vice versa. And the peace that this "justice" generates is no mere absence of strife but the positive and all-embracing *koinonia* to which the word *shalom* refers.

The apostle Paul described participation in the divine life as "being true in love" *(aletheuein en agape).* As such, it involves sharing in a dynamic of forgiveness that transforms and reschematizes us for the discernment of truth. Though vulnerable and open to abuse, this way of *being true* to our enemies in love serves to reconcile diverse perspectives, change perceptions, and heal memories. In these ways it describes a political realism by which God not only delivers human history from its brokenness but redeems, renews, and re-creates it, opening up possibilities that would otherwise be inconceivable.

# Notes

Much of this material was originally given in a paper to a conference on reconciliation organised by ECONI (now known as the Centre for Contemporary Christianity in Ireland) on October 25, 2003, in Belfast.

1. For a detailed, balanced, and in-depth analysis of the difficulties, debates, and dilemmas surrounding the modus operandi of the South African Truth and Reconciliation Commission, see the essay by Mark Amstutz in this volume (ch. 6).

2. One of the impressive features of recent papal encyclicals on anthropological and ethical issues has been his commitment to doing precisely this. Pope John Paul II's encyclical letter *Evangelium Vitae* is particularly noteworthy in this regard.

3. Here I am referring to the Greek words that the apostle Paul uses in Rom. 12:2.

4. 1 John 4:20.

5. The following discussion of covenant and contract summarizes James B. Torrance's (my father's) research published in the *Scottish Journal of Theology* and elsewhere. Material cited in this section can be found in the following: "Covenant and Contract: A Study of the Theological Background of Worship in Seventeenth-Century Scotland," *Scottish Journal of Theology* 23 (1970): 51–76, "The Concept of Federal Theology: Was Calvin a Federal Theologian?" in *Calvinus Sacrae Scripturae Professor,* ed. Wilhelm H. Neuser (Grand Rapids, MI: William B. Eerdmans, 1994), 15–40, and "The Contribution of McLeod Campbell to Scottish Theology," *Scottish Journal of Theology* 26 (1973): 295–311. See also his book *Worship, Community and the Triune God of Grace* (Downer's Grove, IL: InterVarsity Press, 1996).

6. This section continues to summarize and develop James Torrance's argument as found in the articles cited above.

7. This is not to deny that breach of contract constitutes serious problems in the real world. See, for example, O. Hart and J. Moore, "Theory of Debt Based on the Inalienability of Human Capital," *Quarterly Journal of Economics* 109 (1994): 841–79. As Nancy Cartwright summarizes, "The central idea behind the model is that crucial aspects of debt contracts are determined by the fact that entrepreneurs cannot be locked into contracts but may withdraw with only small (in their model *no*) penalties other than loss of the project's assets. That means that some debt contracts may be unenforceable and hence inefficiency may result." *The Dappled World: A Study of the Boundaries of Science* (New York: Cambridge University Press, 1999), 145–46.

8. Any such attempt generates a regressive circularity, as I discuss in "The Self-Relation, Narcissism and the Gospel of Grace," *Scottish Journal of Theology* 40 (1987): 481–510.

9. This self-giving generosity includes the presence of the Spirit who gives us the eyes to recognize this grace.

10. The law is fulfilled in loving God and our neighbors as ourselves. Moreover, we love God because he first loved us—and *can* love to the extent that we are brought to perceive through the Spirit (and by that same love) that he first loved us.

11. Oliver O'Donovan, *Resurrection and Moral Order: An Outline for Evangelical Ethics* (Grand Rapids, MI: William B. Eerdmans, 1986).

12. I should add that in 1831 the General Assembly of the Church of Scotland found him guilty of heresy and he was removed from his cure.

13. Murray Rae, *By Faith Transformed: Kierkegaard's Vision of the Incarnation* (Oxford: Clarendon Press, 1997).

14. This was a group of theologians who were united around Thomas Boston and his enthusiasm for a work entitled *The Marrow of Modern Divinity.* This was published in the early seventeenth century and proved anathema to the legalistic orientation of the 1720 General Assembly of the Church of Scotland, who consequently condemned the book as heretical and antinomian.

15. Paul expressly wished he could give up his own salvation for that of his own people. Cf. Rom. 9:3.

16. Intrinsic to Paul's argument is an "I, yet not I" character of the Christian life— "I live, yet not I, Christ lives in me." Cf. Gal. 2:20.

17. Luke 19:1–10.

18. Kenneth Bailey, *Poet and Peasant* (Grand Rapids, MI: William B. Eerdmans, 1976). See ch. 6 for a detailed exposition of the cultural implications of Luke 15.

19. Ibid., 181.

20. Cf. Rom. 12:2, "Be transformed (*Metamorphousthe*) for the discernment of truth and do not be schematized by the secular order (*Me suschematizesthe*)!" The imperative needs to be construed as a performative utterance—that is, as an utterance made in such a way as to engender the intended result. "Be transformed!" is not instructing us to turn in upon ourselves and engage in self-transformation. Like "Repent!" it serves to effect what it intends but also in such a way that what is intended is simultaneously communicated—much as when a parent exhorts her child with the words "Wake up!" No parent thinks that the child can hear these words in her sleep and then determine to wake herself up.

21. This is an issue I explored in an article on the sociopolitical ramifications of forgiveness, entitled "Forgiveness," *Journal of Theology for Southern Africa,* no. 56 (September 1986): 47–59.

22. Cf. John McLeod Campbell, *The Nature of the Atonement* (Grand Rapids, MI: William B. Eerdmans, 1996).

23. By *methodological naturalism,* I mean the assumption of "naturalism" in our methods of political analysis, interpretation, and planning. Philosophical naturalism assumes that God does not exist and that it is inappropriate, therefore, to allow any consideration of the nature and purposes of God to feature in the business of political analysis and interpretation.

24. St Anselm, *Cur Deus Homo,* bk. 1, ch. 12 (p. 25). See also pp. 26, 46, and 60.

25. Although such an approach is argued to be more honoring of the victim than one that forgives, precisely the opposite is the case.

26. Miroslav Volf, *Exclusion and Embrace: A Theological Exploration of Identity, Otherness and Reconciliation* (Nashville, TN: Abingdon Press, 1996), 121.

27. The whole point of the predicament of partiality is that, as human beings, we are invariably blind to an objective, detached, neutral perception of complex historical situations. We always interpret events, see events "from a perspective." We can see that perspective for what it is only when we are given a new perspective—and that is not something we can give ourselves. The concept of "natural justice" will invariably struggle to offer a way out of this predicament—it presumes that we have an ability objectively to assess and to weigh up all the relevant natural evils in a situation. It is not clear that this is possible either for individuals or for society as a whole. History offers a plethora of illustrations of genuinely collective blindness—to the evils of torture, slavery, classism, racism, patriarchy, and the oppression of women. Future generations will operate with perspectives from which they will doubtless be able to assess the blindnesses that characterize our present perspectives.

28. Volf, *Exclusion and Embrace*, 121.

29. Hannah Arendt, *The Human Condition: A Study of the Central Dilemmas Facing Modern Man* (Garden City, NY: Doubleday, 1959), 212 ff., cited in ibid.

30. Volf, *Exclusion and Embrace*, 122.

31. An interesting question emerges at this point as to whether the view that the suffering intrinsic to punishment is a means to such an end makes retributivism a form of consequentialism where the end, to which it is a means, is the restoration of nature to its proper balance. To avoid this, therefore, they have to hold that the punishment (and the suffering that attends it) is *intrinsically* good.

32. It is important to note here that the intention of this injunction in the Old Testament may well have been to stop revenge, meaning that only one tooth should be taken as a retributive punishment for losing a tooth and not a set of teeth.

33. Under tragic circumstances, a friend of ours was appointed to a position in a British Embassy in Southeast Asia. She was appointed to replace a young man who had returned to the United Kingdom with his wife and son. The reason for this was that he had been out for a drive with his family when his car hit a young girl who ran out in front of them. He stopped to help the girl, who was unconscious. A crowd gathered, mistakenly assumed that the young girl was dead, and determined that, as the driver responsible, he should be punished accordingly. Consequently, they dragged his young daughter from the car and cut her throat. A short while later the girl who had been knocked down revived. Would a final balancing of the scales of justice require taking of the life of the child of the hasty executioner?

34. See McAdams's fascinating discussion, in ch. 5 of this volume, of Gauck's view that "the exposure of wrongdoing and clarification of murky events from the GDR past may actually constitute a blessing for the perpetrators." Through the appropriate pursuit of justice by the state (and public truth telling in *certain* circumstances may be

integral to this), the dignity of the perpetrator of past injustices stands to be affirmed. As Gauck notes, it is possible, indeed, for the process to be liberative for the guilty. That having been said, it is possible for "truth telling" to constitute a form of revenge—a means of the deliberate and destructive humiliation of the guilty. Such an approach is no more liberative of the victim than of the guilty. Here, by contrast, the relevance of Schorlemmer's vision of justice comes into its own. McAdams summarizes his position as suggesting that "it is up to the victim to reach out to the victimizer and, when push comes to shove, to adjust his or her expectations of achieving justice accordingly." Clearly, the form of justice that this attitude seeks is likely to be more creative and enduring than that which requires a full and complete "payment of dues."

35. One argument used for the death penalty is that the punishment "fits" the crime—it echoes or reflects it.

36. Again, an argument of this kind would be that if a murderer denied his victim thirty years of life, he should be denied thirty years of freedom—be sentenced for life.

37. See Gavin D'Costa, "The Impossibility of a Pluralist View of Religions," *Religious Studies* 32 (1996): 223–32.

38. Michael Ignatieff, *The Warrior's Honor: Ethnic War and the Modern Conscience* (London: Chatto and Windus, 1988), 188. This quotation is cited in a paper that Stanley Hauerwas originally presented in Northern Ireland, "Why Time Cannot and Should Not Heal the Wounds of History but Time Has Been and Can Be Redeemed," *Scottish Journal of Theology* 53, no. 1 (2000): 33 ff.

39. Fyodor Dostoyevsky, The *Brothers Karamazov,* cited in Jürgen Moltmann, *The Crucified God* (London: SCM, 1974), 220.

40. It has been said that the ultimate test of the ethics of a society is whether it stands by the wishes expressed in a person's last will and testament. Clearly, the situation here is not unrelated.

41. Simon Wiesenthal, *The Sunflower: On the Possibilities and Limits of Forgiveness* (New York: Schocken Books, 1998), 76.

42. Ibid., 14–15.

43. Ibid., 42–43.

44. Ibid., 55.

45. *Phaedo,* 114, A–B.

46. It has been suggested that there was customary sexual abuse of prisoners prior to crucifixion and that this was suggested to the early church in the reference to Jesus' being stripped naked. See David Tombs, "Crucifixion, State Terror and Sexual Abuse," *Union Seminary Quarterly Review* 53 (Autumn 1999): 89–108.

47. Volf cites Nietzsche's statement that "no deed can be annihilated"—the offense associated with a crime is eternal and unalterable, it cannot be undone. For this reason, he argues, "All punishments, too, must be eternal." But then again, "even an eternal hell" for the guilty still could not "put right," could not cancel out what has been done. The suffering of the father, the mother, and the child as they jumped in terror to a brutal death cannot be "undone." See Volf, *Exclusion and Embrace,* 122.

48. It is imperative that we distinguish here between the Pauline and Platonic use of *metechein* (participation). When Paul uses *metechein* and *koinonein*, he is articulating a profoundly personal ontology grounded in a concept of interpersonal communion that attaches absolute value to the particular and the personal. When Plato speaks of *methexis* (participation), he is referring to the participation of particulars in the impersonal universals in which their reality is to be found.

49. It is important to recognize that the nature of oppression is such (as is all too often illustrated in cases of the sexual abuse of children) that victims often come to regard themselves as deserving the misery they suffer, to feel that they are responsible for their situation and that their sense of guilt is somehow appropriate. The diminishment of their sense of self-worth is such that they are unable to see the sin against them for what it is.

50. Cf. Karl Barth, *Church Dogmatics*, vol. 1, pt. 1 (Edinburgh, T. and T. Clark, 1975).

51. That same love that suffers concretely and particularly with the victim also forgives the SS, the *cetniks*, the Hutu murderers, the South African racists, and, indeed, the rest of us. Their hope is no different from our hope.

52. Wiesenthal, *Sunflower*, 269.

53. It was sobering to witness on television interviews with the relatives of the victims of Carla Faye Tucker who were supporting her controversial execution in the state of Texas. One had no sense from their reactions that those who demanded the death penalty would find the healing they craved in and through this act of retributive justice. Those relatives, however, who had found within themselves the ability to forgive and who pled for amnesty were clearly being healed in and through their commitment to forgive—a process that could only be obstructed by her execution. It is interesting to note the growing body of literature and Internet sites advocating the therapeutic value of forgiveness.

54. Wiesenthal, *Sunflower*, 267–68.

55. Antjie Krog, *Country of My Skull: Guilt, Sorrow and the Limits of Forgiveness in the New South Africa* (New York: Random House, 1998).

56. Ibid., 338–39.

57. Ibid., 340.

58. Ibid., 212.

59. Ibid.

60. The book concludes with a poem:
    I am changed forever. I want to say:
    forgive me
    forgive me
    forgive me

    You whom I have wronged, please
    take me

    with you.
    (Ibid., 365)

61. Here I am borrowing Volf's summary of Welker in *Exclusion and Embrace*, 123.

# CHAPTER THREE

# The Place of Forgiveness in the Actions of the State

## NICHOLAS WOLTERSTORFF

One of the most perplexing problems facing states is that of so-called transitional justice: how to move forward from a period of gross and pervasive injustice to a period of just and peaceful stability. One option is to ferret out the offenders and bring them before the bar of retributive justice for their offenses. Another is to forego ferreting out the offenders and declare a general amnesty for whatever may be the offenses. A third is to ferret out the offenders and forgive them for their offenses. Naturally there can be combinations among these.

The fact that in the latter half of the twentieth century a rather large number of states found themselves in situations of transitional justice has stimulated a lively debate among theorists and practitioners as to which of these options is morally tenable and, if two or more are morally tenable, which is to be preferred. There has also been a debate over whether forgiveness is even the sort of thing that a state can do. In the essay that follows I will argue that forgiveness is sometimes not only morally tenable but obligatory, that it is the sort of thing a state can do, and that sometimes it is desirable for the state to forgive. Since the issues are deep and complex, my treatment will be far from exhaustive. I will look first at what forgiveness is, and then at its place in the moral life of agents, whether those agents are individuals, groups, or institutions.

## Jesus Enjoins Forgiveness

In her book *The Human Condition,* Hannah Arendt made the now-famous claim that Jesus discovered "the role of forgiveness in the realm of human affairs."[1] To this she added, "The fact that [Jesus] made this discovery in a religious context and articulated it in religious language is no reason to take it any less seriously in a strictly secular sense."[2] What will emerge from our discussion is a variant on Arendt's second thesis: though Jesus set the concept of forgiveness within a religious context and articulated it in religious language, that is no reason to take it any less seriously *in our thinking about the political.*

Arendt's claim that Jesus discovered the role of forgiveness in human affairs cannot be sustained; forgiveness had a role in the Scriptures that Jesus was familiar with, viz., the Hebrew Bible. What is true is that Jesus assigned a far more important place to forgiveness in the relation between God and human beings, and among human beings, than anyone before him, and that his doing so was decisive in giving to forgiveness the prominent place in human thought that it has occupied ever since.

Let us begin by reminding ourselves of some of what Jesus said. "Forgive us our debts," Jesus taught his disciples to pray, "as we forgive our debtors." And he told a parable about an unmerciful servant who, after having his own huge debt forgiven by his king, refused to forgive the minor debt of one of his own servants.

Therefore the kingdom of heaven may be compared to a king who wished to settle accounts with his servants. When he began the reckoning, one was brought to him who owed him ten thousand talents; and as he could not pay, his lord ordered him to be sold with his wife and children and all that he had, and payment to be made. So the servant fell on his knees, imploring him, "Lord, have patience with me, and I will pay you everything." Out of pity for him the lord of that servant released him and forgave him the debt. But that same servant, as he went out, came upon one of his fellow servants who owed him a hundred denarii; seizing him by the throat he said, "Pay what you owe." His fellow servant fell down and besought him, "Have patience with me, and I will pay you." He refused, and put him in prison till he should pay the debt. When his fellow servants saw what had taken place, they were greatly distressed, and reported to their lord all that had taken place. Then his lord summoned him and said to him, "You wicked servant! I forgave you all that debt because you besought me; and should you not have had mercy on your fellow servant as I had mercy on you?" In anger his lord delivered him to the jailers, till he should pay all his debt. So also my heavenly Father will do to every one of you, if you do not forgive your brother from your heart. (Matt. 18:23–25)[3]

A few brief comments are in order. The situation of both debtors was that payment of the debt was due. Had that not been the case, the debtors, rather than pleading for patience, would have reminded their creditors that the debt was not yet due; had the king nonetheless insisted on being repaid then and there, it would have been a parable about the unjust king. Second, though in each case the debt was due, in each case the debtor found himself incapable of repaying the debt. Only about the major debtor is it explicitly said that he could not pay; but surely we are to understand that this was also the situation of the minor debtor. Last, in each case the consequence of being required to pay on the spot was, or would have been, calamitous. In the case of the major debtor, he and his entire family and all their possessions would have been sold; in the case of the minor debtor, he was tossed into debtor's prison.

The reason for getting clear on the situation of creditors and debtors in the parable is that thereby we avoid a rather natural misinterpretation of Jesus' final words. Those final words, all by themselves, might suggest that debts are always and everywhere to be forgiven. Consider the following scenario: I go into a shoe store and, after trying on a number of pairs, find a pair that I like. The owner takes the shoes and rings up the sale on the cash register. I hand him the money, thereby putting him in my debt. But he, discerning that I am a soft touch, refuses to hand me the shoes and also refuses to return my money. The relation of creditor and debtor in this scenario is obviously very different from that of creditors and debtors in the parable; I do not interpret Jesus as holding up the forgiving king as a model for how I ought to act in this situation. He is not suggesting that I should cheerfully walk out minus both money and shoes after remarking to the owner, "I won't hold it against you." Were debts always and everywhere forgiven, an economy would be impossible. We are to forgive our debtors in situations relevantly similar to those of the debtors in the parable. What exactly are the relevantly similar ways, we are not told; Jesus leaves that for us to figure out.

The point of the parable, however, is not instruction in how to handle financial debts but instruction in how to handle moral debts. It is interesting that Jesus takes for granted that the forgiving of financial debts is a genuine case of forgiveness and not, as some contend, forgiveness only in a stretched sense of the word.[4] But clearly what Jesus had his eye on was the forgiveness of the person who is morally in one's debt. What he says about the propriety of forgiving financial debts is meant to illuminate the propriety of forgiving those who are morally in one's debt. Of course, Jesus did not think that financial transactions were exempt from moral considerations; that is why the move in the parable from the former to the latter is made without question.

When someone is morally indebted to us, in a situation relevantly similar to that of the creditors in the parable, we are to forgive. We are to do so out of mercy. The reason, at bottom, that we are to forgive out of mercy is that thereby we imitate our heavenly Father. The parable has often been called "the parable of the ungrateful servant." There is no reason in the text of the parable to infer that the major debtor was ungrateful; I would suppose, to the contrary, that he was *extremely* grateful. His failure was not that he was ungrateful but that he egregiously failed to imitate his lord in his lord's exercise of mercy. "Should you not have had mercy on your fellow servant *as I had mercy on you?*" is the question posed. Jesus does not here say why God forgives, nor why God wants us to imitate him in forgiving. What the goal of forgiveness might be is a point that I will be coming back to later.

## What Is Forgiveness?

Though there is a great deal of disagreement in the literature as to the nature and conditions of forgiveness, I judge that there is consensus over the core of the concept: forgiveness is the foregoing of one's right to retributive justice, in some way and to some degree.

Forgiveness becomes relevant when someone or something has been treated unjustly—when they have been wronged, when their rights have been violated, when they have been deprived of what is due them, of what they are entitled to.[5] I regard these diverse locutions as alternative ways of expressing the same idea. The wronged party may be a person, obviously; but it may also be a group or institution—or possibly some plant or animal. And not only persons but also groups and institutions may do the wronging. For the sake of rhetorical economy I will usually use personal pronouns for the entity that wrongs and for the one that is wronged; but it is to be understood throughout that wronging and being wronged are not confined to persons. The point will become important when we get to a discussion of forgiveness in the political realm.

Very often, when A wrongs B, a new right enters the situation that was not there before. The initial situation was that B had a right to certain life-goods. A was then responsible for B's not enjoying those goods; A wronged B. And now, on account of having been wronged by A, B has a right to A's undergoing certain evils—to use the traditional word.[6] B now has a right to retributive justice. Retributive rights are rights that one has to someone's undergoing something that is an evil for him. Such rights are always acquired; they are not to be found among one's natural rights. The only way to acquire such a right is to be wronged by someone. And the only person against whom one acquires retributive rights is the person who wronged one.

That to which one has a right is always something that is a good in one's life; for example, I have the right to the life-good of walking in the park unmolested. In the case of retributive justice, the life-good to which one has a right is that the person who has wronged one should undergo a life-evil—something that is a bad thing in his life, an undesirable thing. It is this feature of retribution that has over and again made it seem questionable. Be it granted that, in this interlocking world of ours, a good in my life may sometimes be an evil in the life of another. How can it be that I have a *right* to such a good?

The offender has deprived me of some life-good to which I had a right— some life-good that was due me, to which I was entitled. Thereupon I acquire the right that certain bad things, certain life-evils, come his way. How are we now to describe the offender's situation? We cannot say that he now has a *right* to those life-evils; our concept of a *right to* something is tied inextricably to that something's being a good. But if he does not have a right to those things that are evils in his life, what relation then does he have to those things?

They are things he deserves. Let me stretch ordinary English a bit and say that he has a *desert* to those life-evils. When one person wrongs another, then each party has something due him on account of the action of wronging. The wronging party has a desert to certain life-evils; that is what is due him. The wronged party has a right to certain life-goods; that is what is due him. And those things that are life-evils for the wrongdoer, to which he has a desert, are the very same as those that are life-goods for the wronged party, to which he has a right. The situation in primary justice is that one party is due some life-good; the situation in retributive justice is that two parties are each due something, that something being exactly the same thing.[7] That something is, however, a life-good for the one party and a life-evil for the other.

What, then, is forgiveness? Well, begin by noticing that rather than enjoying or claiming some life-good to which one has a right, one may forego doing so.

I may, for example, forego taking possession of the item that is mine by right for having won the contest. Perhaps Meissen porcelain is not to my taste; I will content myself with the satisfaction of having won. Notice that to forego enjoying or claiming some life-good to which one has a right is not, so far forth, to lose one's right to that good, to alienate it. To forego the good of walking unmolested in Central Park is not to give up one's right to that good. The phrase "foregoing one's right" is not to be understood as giving up one's right but as foregoing enjoying or claiming the life-good to which one has a right. Of course, in many cases it is possible not only to forego enjoying or claiming some life-good to which one has a right but to alienate one's right to that good.

Among the life-goods that one can forego enjoying or claiming are those to which one has a retributive right. One might do this out of indifference to having been wronged. One is too lazy to be bothered, or preoccupied with more important things, or scornful of the wrongdoer: "I won't be bothered with scum like that." But one can also forego enjoying or claiming the goods to which one has a retributive right without being at all indifferent. And then, depending on what exactly one has a retributive right to, one may forego one's retributive right either by refraining from doing something or by actively taking steps. One may let it happen that the person who wronged one is not punished, or one may work to prevent his being punished—as one may also work on oneself to eliminate one's anger at him for having wronged one.

The example just given makes clear that foregoing enjoying or claiming the goods to which one has a retributive right is typically something that comes in different forms and degrees: I may forego punishment of the offender while still harboring my anger, or I may forego both his being punished and my anger. Alternatively, I may work at eliminating my anger while nonetheless insisting that he be punished.

We can now say what constitutes forgiveness: in a situation in which one recognizes that one has been wronged and is not indifferent thereto, forgiveness is the enacted resolution to forego enjoying or claiming some or all of the life-goods to which one has a retributive right. Only the wronged party can do the forgiving and only the wronging party can be forgiven. B cannot forgive A for the wrongs A perpetrated on C, only for the wrongs A perpetrated on B.[8] What must be added is that it is possible to forgive by way of an authorized representative acting on one's behalf.

There is a big dispute in the literature as to the role of resentment in forgiveness—*resentment* being Nietzsche's word for what I have described, more accurately I think, as anger. Is forgiveness all about the overcoming of resentment, not at all about the overcoming of resentment, or somewhere in between? My own position was hinted at above. By virtue of having been wronged, one has a right to various of the moral emotions, prominent among them being anger. *On account of* being wronged, one has the right to be angry with the person who wronged one *for* his having wronged one.[9]

In saying this, I am making two controversial assumptions. I am assuming, in the first place, that B's anger at A is an evil in A's life. Though B's anger at A may have good consequences in A's life, it is *as such* an evil in A's life. Among the things that make a person's life less admirable than otherwise it would be is that there are people angry at him or her. This is so even if B keeps his anger entirely to himself and even if his anger has no adverse impact on A's experienced well-being. The evil in the life of the wrongdoer to which the wronged party has a retributive right is not to be cashed out entirely in terms of impairments to the experienced well-being of the wrongdoer, nor is it to be cashed out entirely in terms of impairment of A's interests. It may be that A is entirely indifferent to whether B is angry at him; he has no interest whatsoever in B's not being angry at him. It remains the case, nonetheless, that B's anger at A is, as such, an evil in A's life. It makes his life less admirable, less estimable, less excellent, whether he thinks so or not.

I am also assuming that anger over being wronged is a good thing in the emotional life of the victim. Nursing one's anger may not be a good thing; it may be better to arrive eventually at the place where one forgives and puts one's anger behind one. But anger is the emotional recognition of having been treated unjustly. There is something sadly defective about people who fail to recognize when they have been wronged, or whose recognition is so purely intellectualistic that they are emotionally indifferent. Such people are either unaware of their worth, indifferent to their worth, or imperceptive of when they are being treated with disrespect for their worth. Needless to say, oppressors find such people ideal for their purposes; they do what they can to produce them.

Earlier we noted that foregoing one's retributive rights may come in degrees; accordingly, contrary to what is usually assumed, forgiveness also comes in different degrees and different forms: different degrees because one can resolve to forego enjoying or claiming more or fewer of the goods to which one has a retributive right, different forms because one can pick and choose from among the goods to which one has a retributive right those that one will forego enjoying or claiming. On account of your having wronged me, I am now entitled to being angry at you, to criticizing you in public for what you have done, to your being punished, and so forth. I can enact the resolve to forego enjoying or claiming any or all of these.

At this point I am again making a controversial assumption. I am assuming that though punishment of the offender will often be among the retributive rights of the victim, it is not always the case that punishment of the offender is a duty on the part of someone or other. In their papers in this volume, both Amstutz (ch. 6) and McAdams (ch. 5) note that a good many theorists, especially those in the liberal tradition, hold that punishment of wrongdoers is a duty.[10] If it were a duty, then forgiveness either would be immoral or would never include foregoing punishment. Here I cannot enter into the arguments in favor of the position that wrongdoing requires punishment. I shall have to content myself with observing that the moral vision of the Christian and Hebrew Scriptures, on my understanding of it, holds that God's forgiveness of the sinner includes the foregoing of just punishment.[11]

In her book *Pardons: Justice, Mercy, and the Public Interest,* Kathleen Dean Moore argues that forgiveness is a certain "attitude of one who has been injured toward the one who has inflicted the injury. The attitude of forgiveness is characterized by the presence of good will or by the lack of personal resentment for the injury."[12] Moore makes explicit that on this understanding of forgiveness one can punish while forgiving. I reach the same conclusion, that one can punish while forgiving, but by a different route. Forgiveness, so I have suggested, is not an attitude but an enacted resolution: the enacted resolution to forego enjoying or claiming the goods to which one has a retributive right, *whatever those goods may be.* Typically the life-goods to which one has a retributive right include feeling angry with the wrongdoer for his having wronged one; but typically they also include the wrongdoer's being punished. About the person who stops the punishment but nurses the anger, we would say that though she has forgiven, she has not *fully* forgiven; she has forgiven *insofar as* she stops the punishment but not *insofar as* she still nurses the anger. I judge that we would think and speak the same way about the converse situation. Though that person has forgiven who no longer harbors anger toward the wrongdoer but nonetheless supports the punishment, she has not *fully* forgiven. She has forgiven *insofar as* she no longer harbors anger but not *insofar as* she still supports the punishment.

Whereas I have analyzed forgiveness as the enacted resolution to forego some or all of the goods to which one has a retributive right, P. E. Digeser, in his already-mentioned book *Political Forgiveness,* analyzes it instead as an illocutionary act. More accurately, he analyzes *political* forgiveness thus. This seems to me incorrect. In the first place, whereas an illocutionary act consists of saying something, one can forgive someone without saying anything; one can just *do* it. In place of the concept of an *illocutionary act* I have proposed the concept of a *resolution.* A resolution may or may not get expressed in some illocutionary act. But second, mere resolution is not enough, nor would mere illocutionary act be enough if that were the core concept rather than resolution. If one does not act on one's resolution, one has not forgiven—just as one would not have forgiven if one performed the illocutionary act of announcing that one was foregoing one's retributive rights but then did nothing. Forgiveness requires *actually* foregoing.

On the other hand, mere foregoing is also not sufficient. One may forego enjoying or claiming the goods to which one has a retributive right because one is lazy, or distracted: a terrorist airplane slams into the World Trade Center and the insulting remark directed at one the moment before flies forever out of mind. Forgetting and not bothering are not forgiving. Forgiving consists in the enacted *resolution* to forego, actively or passively, enjoying or possessing at least some of the goods to which one has a retributive right. The forgiving may be done entirely in one's heart; it may, for example, take the form of enacting the secret resolution to overcome one's rightful feelings of anger. Or it may be entirely public, taking the form of getting the wheels of justice to stop grinding against the one who has wronged one—perhaps announcing why one is doing that, perhaps not.

Connected with the fact that forgiveness neither is as such an illocutionary act nor requires to be expressed in such an act is the fact that the one forgiven may not know that she has been forgiven. If one enacts the resolution to forego at least some of those goods to which one has a retributive right, then one forgives whether or not the forgiven party knows this. Of course it may be that if one is to achieve the end one had in mind with forgiving—reconciliation, let us say—one's forgiving must become known by the forgiven party. It is also the case that one may forgive even though the one forgiven refuses to accept one's forgiveness, on the ground that he has done nothing to be forgiven for; the other person has, so he insists, no retributive rights against him. Forgiveness of the wrongdoer is not contingent on the remorse or repentance of the wrongdoer—though in this case too, the end one hoped to achieve by forgiving may well be frustrated by lack of remorse.

The articulation of forgiveness that I have articulated also differs in some ways from that offered by Mark Amstutz in his essay in this volume. Amstutz says that "forgiveness depends upon a number of core elements, including consensus about past wrongdoing, remorse and repentance, renunciation of vengeance, cultivation of empathy, and mitigation or cancellation of a deserved penalty." On my analysis, forgiveness itself does not depend on consensus about past wrongdoing, nor on remorse and repentance. Almost always, if these are lacking, the one who has been wronged is frustrated in what he wants to bring about by way of his forgiveness, namely reconciliation of some sort and to some degree; his forgiveness is left hanging in the air, as it were. But he may nonetheless have forgiven. Likewise, on my analysis forgiveness as such does not require cultivation of empathy and mitigation or cancellation of a deserved penalty. It requires foregoing some of one's retributive rights, but not necessarily those. Whether it requires the renunciation of vengeance depends on what one understands by "vengeance."

## Can One Have a Right to Be Forgiven?

In the nature of the case the wrongdoer, if one considers just his wrongdoing, has no right to be forgiven. On account of his wrongdoing he now has a desert to certain life-evils befalling him; hence perforce he does not have a right to the good of those evils not befalling him. In particular, he does not have a right to the good of those evils not befalling him because of the forgiveness of the wronged person. Considering just his wrongdoing, he is not wronged if he is not forgiven. Yet Jesus, in the passage quoted, was clearly instructing his followers that it was their *duty* to forgive. This, then, is a case in which one has a duty to treat someone a certain way even though that person has no right against one to one's treating him or her that way. It is an intriguing question how this can be. What is it that *requires* this action of me if my failure to perform it does not amount to, or result in, my wronging you? This question too will have to be left unanswered on this occasion.

Some Gospel passages reporting what Jesus said about forgiveness are plausibly interpreted as suggesting that there is one circumstance in which one's duty to forgive someone does have, as its correlative, the right of that person to be forgiven. In the course of his instructions on forgiveness in Matthew 18, Jesus said that

[i]f your brother sins against you, go and tell him his fault, between you and him alone. If he listens to you, you have gained your brother. But

if he does not listen, take one or two others along with you, that every word may be confirmed by the evidence of two or three witnesses. If he refuses to listen to them, tell it to the church; and if he refuses to listen even to the church, let him be to you as a Gentile and a tax collector. (Matt. 18:15–17)

Supplement that passage with this one:

Take heed to yourselves; if your brother sins, rebuke him, and if he repents, forgive him; and if he sins against you seven times in the day, and turns to you seven times, and says, "I repent," you must forgive him. (Luke 17:3–4)

One way of fitting these passages together with the one quoted earlier would be this: just as the straitened circumstances of the wrongdoer impose on Jesus' followers the duty to forgive without the wrongdoer's having a right to be forgiven, so too the repentance of the wrongdoer imposes on them such a duty. This strikes me as a possible but not very plausible interpretation; it brings the thought of the passages closer together than the text justifies.

Notice that, in contrast to the passage with which we began, Jesus here says nothing about forgiving out of mercy. One can see why. Mercy may not be relevant. The repentant person may not be in the sort of straitened circumstances in which the two debtors in the parable found themselves. In the earlier passage, Jesus spoke of imitating one's heavenly Father by forgiving one's brother out of mercy; here he says nothing of the sort. Instead he says that if the wrongdoer repents, "you must forgive him."

I suggest that the thought in the two passages just cited is that repentance introduces a morally significant change into the situation that confronts the wronged party. Previously the moral situation confronting the wronged party was that the other person had wronged him. Now what confronts him is this more complex moral situation: the other party wronged him *and that other party now repents of having done so.* The morally significant difference between the two situations is that repentance added to wrongdoing gives the wrongdoer the *right* to be forgiven. The victim's duty to forgive is now grounded in the right of the other person to be forgiven—grounded in the fact that were he not to forgive, the repentant wrongdoer would be wronged. Given that forgiveness comes in different modes and degrees, an obvious question to raise is what mode and degree of forgiveness are made obligatory by repentance. Jesus does not say. One surmises that the core of the forgiveness that repentance makes obligatory is the eradication of one's moral emotion of anger.

The disciples found Jesus' teaching on this matter hard to swallow. Peter, playing the role of the philosopher, thinks he has spotted the possibility of deriving a *reductio ad absurdum* from Jesus' teaching. "Lord," he says, "how often shall my brother sin against me and I forgive him? As many as seven times?" Instead of conceding that it would indeed be absurd to forgive someone seven times, Jesus, by his hyperbolic response, makes explicit what before was only implicit: we are obligated to forgive the wrongdoer *whenever* he repents. "I do not say to you seven times, but seventy times seven," Jesus replies to Peter.

## Motives and Goals of Forgiveness

Forgiveness, as I have analyzed it, can be performed out of a variety of distinct motives. Jesus enjoined his listeners to imitate our heavenly Father in forgiving out of mercy those who have wronged us; forgiving out of mercy is one among many motives for forgiving. Fear is another: the prospect of exercising one's retributive rights is just too frightening. Likewise, forgiveness can be performed with a variety of distinct ends in view—states of affairs that one intends to bring about by means of the forgiving. Prominent among these is surely reconciliation.

Very often the wronged party forgives so that he and the wrongdoer may be reconciled. The expected or hoped-for reconciliation may not come about; the intention of the forgiver may be frustrated. Nonetheless, the forgiving has taken place. It is not a necessary condition of forgiving that one's intention in forgiving, the end for the sake of which one forgives, actually come about.

Let us take just a bit of time to look into this phenomenon of forgiving as a means to reconciliation, beginning with a somewhat deeper scrutiny of retributive justice. Why is it that, on account of your having wronged me, I now have the right to that strange good for myself of an impairment of your good? The traditional answer, which seems to me on the right track, though in need of a lot of fleshing out, is that your wronging me upset without just cause the proportion holding between you and me in the life-goods that we each experience and possess and that punishment restores the proportion to roughly what it was before you wronged me. Your wronging me impaired my life-good for me without impairing yours. Your punishment, assuming it is appropriate, then impairs your life-good in a roughly equal way, so that now we are in roughly the same relation that we were before you wronged me. The ancient saying "An eye for an eye and a tooth for a tooth" is too crude in its simplistic insistence on identity; nonetheless, it points to an important truth. The impairment of my life-good that your wronging of me brought about calls for being matched by an equal, though not necessarily identical, impairment of your life-good. Punishment restores the *status quo ante* in the following sense: you are now a loser in rough equality with me. I am still a loser; there is no undoing the wrong you have done me. But now we are more or less equally losers. The evil, the impairment of your good, that is now visited on you is roughly equal to the evil, the impairment of my good, that you perpetrated on me. Why, in turn, the attainment of this sort of equality should be morally desirable, perhaps even obligatory, is another of the questions I cannot here consider.[13]

Once the restoration to the former proportion has occurred, we are to shake hands and say to each other, "Let bygones be bygones." You have paid the fair price; we are back to where we were before you did what you did. Our expression "getting even with you" has a sinister tone; but the underlying thought is correct: we are even. And since I no longer have anything that I can rightly hold against you on account of what you did—you have paid the fair price—I am to be reconciled with you. In particular, I, the wronged party, am no longer to harbor feelings of anger and resentment toward you, the wrongdoer. The point of punishment, in short, is to release the wrongdoer from the social burden of his past wrongdoing; its point is to stop his past wrongdoing from forever haunting his social future.

When appropriate punishment has been exacted, the person wronged is to remember the wrongdoing no more. Not in the sense that he forgets that it happened—often that will not be possible—but in the sense of "remembering" that worried parents use when their young son leaves for the big seductive city and they say, "Remember what we taught you." They do not just mean "Don't forget what we taught you." They mean "Keep what we have taught you fresh in your mind and formative of your actions." In that sense, after the wrongdoer has been punished, the wronged person is to remember no more the wrong done him. This nonremembering is a key component in how the one wronged and the one wronging are to interact with each other henceforth.

A deeply lamentable feature of how punishment is currently thought about and practiced in the United States is that the obligation of the wronged party to eliminate feelings of anger and resentment once the full punishment has been exacted is completely ignored. Citizens feel entirely within their rights in harboring negative feelings toward the wrongdoer even after full time has been served.

Punishment as a means to social reconciliation has serious defects, however. Many of the wrongs we suffer in the course of daily life—slights, insults, being put down—are such that it is hard to see what sort of punishment would be appropriate. Yes, I am within my rights in feeling angry; but when has my anger endured sufficiently long for the wrongdoer to have paid the right price for this sort of impairment to his good? It is hard to make any sense of the idea. Add that if every wrong were punished, there would be far too much punishing going on for society to function. In addition, sometimes the wrongdoer is not available for punishing; he is dead. And for some crimes, the very notion of a "fitting" punishment is inapplicable. Even if those who caused the death of some three thousand people in the terrorist attack on the World Trade Center were still alive, what would be a "fitting" punishment?

In their essays in this volume, Amstutz, McAdams, and Wells (chs. 6, 5, and 7 respectively) all note in some detail a problem of a rather different sort with punishment as a means to reconciliation. Whereas it may eventually yield in the wronged party the nonremembering of which I spoke above, often it stirs up in the punished wrongdoer and his associates the very same negative emotions of anger and resentment that the wronged party is to eliminate when the punishment has been fulfilled. This happens when the punished party believes that he has not in fact wronged the aggrieved party—or has not wronged her so seriously as to deserve such punishment. When the opportunity arises, he "gets even" with the one who punished him, whereupon that party now sees herself as once again wronged and seizes such opportunities as arise to "get even" a second time—and off they are on a cycle of revenge in which each party sees itself only as wronged and never as wronging. Present-day Israel-Palestine is a painfully vivid example of the point: if we are to believe each party's self-description, neither Israelis nor Palestinians ever initiate any violence, each only responds with justice to the violence initiated by the other.

If B believes she has been wronged by A while A refuses to concede this, then punishment has no chance of effecting reconciliation. Perhaps B no longer harbors feelings of anger and resentment, but now A does. In all such cases, something else than retribution is required if there is to be reconciliation. That something else is forgiveness. Perhaps mutual forgiveness: B forgiving A for having wronged her, and A forgiving B for mistakenly—as A sees it—believing that he has wronged B and for B's wrongly punishing him.

## Is Forgiveness Possible?

Could it be that we too glibly assume that forgiveness is possible? May it be that full forgiveness is not possible? Here is a reason for wondering. Full forgiveness includes, so I have argued, the elimination of one's negative feelings toward the wrongdoer; I have not fully forgiven you if I am still angry with you for the way you wronged me. But forgiving you for what you did to me is not, so it is standardly held, *forgetting* what you did to me; forgiving is not forgetting. Without forgetting what you did to me, I nonetheless fully forgive you, eliminating from my mind and heart all negative emotions that I feel toward you on account of your having wronged me. Is that a possible scenario?

I am myself much attracted to the theory of emotions recently developed by Robert Roberts.[14] An emotion, says, Roberts, is a "concern-laden construal." A *construal* is an interpretation; and it is a *concern-laden* construal if I am *invested* in what I interpret as being the case. My interpretation of your remark as wronging me—perhaps I interpret it as an insult—is an emotion, given my concern that I not be wronged. The concern-laden construal, on this account, does not *result* in an emotion; it *is* an emotion. As long as I hold in mind your having wronged me, I am at least somewhat angry with you. And if I continue to feel some tinge of anger, I have not fully forgiven you. Full forgiveness looks impossible.

There appear to me to be only two conditions under which full forgiveness can take place. One is, putting out of mind or forgetting. As long as I harbor the memory of your having wronged me—as long as I have not put it out of mind or forgotten it—I have not fully forgiven you. The standard dichotomy between forgiving and forgetting is too crude. It is true that one may forget without forgiving. Nonetheless, forgiveness requires that one either forget the wrong done one or put it out of mind if one has not forgotten it.

Second, if you repent of what you did to me and I know that you do, that changes things. Full forgiveness without putting out of mind or forgetting what you have done to me seems possible in such a case. My concern-laden construal of that more complex situation, your having wronged me and now being repentant, is surely not anger or resentment if I concentrate as much on the repentance as on the wronging. How to describe it instead, I do not know; but whatever it is, it seems to me not to be an evil for you. If this is correct, then what we have here is another aspect of the significance of Jesus' insistence on the relevance of repentance to forgiveness.

What is repentance? Well, at its core it is the acknowledgment that one has done wrong to the other person. So here is where we are: if the person who has wronged one refuses to concede that he has done so, then it is impossible fully to forgive him without putting out of mind the wrong he has done one or forgetting it; failure to do one or the other of those means that one still harbors at least a tinge of those negative emotions that are evils for the other person. If, on the other hand, the other person acknowledges that he has done wrong, then full forgiveness without either putting out of mind or forgetting is a genuine possibility.

Two ancillary points are important. Not infrequently partial forgiveness evokes repentance, thereby making full forgiveness a possibility. And second, forgiveness in the absence of repentance, achieved by putting out of mind or forgetting, is typically fraught with moral ambiguity. The husband has been unfaithful to his wife. She knows that he has been, and he knows that she knows. But he is not at all repentant, nor does she think he is. Nonetheless, she tries to forgive, perhaps because everyone is telling her that it's the "wifely thing" to do, perhaps because she judges that there is no other way for her to go on. Let bygones be bygones, she says, even in the face of all lack of remorse on his part. Reconciliation may eventually be within reach if she is successful in her attempt at amnesia; but it is reconciliation of a most imperfect sort. It is this sort of forgiveness that has given forgiveness a bad name among feminists—and rightly so. This is being a doormat. Sad to say, sometimes the reconciliation made possible by amnesia is the best the wronged party can achieve.

## Can States Forgive?

Can and should the concept of forgiveness be applied in the political order? The question has a number of distinct facets: Can and should states forgive individuals, can and should individuals forgive states, can and should states forgive states, can and should individuals forgive individuals for political acts? Here I must confine myself to dealing with just the first of these, this being the one that is theoretically most problematic, namely, can and should states forgive individuals? (This is also the question on which Amstutz concentrates, whereas McAdams and Wells concentrate on whether individuals can and should forgive other individuals for political acts.)

An important preliminary issue that arises here, almost entirely ignored in the literature on political forgiveness, is how we are to understand the relation between the people and its government when the state acts. Take, for example, a declaration of war issued by the executive of some state. Is this to be understood as *the state* declaring war, by way of the declaration of its executive? Or is it to be understood as *the people* declaring war, by way of what its state does (and that, in turn, by way of what its executive does)? On the latter interpretation, the people are the primary agent. The right to declare war is vested in them; the state is simply their public voice and executive. On the former interpretation, the state is the primary agent; the right to declare war is vested in it. Classical contract theory would say that the state has acquired that right by transference: the right, originally vested in the people, was somehow transferred from them to their state. The people alienated to the state their own nonderivative right to declare war. Be that as it may: on this account the state is understood not as the voice and executive of the people but as itself the primary agent of such acts as declaring war. I use the example of declaration of war only to illuminate the two ways of understanding the situation; other examples could have been used as well.

Here is how the distinction pertains to our reflections here: When a crime has been committed in a society that enjoys the rule of law, is it a crime against the people or a crime against the state? Usually, of course, there is also an individual or group of individuals against whom it is a crime. But fundamental to our sort of rule-of-law society is the assumption that it is also a crime against either the people (the community) or the state. But which: people or state? The counterpart question arises when the wrongdoer is convicted and punished: Is it the state that convicts and punishes or the people that do so, the state being merely the voice and executive of the people?

The issue is obviously deep and complicated; as with a number of other issues that I have highlighted, here is not the place to enter into it. The standard assumption in the literature on political forgiveness appears to be that the state, rather than the people as a corporate body, is the victim of crime and the agent of punishment. I think it is not at all obvious that that assumption is correct; nonetheless, let me go along with it on this occasion.

The literature on the issue of whether states can forgive individuals has focused on three issues. Do states have the sort of status that is required for forgiveness to be relevant; that is, can states acquire retributive rights on account of having been wronged? Supposing they do, then second, do states have the sort of agency that is required for forgiving—that is, can states enact the resolution to forego enjoying or claiming some or all of the goods to which they have a retributive right? And third, supposing states do possess both the requisite status and the requisite agency, can they satisfy whatever are the conditions necessary for forgiveness?

Given the assumption just mentioned, the first two questions have easy answers. The whole system of criminal justice in our sort of rule-of-law society takes for granted that the state can be the victim of an act of wrongdoing and that it acquires retributive rights on account of being the victim. Likewise it is taken for granted by the system that the state has whatever powers of agency may be required for convicting and punishing wrongdoers and for foregoing those. The only interesting question, given the assumption, is the third: Can the state satisfy the conditions necessary for forgiveness?

Why would there be doubts on the matter? If one grants that the state can convict and punish, and can forego convicting and punishing, what reason could one have for doubting that it can also forgive? What more is required? The point most frequently raised is that, since states are incapable of feeling the negative moral emotions appropriate to being wronged, they are perforce also incapable of effecting what is essential to forgiveness, viz., the elimination of such moral emotions. The most prominent exponent of this line of thought is probably Kathleen Dean Moore in the book already mentioned, *Pardons: Justice, Mercy, and the Public Interest.*

The strategy P. E. Digeser adopts for replying to this objection is to frame a concept of *political forgiveness* that states can satisfy and that, as he sees it, is distinct from, but related to, our ordinary concept of forgiveness. He frames the concept with an eye on pardons and debt forgiveness. The problem with such a strategy is that one leaves oneself wide open to the objection that, yes, of course, with an eye on what states can and cannot do, one can formulate a concept of something states can do that is rather like the ordinary concept of forgiving, and one can call it a concept of *political forgiveness.* But one does not thereby establish that states can *forgive;* all one establishes is that states can satisfy this new concept of something that is rather like forgiveness.

My own answer to the objection makes use of the ordinary concept of forgiveness. It has two parts. In the first place, as I argued earlier, it is not a condition of the exercise of forgiveness by some individual that she eliminate her feelings of anger toward the wrongdoer for the wrong he did her. I concede that that is a condition of *full and complete* forgiveness; but one can forgive without forgiving fully and completely. The assumptions behind this claim of mine about full and complete forgiveness are that one typically has retributive rights to a number of distinct goods when one has been wronged, that one can enact the resolution to forego enjoying or claiming one or more of the goods to which one has a retributive right without enacting the resolution to forego all of them, that in particular one can enact the resolution to forego a good many of them without enacting the resolution to get rid of one's negative moral emotions, and that it is simply not true that our concept of *forgiveness* requires us to say that one has not forgiven *at all* unless one has enacted the resolution to get rid of one's negative moral emotions.

That, I say, is one part of my answer. The other part is that since states are not the sorts of entities that are capable of having emotions, they also do not possess the retributive right to such moral emotions as anger and resentment, upon being wronged. That is not the sort of right they can have. Accordingly, a state may *entirely* forego the retributive rights that it has acquired on account of being the victim of wrongdoing *without* doing anything at all to get its negative emotions under control; it has no such emotions to *get* under control. If it is thought to be a condition of forgiveness that the forgiver not harbor such emotions, then states automatically satisfy that requirement![15]

The reason states have no emotions is that they have no mind. Having no mind, they cannot entertain the concern-laden construals that emotions are, on Robert Roberts's analysis. And this implies that the issue of whether the victim is harboring or forgetting such construals cannot even arise. States do not have to forget in order to forgive; because they cannot remember they cannot forget. Rather than its being problematic whether states can forgive, it is easier for them to forgive than for individuals to do so.

## States Do in Fact Forgive

But is it ever a *good thing* for a state to forgive? The state can forgive; but *should* it? Begin by noticing that states do in fact forgive—all the time. The great bulk of the cases appear to me to fall under four headings: states forgive out of expediency, they forgive out of mercy for the offender, they forgive out of admiration for the character or social contribution of the offender, and they forgive for the sake of reconciliation. Let me offer examples of each.

Given that the attorney general of any government has only limited prosecutorial resources at her disposal, she must constantly make decisions as to when to prosecute and when not. If she thinks it unlikely that she will win the case, she usually does not prosecute. But even when she thinks she will win, she often does not prosecute. The offense is too minor; she has to husband her resources for more important infractions. She enacts the resolution to forego punishment of the transgressor. Thereby the state forgives—out of expediency.

Second, states now and then forgive financial debts owed them by foreign countries; if we take at face value their explanations of why they do this, it is done out of mercy for the foreign country that finds itself in a financially straitened condition. Likewise state executives now and then out of mercy pardon prisoners who are terminally ill. Thereby the state forgives.

Third, executive pardons are sometimes issued on the ground that, though the person has indeed fallen afoul of the law and deserves to be punished, his character overall is so admirable, or his past contributions to society are so estimable, that it would be a good thing to forego full punishment. In general, executive pardons given for reasons other than that justice has misfired constitute acts of forgiveness by the state.

Last, there is forgiveness for the sake of reconciliation. Gerald Ford explicitly stated that his pardon of Richard Nixon—strictly, the American state's pardon of Nixon—was for the sake of reconciliation. He judged that were Nixon to be punished, the poisonous atmosphere engendered by Nixon's actions and by the conflicting judgments thereon would last for years and years; best to get the whole thing behind us. So too for South Africa's Truth and Reconciliation Commission, discussed in some detail by Amstutz. Though the commission did not require forgiveness on the part of individuals who were victims, I find the argument of P. E. Digeser compelling that, for the most part, what it itself exercised on behalf of the state was not amnesty but forgiveness.[16] Forgiveness, to say it once again, is the enacted resolution to forego enjoying or claiming some or all of the goods to which one has a retributive right. Forgiveness thus understood presupposes clarity on the part of the forgiver as to the nature of the offense. If I do not know what you have done, then I also do not know what are the goods to which I have a retributive right; and if I do not know what those are, I cannot resolve to forego enjoying or claiming them. By contrast, one declares amnesty when one does not know in detail what was done by whom, only that something wrong was done.[17] The actions of the Truth and Reconciliation Commission came closer, by and large, to forgiveness than to amnesty; and their stated goal was reconciliation.[18]

It is commonly held that the business of government is justice. When one scrutinizes what governments actually do, one discerns that the rendering of retributive justice is superseded by forgiveness far more often than one would have supposed in advance.

## When State Forgiveness Becomes Problematic

It would be interesting to go beyond the point just made, that states as well as individuals can and do forgive, to explore the similarities and differences between forgiveness as exercised by these two, very different, sorts of agents. For example, do states as well as individuals have the duty to forgive when the wrongdoer repents, by virtue of the repentant wrongdoer's then having a right to forgiveness? Judges sometimes take into account the penitence or impenitence of the wrongdoer when imposing sentence, as do parole boards when determining probation and release; otherwise, the criminal justice system takes no account of repentance. Is that the way it should be? And do states in stable, well-ordered, rule-of-law societies have a duty to punish, or should they regard punishment and forgiveness as two alternative paths to the same goal of reconciliation, choosing between them on a case-by-case basis? We must resist all these important and interesting bypaths and conclude our discussion by considering the role of state forgiveness in extreme, non-normal situations of transitional justice.

There is an inherent peculiarity of state forgiveness that makes it problematic, commonplace though it may be in certain of its forms. The great bulk of crimes committed in a rule-of-law state have victims of two sorts: a person or group of persons on the one hand and the state on the other. Now if the state and the person join in forgiving the wrongdoer, no problem. But suppose they do not. Specifically, suppose the state decides, out of its own interest in social reconciliation, to forgive, whereas the person does not forgive. Perhaps the person is dead and cannot forgive; or perhaps the person is very much alive but refuses to forgive. It would appear that for the state to proceed with forgiveness in such a case would be perforce to perpetrate injustice on the person who was already a victim; the state against her will would deprive her of her right to retributive justice. Typically in such cases there is also an issue of equity: Why forgive these and not those? But the fundamental problem, over and over, is that it appears that the state, rather than securing justice for its citizens, deliberately perpetrates injustice on those who are already victims. They become victims twice over. It appears that the state, when it forgives, rather than ensuring that the one deprived of the goods to which she had a primary right will at least enjoy those to which she has a retributive right, further victimizes her by now itself depriving her of those retributive goods against her will.

Often the consequence will be that the wronged party and those who take her side are not only angry at the criminal for the wrong he perpetrated on her but angry at the state for the wrong it perpetrated on her of depriving her of her retributive rights by forgiving him. To both of these angers, she and those who take her side will apparently be entitled. This will especially be the case when the state forgives in the absence of any sign of repentance and remorse on the part of the wrongdoer. Hardly the path toward reconciliation that the state supposed it was treading!

For the state to forgive the wrongdoer over the protests of the victim and/or those who take her side is — so it would appear — for the state to break faith with its citizens. Citizens in a well-ordered state trust the state to protect them against crime and to punish those who commit it; both the moral legitimacy of the state and its stability depend on its keeping that trust. State forgiveness appears to break that trust.

So far as I can see, the only possible response to this case for the moral unacceptability of state forgiveness goes along the following lines. The goods to which one has a retributive right are strange goods; they are goods for oneself of certain evils befalling the other person: restricted movement, the infliction of physical pain, social opprobrium, and the like. Part of what is strange about many of these goods is that to be deprived of them is to have, not one's own experiential well-being impaired, but that of the other person. I now have a right to the movements of the wrongdoer being constricted; but if they are not, that may well make no difference whatsoever to my own experiential well-being. When the crime is such that restitution can be made, then if restitution comes my way, that does of course makes a difference to my experiential well-being. But punishment of the wrongdoer often does not. In fact, harboring feelings of anger and resentment often *impairs* the experiential well-being of the victim. My first point, then, is this: if there are any (prima facie) rights such that in some circumstances it is acceptable for a person to be deprived of the goods to which he has the right, it is likely that they will be found among these strange retributive rights.

Second, let us remind ourselves of the traditional reason for supposing that there are these peculiar goods to which one has a right when one has been wronged: goods for oneself of the other person being deprived of goods. The idea was that if your good is impaired to roughly the same degree that you impaired my good, then we are once again in roughly the same relative position with respect to our life-goods that we were before you wronged me; we ought, accordingly, to put the whole matter behind us in our interactions with each other. I am to accept the price you have paid as a fair price for the life-good you deprived me of.

Forgiveness, as we observed earlier, is an alternative strategy for achieving the same goal. When I forgive, I resolve that I will forego whatever is the fair price for the good you deprived me of. I will not charge you for it. Having foregone charging you for it, what you did is now behind us in how we henceforth engage each other.

The final step is this: recall that, as we saw earlier, it may sometimes be an obligation to forgive. It may be an obligation even though the wrongdoer does not have a right to be forgiven.

I think the only way for state forgiveness in situations of transitional justice to not be the compounding of injustice is for the personal victim to have the duty to forgive when the state correctly judges that punishing the wrongdoer, if that is a possibility, would make it impossible in the foreseeable future to bring about the reconciliation required for establishing a just and harmonious society. Sometimes states do find themselves in this far-from-ideal situation. When they do, I suggest, it is the duty of the wronged individual to go along with the state and forgive. If the good of living henceforth in a just and harmonious society is in conflict with the retributive good of the wrongdoer being punished, then the wronged person has a duty to choose the greater good. (This amounts to what McAdams, in his analysis of the East German situation, calls "the victim-centered approach.") When it is the duty of the individual, in these painful situations, to forgive if the state does so, then the state is not wronging the wronged in doing so.

## Is State Forgiveness the Better Way for Transitional Justice?

I have argued that states of the modern world regularly offer forgiveness of various sorts to offenders. I would guess that this is one of the ways in which Christianity has shaped our political order. It may be that states also offer forgiveness in parts of the world where Christianity has had little or no impact. But it seems to me beyond doubt that one of the long-term influences of Christianity on our polities has been the tempering of the demands of retributive justice with forgiveness. There have been those in the Christian tradition who have opposed such tempering; mercy and forgiveness, they have said, is for the church; justice is the business of the state. It would be worth uncovering and evaluating the reasons they have for such a view. Their view has not, however, won the day: over and over Christians in positions of political power or authority have yielded to their Christian impulse to forgive.

What has placed forgiveness on the agenda of contemporary political theory is not, however, that long quiet tradition of pardoning offenders, forgiving debts, and so forth, but the judgment of various states in Africa and Latin America that the most promising way, if not, indeed, the only possible way, to move forward from a period of deep injustice to a situation in which the members of society are sufficiently reconciled to make possible a just and stable polity is for the state to forgive a good many of the perpetrators of injustice.

The verdict is still out on how promising forgiveness on this large scale really is—or more precisely, on the conditions under which it can be successful. Amstutz's analysis of the two cases of Argentina and South Africa is evidence for the conclusion that state forgiveness, at least when part of a quite self-conscious use of restorative justice strategies, is much better for healing wounds and getting on to the business of constructing a new society than is the traditional strategy of holding trials and dealing out punishments. Whether that conclusion holds up when other examples are brought into the picture is something that awaits further analysis. Here I have addressed myself not to the relative effectiveness of state forgiveness for achieving the reconciliation needed for constructing a new society but to the prior questions, Is it possible and is it morally defensible for states to forgive? The conclusion that has emerged is that states *can* forgive, in the ordinary sense of the word *forgive,* and that in certain situations it is morally tenable for them to forgive, namely, when it is the obligation of the victims and/or their supporters to join the state in forgiving.

## Notes

1. Hannah Arendt, *The Human Condition* (Chicago: University of Chicago Press, 1958), 238.

2. Ibid.

3. I have slightly adapted the RSV translation.

4. For references, see P. E. Digeser, *Political Forgiveness* (Ithaca: Cornell University Press, 2001), 19.

5. The forgiveness of financial debts requires a slight qualification to this thesis. If the debt is forgiven after the debtor has defaulted, then the thesis applies as formulated. But it is also possible to forgive a debt when the debtor has not yet defaulted but is about to do so, or when it becomes clear that it will be very difficult for him not to do so. Thus forgiveness is also sometimes relevant when one is about to be deprived of what is due one or when it is very difficult for the other party not to deprive one of that.

6. We do still speak of "natural evils," meaning by this bad things befalling a person rather than immoral things done by or to a person.

7. One might wonder whether this identity of what the wronged party has a right to, and the wronging party has a desert to, holds in the case of restitution. The wronged party has a right to restitution; the wronging party does not have a desert to restitution. My reply is that *restitution* does not fully describe what the wronged party has a right to. The wronged party has a right to *the wrongdoer paying restitution*. And to this the wrongdoer has a desert.

8. I can now explain why I disagree with those who hold that the forgiving of financial debt is not a true case of forgiveness but forgiveness only by analogy—and why I regard Jesus as correct in taking the forgiveness of financial debt as a special case of forgiveness in general. When a debtor fails to pay a loan at the agreed-upon time, the creditor acquires certain retributive rights against the debtor on account of that failure. For the creditor to forgive the debt is for him to enact the resolution to forego the goods to which he has a retributive right. One wonders whether the ability of bankruptcy courts to forgive debts (to some extent) is an exception to the principle enunciated in the text above, that only the wronged party can forgive the wrongdoer. I doubt it; I think this is to be understood as a very special case of someone forgiving on one's behalf.

9. There is an excellent discussion and defense of this claim in Jeffrie G. Murphy and Jean Hampton, *Forgiveness and Mercy* (Cambridge: Cambridge University Press, 1988).

10. There is also a long tradition of Christian theology that holds this view. See, for example, chs. 9 and 10 of Anselm's *Proslogion.*

11. I do address the arguments in my essay "Does Forgiveness Undermine Justice?" in *God and the Ethics of Belief,* ed. Andress Chignell and Andrew Dole (Cambridge: Cambridge University Press, 2005.).

12. Kathleen Dean Moore, *Pardons: Justice, Mercy, and the Public Interest* (New York: Oxford University Press, 1989), 184.

13. I do consider it in Wolterstorff, "Does Forgiveness Undermine Justice?" There is a fine discussion of the issues in Murphy and Hampton, *Forgiveness and Mercy.*

14. Robert Roberts, *Emotions* (Cambridge: Cambridge University Press, 2003).

15. In his essay in this volume (ch. 6), Amstutz allies himself with a number of thinkers who hold that a people—in distinction from its state—is the sort of entity that can have emotions. Here, then, we get a glimpse of the importance of the issue as to whether, in a rule-of-law society such as ours, the state or the people is the victim of wrongdoing and the possessor of retributive rights.

16. See Digeser, *Political Forgiveness,* 74.

17. Ibid.

18. Amstutz, in ch. 6 of this volume, says that the South African TRC "promised amnesty to perpetrators who confessed their wrongdoing." If amnesty is indeed what I take it to be, then the attempt of the TRC to ferret out wrongdoers and their wrongdoing means that what they extended was not amnesty, strictly speaking, but forgiveness.

# CHAPTER FOUR

# Interfaith Perspectives on Reconciliation

## DAVID B. BURRELL, C.S.C.

Societies in transition from regimes that managed to shred the very fabric of that society, and that often found support for their destructive policies by using religious identity markers, will need to discover resources in their religious bodies to reweave that torn fabric. These reflections will attempt to show how that societal crisis can be a blessed opportunity for the religious groups in question to come together to discover their enhanced potential to foster reconciliation within the larger society. For as they overcome their endemic hostility to one another as "other," that witness may well be catching. Given my context in the Holy Land, the religious groups that figure in these reflections will be the Abrahamic faiths, Judaism, Christianity, and Islam, but other milieus could proffer other examples.

Let us begin with the Gospels. Just after Jesus had (according to Luke's account) "set his face towards Jerusalem" (9:51), he excoriated the people among whom he had lived, announcing to "the seventy disciples: 'Woe to you, Chorazin! Woe to you, Bethsaida! For if the deeds of power done in you had been done in Tyre and Sidon, they would have repented long ago'" (10:13). Moreover, he had just rebuked two of his closest disciples, James and John, when they asked him (in the spirit of Elijah): "Do you want us to command fire to come down from heaven and consume [these Samaritans who refused us hospitality]?" with the words: "You do not know what manner of spirit you are. The son of man came to save souls, not destroy them" (9:55). It is a prominent feature of the Gospels that Jesus' closest associates—whom he would remind, on the eve of their slinking away, that they were rather friends than servants—kept missing the point. Indeed, the rare ones who got it were a Samaritan woman, a pagan woman from the very region of Tyre and Sidon, and a Roman centurion: "I have not found faith like this in Israel" (Luke 7:10). Ironically enough, remarks like these were often construed by the successor community to belittle the Jews for their rejection of Jesus, while their manifest intent has to be to warn any in-group that the out-group may be better positioned to recognize the disruptive truth in what they have come to assimilate as their revelation. Had not Jesus, just before rebuking James and John, had to address some disciples intent on maintaining the boundaries of their group—"Lord, some people were casting out demons in your name and we told them to stop," insisting: "Let them alone; whoever is not against you is for you" (Luke 9:50)? Finally, if the Gospels are more proclamation than they are history, "the Pharisees" refers less to an historical group then it presages any set of religious leaders intent on preserving the integrity of their community, as they construe it.

So we are led inescapably to conclude that religious "others" will often provide the key to understanding the reaches of the faith that we espouse, and even more strongly that if we link our adherence to that faith with a concomitant rejection of these "others," then we will have missed the point of the revelation offered us. Can our failure to recognize the crucial role that "other-believers" play in our own faith commitment be one of those cases where a clear Gospel teaching has remained obscure until events conspired to force us to acknowledge it?[1] For we have freely traded the epithet of "infidel" with Muslims from the Crusades until quite recently, leaving it to Western political leaders to resurrect now. Yet the prescient document from the Second Vatican Council, *Nostra Aetate,* renounced all that (while reminding us that Jews remain God's covenanted people) by asserting that "Muslims . . . worship God, who is one, living and subsistent, merciful and almighty, the creator of heaven and earth, who has also spoken to [human beings]. They strive to submit themselves without reserve to the hidden decrees of God, just as Abraham submitted himself to God's plan, to whose faith Muslims eagerly link their own."[2] Indeed, I would hope that a fringe benefit of these reflections could be to realize that the import of that singular document lies in bringing Christians to a keen appreciation of the role that those of other faiths can play in articulating our own, rather than offering counsel on the nugatory question of whether other-believers can be saved. For whatever "salvation" might mean—and its sense differs from one faith tradition to another—it is clearly God's business and not ours.[3]

But how can we best portray the role that other-believers play in helping us to articulate our faith traditions, and how can it contribute to our subject of reconciliation? I shall argue that these two questions lead to a single answer: only by recognizing the role that other-believers play in enhancing and confirming our faith—whoever "we" might be—can we activate the powers latent within that faith for reconciling differences, precisely where our standard responses to difference have proved so deadly. That has of course been in the domain of political life and interaction, where religious difference seems to exacerbate rather than temper animosity. Rather than simply remark that *corruptio optimi pessima est,* however, can we trace the reasons for that to our need to reduce religious heritage to our possession? Karl Barth liked to call it the devolution of *faith* into *religion,* yet while he would have wished to restrict the term *faith* to Christian revelation, we may well find similar correctives in each of the Abrahamic faiths. Correctives, that is, to the propensity of staunch believers to feel that they have grasped the import of their faith tradition and would certainly need no help from others—especially "other-believers"—to improve their grasp of their own faith.[4] Indeed, the philosophical dimension of my response will remind us how faith cannot be something that we grasp but rather must grasp us, but let us first be reminded by the Gospel.

Shortly after having reminded the disciples that they were ignorant of "what manner of spirit they were," Luke tells us that Jesus "sent them on ahead of him in pairs to every town and place where he himself intended to go," admonishing them to "cure the sick who are there and say to them: 'the kingdom of God has come near to you'" (10:9). Then when "the seventy disciples returned with joy, saying 'Lord, in your name even the demons submit to us!'" Luke relates a reflective turn on Jesus' part quite uncharacteristic of the synoptics: "At that hour Jesus rejoiced in the Holy Spirit and said: 'I thank you, Father, Lord of heaven and earth, because you have hidden these things from the wise and intelligent and have revealed them to infants; yes, Father, for such was your gracious will'" (10:21). Since we are clearly the "wise and intelligent," I want to suggest that Jesus is identifying an epistemological failure we all share when it comes to appropriating a God-given revelation by faith. My guide to exposing this failure will be Aquinas, but my chosen commentator will be Oliver Sacks. What recommends the author of *The Man Who Mistook His Wife for a Hat* for this task is not only his luminous prose but his reflections (introducing Part One) on "deficiencies," acutely displayed in the way in which he practices neurology.[5] For neurologists, he reminds us, are preoccupied with *deficiencies,* often those induced by injury or trauma. Yet what came to fascinate Sacks were the ways those deficiencies opened his patients to modes of understanding un-available to us who regard ourselves as whole and complete. This practitioner of neurology recovered the art of medicine at the precise point where he came to recognize the limits of his science. Or, put more positively, his scientific acumen led him to a point where he could identify yet other powers of a human person shining through what were manifest deficiencies. And what should interest us is the way he allowed himself to be carried beyond the limits of what he could claim to know, only to learn from these "deficient" persons something that they alone could teach him. What can such remarkable commentary on Jesus' words of praise to his Father tell us about the inner structure of faith and its endemic need for "others" to illuminate its import for us believers?

Aquinas's initial answer is simple and straightforward: in speaking of God (and the "things of God") we can at best but "signify imperfectly."[6] His generous account suggests the "glass half-empty, half-full" dilemma. For it means, of course, that we will get it wrong much of the time, and especially when we think we have it right! So we will ever be in need of correction when attempting to articulate the content of a purportedly divine revelation. That does not militate against what Robert Sokolowski identifies as the central task of theology: "working out terminal distinctions" to secure the grammar proper to discourse about God.[7] But it may take generations to explore the import of those distinctions. Here lies the special role of interfaith encounter. As Jean Daniélou noted fifty years ago, the prevailing story of Christian missionary activity—bringing Christ, say, to India—failed to capture the effective drama of mission practice. Indeed, it would be more accurate to say that we meet Christ there.[8] The explanation is as simple as "reader-response" criticism: try to speak of Jesus to people formed as Hindus, and the questions they raise will force us to a new perspective on the life and mission of Jesus. What ensues is our discovering a fresh face of Jesus, or, even better, another face of God reflected in Jesus. Indeed, such an encounter can open a new chapter in theology, as Sara Grant's Teape lectures show eloquently.[9] By constructing a conversation between Aquinas and Shankara, she shows just how unique the relation between creation and its Creator must be. Once we attend to the import of his formula for creation as "the emanation of the being entire from the universal cause of all being" (*ST* 1.45.1), we find that we cannot speak of Creator and creation as two separate things. What Sokolowski calls "the distinction" of God from God's creation is real enough, certainly, to block any naïve pantheistic images; yet we can hardly speak of two separate things, since the very being of creatures is a "being-to" God (*ST* 1.45.4). So the term adopted by Shankara and so redolent of Hindu thought—*nonduality*—turns out to render the elusive Creator/creature distinction better than anything else. But it took a person whose study of Shankara's thought had been augmented by years actively participating in an ashram in Pune in India to bring to light the treasure latent in the Christian doctrine of creation.

Read in conjunction with Rudi teVelde's *Substantiality and Participation in Aquinas,* Sara Grant's slim volume offers a contemporary perspective on Aquinas's recourse to this instrument of Neo-Platonic thought to render coherent the radical introduction of a free Creator into Hellenic metaphysics.[10] Yet that was only accomplished, in fact, in conjunction with Avicenna and Moses Maimonides: an Islamic philosopher who introduced a distinction that would prove key to Aquinas's elaboration of the Creator as "cause of being" and a Jewish thinker steeped in "the Islamicate."[11] So what many regard as the classical Christian synthesis of philosophical theology, Aquinas's *Summa Theologiae,* proves in retrospect to have already been an intercultural, interfaith achievement, offering a constructive intellectual demonstration of how faith cannot be something that we grasp but must be something that grasps us; and more positively, of the role those of other faiths can play in articulating one's own. What I want to show now are the ways in which our present generation is called to a fresh appreciation of the need to enrich our faith-perspective with that of others who believe quite differently than we do, as the only hope of reconciling those differences that a self-enclosed view of "religion" can so easily escalate into deadly conflict. What sets the stage for conflict will turn out, in fact, to be notions of the divinity with idolatrous consequences, opposing one another like tribal gods yet all the more deadly in that they presume to have total sway (or, in the case of messianic Jewish groups like Gush Emunim, exclusive hegemony over a piece of land). This is hardly new, of course, since the Crusades might be considered a delayed Western reaction to Islam's spectacular spread within a century of the death of the Prophet, while the later *mission civilizatrice* of colonialism represented a belated Western recovery from the stalemate attendant upon Christian withdrawal from the Holy Land following the demise of the Crusades as well as the later defeat of Ottoman Muslim forces at Vienna in 1529. And the Zionist recovery of that same land fulfills the pattern as well, even though its origins were expressly secular, utopian, and socialist, for the symbolic forces it unleashed have been transmuted into virulently religious forms of nationalism.

When religion can so easily mask and meretriciously legitimate forces intent on dominating land, as well as natural resources crucial to the industrialized world like oil, what hope have we of turning those same religious traditions into forces for reconciliation? Very little, humanly speaking, and each of the Abrahamic faiths deploys its symbolic resources to help us understand that fact. What Christians call "original sin" Jews call *yetzer ra* (inclination to evil), and Muslims *jahiliyya* (state of ignorance). In Islam, this description of Bedouin tribes in the Hejaz before the revelation of the Qur'an "came down" to Muhammad became normative for all human beings bereft of revelation, wandering aimlessly in the desert as they follow the whims of their own wayward desires. Indeed, that parable sounds familiar to Christians as Paul's reminder that "the good that we would do we don't do, and the evil that we would not do we do do"; indeed, nothing can save us from this "body of death" but "the grace of God in Christ Jesus our Lord" (Rom. 7:18), reminding some of us of Chesterton's quip that "original sin is the only part of Christian theology which can really be proved."[12] The inertial pull of *yetzer ra* in Jewish ethos can be detected in any conversation among Jews, particularly those intent on improving the current situation, whatever it may be. Yet the contrary path of Torah observance stands, as Muslims have the living presence of God's creating and healing Word in the Qur'an, and Christians "the grace of God in Christ Jesus our Lord." So a grim diagnosis of the human condition is matched by a strong antidote for its crippling effects. But how effective have these antidotes been for as long as they have been present in the traditions taken separately? Francis of Assisi, whose very life reminded his century of the efficacy of that "grace of God in Christ Jesus," was said to have been as impressed with the faith of the Muslims whom he met at Damietta as he was depressed at the conduct of the crusading knights with whom he had been transported there. Yet it may be that the opening provided by *Nostra Aetate,* together with cultural changes in attitudes catalyzed by increased commingling of cultures, will bring people of faith into alliances that can foster mutual illumination and unveil other dimensions of these faith traditions. In short, what each of us has failed to do separately we may now be given the opportunity to accomplish together.

What I would like to suggest is that the presence of other-believers can help the faithful in each tradition to gain insight into the distortions of that tradition: the ways it has compromised with various seductions of state power, the ways in which fixation on a particular "other" may have skewed their understanding of the revelation given them. Sometimes minority voices within a tradition will make that clear, as Mennonites trace compromising elements in Western Christianity to an early alliance with Constantine, while Sufi Muslims remind their Sunni and Shi'a companions in faith of the crippling effects of a soulless *shari'a*, harkening to the way religious and secular leaders colluded in Baghdad in 922 to dispose of Ibn Mansur al-Hallaj: "his hands and his feet were cut off, he was hanged on the gallows, and then decapitated; his body was burned and its ashes cast into the Tigris."[13] Yet the memory of his martyrdom continues to haunt the Islamic world as a poignant reminder of God's presence among us in holy men and women. In fact, this towering figure became the inner guide of Louis Massignon, the French Islamicist whose life spanned the first two-thirds of the twentieth century, guiding his return to his Catholicism in a way that allowed him to continue to be instructed by the vibrant faith of his Muslim friends.[14] His friendship with Paul VI also allowed his voice to resonate in the way that *Nostra Aetate* directed Catholics to a fresh appreciation of Islam. Indeed, each of the twentieth-century figures who stand out as spiritual leaders in their respective traditions reflects a creative interaction with another faith tradition, from Martin Buber and Franz Rosenzweig in Judaism, to Louis Massignon, Jules Monchanin, and Bede Griffiths among Catholic Christians, and in Islam, the Pathan leader and man of God 'Abdul Ghaffar Khan, who responded to the inspiration of Gandhi to form a hundred thousand Pathan nonviolent soldiers to help bring independence to India. The fledgling state of Pakistan, led by mullahs and military men, could not countenance Badshah Khan, however, so it imprisoned him and brutally suppressed his army of Khudai Khidmatgars.[15] Indeed, traditions usually find it easier to eject those proposing renewal than to accept their challenging invitation.

For in fact, each of our religious traditions displays a shadow side (to borrow an illuminating expression from Jung's psychology) that can easily be manipulated by those intent to harness it to the service of power and that impedes any self-corrective momentum in the tradition.[16] These shadow sides have been reinforced whenever relations among the communities have been governed by polemics, notably the polemics of power. We have seen how centuries of trading the epithet of *infidel* prevented both Christians and Muslims from even thinking the other had anything to offer, while the genocide at Auschwitz culminated eighteen centuries of "teaching of contempt" (Jules Isaac) as ostensibly Christian societies kept Jews as the *other* in their midst, in a seesaw between begrudging toleration and outright persecution.[17] Can it be any wonder that Ashkenazi Jews' relation to Christianity reflected a "know your enemy" scenario? Sephardic Jews, ensconced in the Islamicate, developed a very different set of attitudes, for while they shared a second-class *(dhimmi)* status with Christians, a leader like Moses Maimonides could flourish in his role as court physician to Salah ad-Din, while also serving his own community in countless ways.

(Indeed, articulate Sephardim can bemoan the way Zionism was fostered in the polemical soil of Ashkenazi Judaism, thereby shaping the prevailing attitudes in the subsequent state of Israel.)[18] As recent events have revealed a shadow side of Islam, Western societies have reacted so as to reveal their own, with predictable polemics. What is most significant about this phenomenon is the way it can turn religious traditions into collective idolatries, as they allow themselves to be so fixated on negative features of an opposing community as to block their own access to the revelation given them, with its power to transform hatred and fear. A contemporary Sufi writer has rendered the name *Islam* as "reconciliation with God," so highlighting that any tradition will need to become reconciled with its God concomitantly with reconciling to others, for the shadow side effectively obscures the revealing God from the community called to receive revelation in fruitfulness.[19] The dialectic of love and rejection dear to the Hebrew prophets works itself out in each of the Abrahamic faiths.

The God shared by Jews, Christians, and Muslims is the free Creator of "heaven and earth," whom the Qur'an describes so simply as "the One who says 'be' and it is" (6:73). John Milbank remarks how startling is the biblical account of the origins of the universe in an "original peaceful creation." Yet he also reminds us how that text has become so "concealed . . . beneath the palimpsest of the negative distortion of *dominium*" that the church must continually "seek to recover [it] through the superimposition of a third redemptive template, which corrects these distortions by means of forgiveness and atonement."[20] For the "dominion" to which he alludes extends beyond nature to include other human beings as well, legitimizing force to subdue any recalcitrant group. Islam finds in that free creation the source empowering efforts to restore that original harmony to the world in which we live, while simply presuming that the struggle necessary to move us from this world *(al-dunyâ)* to the next *(al-âkhira)* will inevitably entail using force—not to coerce hearts ("there is no compulsion in religion," 2:256) but to establish "the *political domain* of Islam, so that Islam can work to produce the order on earth that the Qur'an seeks."[21] So this struggle *(jihâd)* will involve "striving with your wealth and your lives in the path of God" (9:41). As we know, the tradition distinguishes sharply between *lesser* and *greater jihâd*, with the "lesser" identified with overt force and the "greater" with the struggle to align one's own heart with the "path of God." Yet the order, the world for which one is striving, will not be realized until the final judgment, so Fazlur Rahman reasons that our current "vision must see through the consequences of [our] actions and aims [to] the end which constitutes the meaning of positive human effort. This is the end which cannot be achieved without *jihâd*, for it is God's unalterable law that He will not bring about results without human endeavor; otherwise those who endeavor and those who do not would become indistinguishable."[22]

So the beginning and the end are intimately connected for the Qur'an: the same One "who says 'be' and it is" will restore our bodily selves to life for a judgment that will ask how well each of us has sought to return everything to the One from whom we receive everything. For that "return" delineates the "path of God" to which all human beings are called, according to their proper revelation, since without revelation they could not hope to find it. Following it will require constant effort *(jihâd)*, but the power to persevere stems from that same source. Fail we shall, but the One in whose name we initiate every action is above all merciful *(b'ism Allah ar-Rahman ar-Rahîm)*, with a mercy that empowers each fresh start. Indeed, the abiding presence of this call to greater *jihâd* shows why the Sufi author Rabia Terri Harris insists that "'Islam' essentially conveys reconciliation with God,"[23] for each of us will always stand in need of that; which also explains why the greater *jihâd* must always accompany the lesser, lest we too readily identify our wayward goals with "struggle in the path of God." So any effort to restore the original peace of creation, whether by Muslims or Christians, will entail uncovering the ways by which each tradition has left room for our own desires to distort the community's aspirations, so warranting the use of force ostensibly "in the way of God" yet along paths we outline ourselves. And since each one of our Abrahamic communities has shown itself less than exemplary in that task, we may find that our best resources lie in learning from each other's relative successes or failures.

Forgiveness and atonement do not play the same role in Islam as they do in Christian doctrine and commended practice. The gracious mercy of God, exhibited in the gift of the Qur'an, can only remind us of the complete freedom of creation, the original grace. But something else is operative, something parallel to the African *ubuntu* philosophy, wherein human beings are invited to see themselves in relation to the others facing them: "I am because you are." From all indications, the power and momentum of the Peace and Reconciliation Commission in South African society stems from this ancestral conviction of solidarity.[24] One might even ask whether the touted sense of "individual responsibility" that Western Christians celebrate as an achievement would not, bereft of its religious roots, actually impede such a process in our societies, were we to have the courage to undertake it! Yet Islamic societies continue to display an active sense of hospitality: the very presence of a stranger elicits a welcoming response from them. It is difficult to try to identify that response. It need not be one of overt assistance; it appears to be an anticipation that your presence represents something offered to me, perhaps an offering of myself to me: in reaching out to you I anticipate that something will be awakened in me. Yet the promise of that awakening is not what moves me to respond to your presence; that would be too calculating. It is rather that your presence activates a profound sense of our being on this journey together. It is not immediately evident how Islam engenders this spirit, but it may have something to do with the call of the Qur'an, the way it calls forth a response from the listener. And since that response takes place in a communal setting, we are linked together as responders to the creating Word of God and so begin actively to participate in what is generated in the synergy between call and response. This represents a "relational ontology" in practice, a living out of the fact that our very existence is (as Aquinas noted) an "existence-*to*" our Creator, for it is continually coming *from* that One. This abiding sense of creation is a palpable reality in Islam, where mention of any sort of future plans is inevitably tempered with "*in sh'Allah!*" So the Islamic path of reconciliation becomes receiving one another under the canopy of God's prevailing mercy, to which all practicing Muslims feel themselves beholden. It is less a matter of making specific amends for personal injury than a mutual recognition that we are walking a path together, along which we all stumble, so that we are each empowered to welcome the other back, even when that means stepping across a divide exacerbated by personal injury.

This mercy-centered reception of others translates personally into a keen feeling for friendship as well as its exigent practice. It is perhaps here that other-believers feel most welcomed, for personal friendships inevitably result in their being received into the bosom of the community, less as *other*-believers than as *believers*. This sentiment clearly animated Louis Massignon's lifelong study of Islam, as he was drawn into one friendship after another with Muslims educated or uneducated, each of whom apparently nourished his own faith in God. In the event, these continuing friendships effected an acute sense of solidarity with the Algerian independence movement, in the face of repression by his own country's military, which he actively protested on the streets of Paris in his late seventies.[25] Indeed, the figure of Massignon may be said to shape our attempt to gain an interfaith perspective on reconciliation. For it was his founding friendship with al-Hallaj, given expression in his countless Muslim friends, that allowed him to recover his own faith and live it subsequently in the unique way he did: as one whose Christian faith was suffused with what he continued to learn from his Muslim friends. I have tried to characterize this dialectic of faith as "interfaith" by reminding us of the peculiar "shadow side" associated with each of the Abrahamic faiths. What interfaith friendships seem to offer is a way of allowing the faith of others, with the access to the divine it represents, to interact with our own faith commitment to draw out dimensions of our faith response that the shadow side of our tradition may have blocked. This is far from a simple "complementarity" approach, wherein one tradition makes up what is lacking in the other. It rather represents a process whereby triangulating from another tradition—not abstractly but through friendships—allows us to activate the critical dimensions of our own tradition, so clarifying what may have become obscured in the revelation we have received. It is my contention that our generation comes along at a prescient time for effecting a mutual illumination of this sort, exemplified in the life of Louis Massignon. How it can also prove possible with the third and originating Abrahamic partner will be explored in subsequent reflections on the way the Holy Land offers a case study in reconciliation; indeed, more taxing than one could ever imagine.

What we dearly need at this point, however, is a ritual way of expressing that "triangulation through friendship." Steps have been taken by couples facing the prospect of interfaith marriages, notably where the faith of each partner is so dear that they sense how fidelity to their respective faiths will prove crucial to their mutual fidelity over a lifetime. Yet even in relationships of far less intimacy, and especially for those who are striving together toward a shared goal, joint ways of prayer will prove crucial. In chapter 7 of this volume, Ronald Wells tells a story of a eucharistic service intended to reinforce faltering efforts to bridge the acrimonious religious divide during the torturous peacemaking in Northern Ireland, in the face of ecclesiastical rules preventing those who wanted to express their shared hope for reconciliation from full participation. At one of these an older Catholic woman took the communion wafer in her own hands to her Protestant counterpart, offering half of it to him with the words: "The body of Christ broken for us." Let us attend to the total symbolism here, for if age bears the fruit of a wisdom born of suffering, being a woman allowed her to bridge the ecclesiastical divide. Indeed, women may best serve to foster reconciliation between forces now dividing our world into Christian and Muslim, much as women's groups helped to defuse the conflict between Christian societies in Ireland. Moreover, the need for ritual expression reminds us forcibly of Jesus' distillation of the multiple commandments of the Torah to two: reconciliation with God will be effected only as we reconcile with one another, and rituals can best express that intertwining.

In his *Holy War, Holy Peace,* Marc Gopin exploits his rabbinic background and conflict resolution training to ask how religion can bring peace to the Middle East. And his sensitivity to the deeply divisive human issues involved culminates in the final section: specific steps toward a new relationship.[26] These specific steps follow upon a recognition of the ways in which traditional practices *(sulh)* adopted from Islamic and Christian Arab society, as well as *teshuva* (repentance) from Jewish religious practice, can contribute to reconciliation by neutralizing abiding obstacles stemming from fear or from insult to honor.[27] So some of the steps he outlines come under the rubric of "myth, ritual, and ceremony."[28] These embody the ritual remembering of events that once poisoned the atmosphere, yet doing so in a context where the ritual can bring a sense of participating in one another's pain and so eliciting a shared hope. Already groups of bereaved parents are meeting together across the divide, teaching one another how much each set of parents needs the other to overcome the chasm caused by the violent death of their children. What is especially significant here is that the bereaved faces are not at all like the stereotypes of those who pulled the trigger or carried the bomb. Rituals may be second best to such face-to-face groups, yet they carry a potency that can reach more widely. Here is the best possible way to invoke, even to exploit, the resources of religious faiths to make a beginning in setting things right after cataclysmic crises.

Moreover, there is mounting evidence that nothing short of the quality of forgiveness at once demanded and facilitated by the Abrahamic revelations will be able to empower people to make a fresh start after the devastation endorsed by the shadow sides of those same religious faiths. For once religion has been misused to reinforce chauvinistic aspirations, and indeed legitimize demonization of others, appeals to fairness and human rights will hardly be able to be heard. Nothing short of mutual acknowledgment of responsibility for the ensuing human disaster will be able to clear the air to the point where the parties in conflict can envision one another sharing a common destiny. And only then, as Alan Torrance reminds us (in ch. 2 of this volume), will Jews, Christians, or Muslims each be freed to act toward the other from the unconditional acceptance rendered to each by the free Creator freely revealed in their respective scriptures. Indeed, short of that, no fresh start will be given a chance, for each attempt will be measured against the accumulated resistance and resentment engendered by protracted conflict. As South Africa's Truth and Reconciliation

Commission has exhibited, and Terri Phelps's literary analysis of the documents so poignantly delineates, only the truth can liberate, compassionately related and received.[29]

# Notes

1. This is the burden of Karl Rahner's celebrated "world-church" lecture, published in *Theological Studies* 40 (1979) as "Towards a Fundamental Interpretation of Vatican II."

2. Second Vatican Council, *Nostra Aetate,* par 3.

3. On this issue, see Augustine DiNoia, O.P., *Diversity of Religions* (Washington, DC: Catholic University of America Press, 1992), Gavin D'Costa, *Theology and Religious Pluralism* (New York: Oxford University Press, 1986), and Paul Griffiths, *Problems of Religious Diversity* (Malden, MA: Blackwell, 2001).

4. What Griffiths calls "the neuralgic point of creative conceptual growth for Christian thought" (*Problems of Religious Diversity,* 97). Why else would it prove "neuralgic" except for this propensity?

5. Oliver Sacks, *The Man Who Mistook His Wife for a Hat* (New York: Simon and Schuster, 1970), 1–5.

6. Thomas Aquinas, *Summa Theologiae* 1.13.5, with an illuminating appendix to the Blackfriars edition by Herbert McCabe on "imperfect signification" (New York: McGraw-Hill, 1965); henceforth cited in the text as *ST.* See David Burrell, "Maimonides, Aquinas and Ghazali on Naming God," in *The Return to Scripture in Judaism and Christianity,* ed. Peter Ochs (New York: Paulist Press, 1993), 233–55.

7. Robert Sokolowski, *The God of Faith and Reason* (Washington, DC: Catholic University of America Press, 1989); for an extended reflection on Wittgenstein's aphorism "theology as grammar," see George Lindbeck, *The Nature of Doctrine* (Philadelphia: Westminster Press, 1984).

8. Jean Daniélou, *Salvation of the Nations,* trans. Angeline Bouchard (Notre Dame: University of Notre Dame Press, 1962).

9. Sara Grant, *Towards an Alternative Theology: Confessions of a Nondualist Christian* (Notre Dame: University of Notre Dame Press, 2002).

10. Rudi teVelde, *Substantiality and Participation in Aquinas* (Leiden: Brill, 1996).

11. See David B. Burrell, *Knowing the Unknowable God* (Notre Dame: University of Notre Dame Press, 1986). The term *Islamicate* was coined by Marshall Hodgson to convey the extensive cultural milieu; *Venture of Islam* (Chicago: University of Chicago Press, 1974).

12. G. K. Chesterton, *Orthodoxy* (1908; reprint, London: Hodder and Stoughton, 1996); excepting radical Calvinist views that have given the doctrine an unacceptable name.

13. Rabia Terri Harris, "Nonviolence in Islam: the Alternative Community Tradition," in *Subverting Hatred: The Challenge of Nonviolence in Religious Traditions,* ed. Daniel L. Smith-Christopher (Maryknoll, NY: Orbis Books, 1998), 101. See Louis Massignon, *The*

*Passion of al-Hallaj, Mystic and Martyr of Islam,* 4 vols., trans. Herbert Mason (Princeton: Princeton University Press, 1975), and Herbert Mason's dramatic précis *The Death of al-Hallaj* (Notre Dame: University of Notre Dame Press, 1979).

14. Mary Louise Gude, C.S.C., *Louis Massignon: The Crucible of Compassion* (Notre Dame: University of Notre Dame Press, 1996).

15. Harris, "Nonviolence in Islam," 103 n. 12; see Eknath Easwaren, *A Man to Match His Mountains: Badshah Khan, Nonviolent Soldier of Islam* (Petaluma, CA: Nilgiri Press, 1984).

16. See my review of two studies by Avital Wohlman: "A Philosophical Foray into Difference and Dialogue: Avital Wohlman on Maimonides and Aquinas," *American Catholic Philosophical Quarterly* 76 (2002): 181–94.

17. Jules Isaac, *Has Anti-Semitism Roots in Christianity?* (New York: National Conference of Christians and Jews, 1961).

18. See David Sasha in *Sephardic Heritage Update,* October 8, 2002, available from slipstein@aol.com.

19. For the relations among Revealer, revealing Word, and receiving community, see my suggestion of the triadic structure of Abrahamic faiths in *Freedom and Creation in Three Traditions* (Notre Dame: University of Notre Dame Press, 1993).

20. John Milbank, *Theology and Social Theory: Beyond Secular Reason* (Oxford: Blackwell, 1990), 317.

21. Fazlur Rahman, *Major Themes of the Qur'an* (Chicago: Biblioteca Islamica, 1980), 63.

22. Ibid., 64.

23. Harris, "Nonviolence in Islam," 101.

24. Richard Bell, *Understanding African Philosophy* (New York: Routledge, 2002).

25. Gude, *Louis Massignon,* 214 ff.

26. Marc Gopin, *Holy War, Holy Peace* (New York: Oxford, 2002).

27. Ibid., 183–94.

28. Ibid., 204–19.

29 . Terri Phelps, *Shattered Voices* (Philadelphia: University of Pennsylvania Press, 2004).

# CHAPTER FIVE

# The Double Demands of Reconciliation

*The Case of Unified Germany*

## A. JAMES McADAMS

In *Exclusion and Embrace,* the theologian Miroslav Volf outlines a model of Christian reconciliation that makes high demands of new democracies struggling with the evils and injustices of former dictatorships. On the one hand, he stipulates that the fragile new societies that are coming into being will never flourish unless their leaders turn the other cheek. Somehow, those who have been wronged in the past must be willing to reach out to the persons who have caused their misfortunes and, if only because of their common humanity, find a place for them in their lives. But on the other hand, he complicates this expectation by insisting that *full reconciliation* will not take place unless this act of "embrace" is conjoined with an "[indispensable] struggle against deception, injustice, and violence." There can be no doubt that the act of including others, even the most noxious and undeserving of others, comes first in Volf's Christian calculus of values, but his argument is unique in explicitly emphasizing the conditionality of the gesture. Embrace itself, he underscores, "cannot take place until the truth has been said and justice done."[1]

At first glance, Volf's approach to one of the central dilemmas of transitional justice might seem eminently unobjectionable to nonreligious observers of the same phenomenon in the social sciences and legal professions. Political scientists, sociologists, and legal scholars alike have routinely acknowledged the desirability of achieving a balance of sorts between these twin objectives.[2] Yet when pressed, many have been quick to point to the numerous occasions in which inclusion and justice have seemingly assumed mutually exclusive proportions. In their supposedly more realistic assessment of the challenges facing the leaders of fledgling democracies, politicians must often decide which of the two values they want most and, in effect, be willing to absorb the consequences of pursuing only one-half of Volf's model of reconciliation. Either, it is assumed, they put aggressive truth seeking and retribution at the forefront of their government's search for identity (and thereby knowingly run the risk of driving a wedge between their citizens), or they deliberately downplay the wrongdoing of the bygone age in the interest of promoting consensual values in the emerging order (and thereby slight the victims).

In fact, the active participants in these controversies as well have frequently turned to a similarly one-sided logic in making the case for those aspects of the transition that matter most to them. For example, the proponents of the more aggressive perspective have been inclined to define reconciliation as, above all, a victim-oriented enterprise, which presupposes that the instigators of injustice have first been forced to own up to their offenses and proven themselves worthy of the trust and respect of full citizenship. In this image, the wronged hold the key to the viability and sanctity of the fledgling order. Presumably, only they can decide whether the acts of contrition and confession that might be won through criminal trials and truth commissions are sufficient to put the horrors of the past to rest.

It is hard to avoid seeing the truth in this perspective. As Nicholas Wolterstorff points out in chapter 3 of this volume, the democratizing state occupies a peculiar role when its leaders decide, for reasons of their own, to forgive the perpetrators of injustice. Any such action, taken on the state's behalf, risks punishing the victims a second time. As Wolterstorff observes, "The state, when it forgives, rather than ensuring that the one deprived of the goods to which she had a primary right will at least enjoy those to which she has a retributive right, further victimizes her by now itself depriving her of those retributive goods against her will."

In contrast to this position, an opposing group of activists has tended to emphasize the inclusionary side of reconciliation. They treat it as a largely offender-based activity that is meant to bring outsiders back into the public fold and to restore harmonious relations among all of society's diverse parts. Given the depth of the wrongs inflicted by the old regime and the unstable social relations it has bequeathed to its successors, these participants regard truth and justice as, at best, secondary pursuits along the path to national unity. Accordingly, they shift the onus of responsibility to the victims, whom they expect to show forgiveness, understanding, and even a measure of forgetting if the new democracy is to thrive.

Do these competing tendencies mean, then, that Volf is being unrealistic in seeking to unite moral and political agendas that are frequently at odds with each other? Certainly, the recent history of democratic transitions confirms that practically every postauthoritarian government of the past two decades has had to wrestle with the potentially destabilizing consequences of pursuing both victim-centered and offender-based strategies simultaneously. Few have been able to escape the necessity of making hard choices between these polarities.

In addition, these regimes' choices are equally telling. A majority of them—including states as varied as Chile, El Salvador, Brazil, Spain, and Poland—have tended to favor the less provocative of the two paths before them: that is, grudging acceptance of wrongdoing rather than the more confrontational avenues to reconciliation implied by such high-profile activities as criminal prosecutions. South Africa is, arguably, the major exception to this rule in that its leaders, although tending to prefer truth telling over justice, kept open the possibility of criminal prosecutions for individuals who failed to own up to their offenses, as well as for those responsible for particularly heinous crimes. Still, doubters of Volf's position would likely contend—rightly or wrongly—that, in the eyes of the victims (e.g., the relatives of murdered activist Steve Biko), the South African approach has primarily been an offender-based strategy designed to placate the would-be opponents of democracy. As the Chilean rights activist José Zalaquett has maintained about what is, to his mind, the comparatively greater desirability of political stability over justice, "[A]ll things being equal, forgiveness and [offender-based] reconciliation are preferable to punishment."[3] Likewise, the political scientist Samuel Huntington has observed that when the long-term viability of the new regime is uncertain, it is unwise to pursue any form of retributive or corrective action: "The political costs of such an effort will outweigh any moral gains."[4]

But are Zalaquett's and Huntington's assessments correct? Though it is undeniable that many of the leaders of new democracies have looked with favor on such risk-averse policies, I am not persuaded that this record makes Volf's aspirations to a more complete form of reconciliation any less defensible. As I shall contend in this essay, by drawing upon the example of retrospective justice in the post-unification Federal Republic of Germany (FRG) in the 1990s, it may be that far from basing their actions on what they consider to be a sober and informed assessment of their options, these politicians have simply followed the course of seeming least resistance at the time. In fact, I shall also suggest that Germany's experience with this challenge can even give us reason to see Volf's prescriptions as a distinctive kind of realism. His view is informed by a deeper understanding of the options that do and do not present themselves to governments in turbulent circumstances.

I shall make this case in the following pages by focusing on one of the most thorny and divisive of Germany's efforts in the 1990s to come to terms with the crimes and abuses of the communist German Democratic Republic (GDR). This involved the opening of the files of the former East German secret police (the *Staatssicherheitsdienst,* or Stasi) and their utilization in assessing the democratic credentials of literally hundreds of thousands of public officials. By comparing the arguments of two of the most vocal participants in the debates over the Stasi's records, Joachim Gauck and Friedrich Schorlemmer, I shall demonstrate that there was no obvious way to resolve this controversy. Political prognosticators would have been absolutely right to predict that it would be tough going to locate a middle ground between the desire to reopen this dark episode in the GDR's past to sustained scrutiny and the countervailing necessity of showing understanding and due restraint in judging the actions of individuals operating in a different political context.

Nonetheless, as we shall discover by examining the FRG's policies over these years, there are two good reasons for casting a skeptical eye on the sorts of assumptions that have typically led social scientists and other informed observers to think that Germany's leaders would, in the fashion of a dispassionate rational actor, simply choose the most immediately palatable approach to this dilemma. The first is that for all of western Germany's vaunted advantages over the crumbling regime in the East, the German government was seldom in the position where it could do everything it desired. Like the leaders of comparable democracies elsewhere, it did not take long for Chancellor Helmut Kohl and his colleagues to discover that, in the prescient words of one historian, although they might have wanted "to make their own history . . . they [could] not make it just as they [pleased], . . . but under circumstances directly encountered, given and transmitted from the past."[5] In any country, policy is rarely like a smorgasbord where one can choose one's options according to taste or fancy.

The second reason, which Volf above all would want to call to our attention, is that even within the limited range of options available to them, these politicians would learn—or on one question, as I shall suggest later, they should have learned—that they could not afford to slight either of the competing paths to fostering reconciliation in the East. Indeed, I shall argue that Volf's argument can be improved by adding another layer of complexity. Transitional justice is seldom a matter of sorting out the guilty from the innocent. If only it were that simple. As we shall find, the fact that multiple audiences could be affected by the decisions or nondecisions of the German government—not only victims and victimizers but also the entire eastern German population and the FRG itself—meant the country's leaders could never afford to lose sight of the unpredictable and sometimes even contradictory consequences of their actions.

## Seemingly Contradictory Paths to Reconciliation

The circumstances that gave rise to the Stasi controversy in the first place are widely known. In mid-January 1990, a crowd of angry demonstrators stormed into the GDR's secret-police headquarters in East Berlin's Normannenstrasse and took control of the most oppressive organ of the East German dictatorship. This act set in motion a train of events that ultimately opened to public debate the fate of the Stasi's millions of previously ultrasecret recruitment files and personal dossiers.

In many ways, the taking of the secret-police *Zentrale* may be likened to other great historical events, such as the storming of the Bastille in France in 1789 or the assault on the Winter Palace in St. Petersburg in 1917. The benefit of the comparison is not so much for the truth value of these well-known occurrences—both of which have been distorted and romanticized beyond the point of factuality over the years—but instead for what they symbolized about the fall of an oppressive regime. As in revolutionary France or Russia, one could already see signs of the weakening of the ideological and institutional pillars of the GDR's ancien regime for many months preceding the breaching of the Normannenstrasse headquarters. In summer 1989, the ruling communist government had been thrown into crisis as tens of thousands of its citizens, long barred from traveling to the West, took advantage of a suddenly reopened border between Hungary and Austria to flee their country for the FRG. By October, this mass exodus was complemented internally by the heretofore unthinkable appearance of mass demonstrations for political reform in many of the GDR's major cities. Hundreds of thousands of the country's previously quiescent citizens went into the streets to defy the state's authority and assert their political autonomy. Then, on November 9, as a result of a series of miscommunications between government officials and a desperate, last-ditch effort to regain political authority, the Berlin Wall was opened. On a direct and deeply personal basis, eastern Germans were finally able to restore unimpeded contacts with their western compatriots.

Yet it was the fall of the Berlin Stasi headquarters that captured, most poignantly, the collapse of the GDR's dictatorial apparatus. For the first time, as curious protestors entered the complex and searched through the vaults holding vast stores of secret information collected by the Ministry of State Security (MfS), what had been inconceivable on a practical level in a closed state become theoretically possible in an open polity. Ordinary Germans (primarily in the East, but also in the West) could read through relevant segments of the approximately 178 km of shelf space devoted to the documents that had been compiled on their lives and seek to uncover, among other things, the names of persons who had violated their most closely held confidences, informed on them, and written covert reports for the secret police. Furthermore, once these wrongdoers had been identified, it became possible for authorities to use the files to review their activities and to reach informed conclusions about the underlying factors that had motivated their behavior. Provided that one demonstrated that a certain threshold of guilt had been crossed, it was conceivable that these offenders could be disqualified from holding a variety of positions of trust and authority in unified Germany, such as administrative posts in the state bureaucracies, the schools, the police forces, and the courts.

Nevertheless, while nearly everyone could agree that the fall of the last and most secretive bastion of the East German dictatorship was a welcome event, there was nearly instantaneous disagreement about whether opening the Stasi's holdings would be the best way to resolve over four decades of antagonistic relations between former victims and victimizers. This rift can be seen in the contrasting arguments of two of the most prominent eastern commentators on the subject. One was Joachim Gauck, the man who, in fall 1990, was named commissioner of the agency charged with controlling access to the MfS archives, the Federal Authority for the Records of the State Security Service of the GDR (BStU or, colloquially, "Gauck agency"). The other was one of his best-known critics, Friedrich Schorlemmer, who would, as we shall see, eventually end up on the losing side of the battle to severely restrict access to the files.

In some respects, the two personalities might otherwise have been thought to have a great deal in common. Both were Lutheran pastors who had established records of passionate involvement in the affairs of their local parishes, the one from the northern trading city of Rostock and the other from the city Luther made famous, Wittenberg. Both were on record as thoughtful and forthright critics of the East German regime before the events of 1989–90, though Schorlemmer was easily the more vociferous of the two. And, after the GDR's collapse and national unification, both would prove to be committed defenders of democratic values. Yet on the specific question of how—or even whether—the Stasi's holdings should be used as a mechanism to bring eastern Germans together again, Gauck and Schorlemmer unmistakably parted ways.

Gauck's perspective is conveniently spelled out in a book compiled from interviews about his experiences with the BStU during the first year of unification, *Die Stasi-Akten: Das unheimliche Erbe der DDR.*[6] In a chapter subtitled "The Painful Path to Reconciliation," Gauck makes it clear that in his ordering of the priorities before his compatriots, contrition and repentance should always come before forgiveness. Indeed, it is instructive that he defines the conditions for meaningful participation in democratic life in such a way that easterners will have no choice but to commit themselves to the aggressive pursuit of truth and the restoration of human dignity. It is an all-too-human fact of life, Gauck advises his reader, that when confronted with the Stasi's records, many of the GDR's former citizens will initially fail to see the point of rehashing disturbing events from their previous lives and, therefore, will recoil at the opportunity to learn from their mistakes. But, he stresses, the region's future depends on their meeting the challenge. If they are ever to free their country from the "psychic chains and tethers" of dictatorship, they must all be willing to confront even their worst memories directly, among them "the entanglements and injuries [that they inflicted on others], as well as the ancient and long-standing fears, nightmares, and anger that they so quickly concealed and repressed after the toppling of the [communist regime]" (98–99). Only through this "great therapeutic process," Gauck concludes, will they ever learn what it means to become self-reliant participants in a democratic society.

Predictably, Gauck reserves the chief burden of responsibility in this, in his words, "process of reconciliation with oneself" for the Stasi's former collaborators and regular officers. In his understanding of the obligation, it is decisive for a meaningful reckoning with the previous system that those implicated in the files be prepared to expose themselves to the full force of public scrutiny and criticism. Naturally, how they do this is important as well. If they are less than candid about their misdeeds when they come forward, Gauck advises, they will be certain to run into a wall of mistrust and hostility. However, if they honestly admit to their failings right away and acknowledge the hard evidence of their complicity, they will at least have a chance of making amends with those they have wronged.

Of course, this victim-centered understanding of reconciliation is also Gauck's *conditio sine qua non* for inclusion. The postauthoritarian order "will exclude no one," he insists, "who is prepared to recognize the point at which he failed in life. For it is much easier to plan the future with such persons than with those who constantly seek to portray as normal and routine [those types of activities, such as Stasi collaboration,] which are anything but normal and routine." Fortunately, he adds, in a note that we will consider later in this essay, honest contrition is fulfilling as well, for only it can be counted upon to "pave the way to true freedom" (100).

Were we to view Gauck's plea on its own terms, the logic behind it would probably appear self-evident. Surely, persons who suffered through the worst indignities inflicted by the Stasi—the sudden loss of their job, for example, or the breakup of their family, as well as the bitter memories of betrayal by close friends and associates—would demand such gestures. How could they realistically be expected to forgive the offenders if the latter were not first willing to admit to their sins and to suffer through the appropriate sanctions?

Yet this is where the contrasting position represented by Schorlemmer shows just how easy it can be for democratizing elites to be pulled in the opposite direction. Significantly, Schorlemmer would never have disagreed with Gauck about the desirability of encouraging the GDR's one-time citizens to come to terms, in some way and at some point, with their own or with others' involvement in the Stasi's crimes and abuses. In his view as well, the victims had a right to expect this. Nor did he ever encourage anyone to downplay the reprehensible nature of these offenses. In fact, although he initially sided with other prominent East German church authorities (e.g., Bishop Gottfried Forck) in seeking to close down the MfS archives altogether, Schorlemmer eventually came around to supporting their deployment in rare cases, such as those involving the rehabilitation of victims or particularly egregious cases of criminal behavior. Still, he and Gauck found themselves at odds over the decisive question of which elements of the population were to take on the main burden of reconciliation. Whereas Gauck stressed what the instigators had to do to restore their relationship with society as a whole, and especially with those they had wronged, Schorlemmer's emphasis—as we can see reflected throughout his articles, sermons, and interviews during the early 1990s—was predominately on the *victims* and on their special role in showing understanding for their oppressors and contributing to societal calm.

We can see evidence of this crucial difference in a 1993 article in which Schorlemmer addresses the matter of reconciliation directly. "Reconciliation," he argues, "can only succeed when there is a readiness on both sides to speak in an open and differentiated manner about who did, or failed to do, what to whom." It is undeniable, he affirms, that this undertaking cannot mean "impairing the victims' sense of honor." But at the same time, what he has to say about those who are being held responsible for the failings of the old system is even more revealing. They must be convinced that they are not "hopelessly closed out of [the new order]."[7]

At least in part, we can account for this very different assessment of eastern priorities by recognizing that Schorlemmer and Gauck were not at all in agreement about the uses to which the secret-police files could be put. While the BStU chief seems to have assumed from the start that these records would provide a more or less straightforward means of reconstructing the truth about acts of personal betrayal and individual dishonesty under communist rule, Schorlemmer found this approach to truth telling to be, at best, akin to seeing through a glass darkly.

As Schorlemmer cautioned on a number of occasions, the Stasi files would need to be treated with care and skepticism if they were to be utilized at all to assign guilt. As he warns in an earlier 1992 article, nothing "would be more fatal than for one to make sweeping judgments" about an issue that could jeopardize a person's future life chances. Indeed, these are not just any documents but the secret holdings of an organization, the MfS, that violated most standards of human decency to collect them in the first place. Moreover, he emphasizes, if one makes the mistake of relying upon them alone in deciding someone's fate, it will be next to impossible to distinguish accurately between the truly guilty and the mere hangers-on, that is, the "big-time scoundrels and the pitiful small fry *(ganz arme Schweine),* the common snoops and the cunningly blackmailed, the seduced and the committed, the sharp and the insecure, the greedy and the ambitious."[8]

Similarly, in Schorlemmer's view, it is just as crucial for those in positions of authority to consider the less than ideal historical circumstances under which many collaborators chose to associate themselves with the secret police. No matter what their level of culpability, he underscores, these people were living under a dictatorship, and their options were never even close to being as propitious for informed choice as those enjoyed by their compatriots in the West. Therefore, to fail to judge them accordingly would be to risk the danger that "the files would be believed but not the context of real life in which they came into being."[9]

Notwithstanding these difficulties, Schorlemmer's greatest concern is that in focusing on the misbehavior of the Stasi, those who are demanding justice in the East have come perilously close to forgetting their own humanity and fallibility. Who can say, he queries in one article, that those easterners who had the good fortune to have never been subject to the Stasi's machinations would have preserved their honor had their luck been otherwise?[10] As if to answer this question, he reminds his reader of the biblical admonition that anyone wanting to point his finger at others should first be required to look in the mirror. "Who has never been guilty of betrayal?" he wonders, ". . . . Who has not known temptation? Who has never violated his own principles and ideals by failing to speak up?"[11]

In this spirit, the lesson that Schorlemmer derives from these judgments is fully in keeping with the inclusionary understanding of reconciliation. It is up to the victim to reach out to the victimizer and, when push comes to shove, to adjust his or her expectations of achieving justice accordingly. Even a Judas Iscariot, he advises, is entitled to the grace of not having to suffer forever under the weight of his guilt (and, Schorlemmer tells us, it was Judas's tragedy not to have had the wisdom to recognize this fact). Correspondingly, we are led to believe that the same logic can be applied to one's treatment of those persons who are identified as agents and collaborators in the Stasi files. "That which God does not regard as final," he insists, "we, too, should not regard as final — despite our anger, despite our wounds, and despite our disappointment."[12] In short, while one might hope to take modest steps to deal with their sins, a big enough challenge for anyone of Christian faith, the more important thing was to begin this process by receiving them back in society's fold.

## The West's Surprisingly Limited Choices

It does not take much imagination to see why German policy makers would have been hard pressed to bring Schorlemmer's inclusionary instincts into sync with Gauck's much more demanding understanding of reconciliation. Whereas one pastor was eager to set the opening tone for the region's reckoning with injustice by reaching out to his fellow human beings, the other's act of "embrace" presupposed a mandatory demonstration of contrition. Does this mean, however, that the ideal-typical social scientist that we described earlier in this essay would have been correct in predicting that the FRG's leaders would resolve the conflict by simply choosing their favored polarity?

In this instance, the reader will be forgiven for jumping to the conclusion — as many experts have done — that just such a choice was embodied in the German Bundestag's long-awaited passage in December 1991 of the so-called Stasi-Records law (*Stasi-Unterlagen Gesetz,* or StUG), which regularized citizen access to the secret-police holdings and provided the final legal framework for the loyalty tests of public officials. For one thing, it is telling how quickly the advocates of an offender-based strategy had lost the ability to dictate political outcomes after the reunification of the Germanies. By this time, some two years after the dramatic opening of the Berlin Wall, Schorlemmer was very much on the defensive. He had already failed to make the case for either keeping the MfS archives under tight rein or restricting their uses to special investigative committees (e.g., those designated by the churches).[13] Additionally, he was increasingly to be found among those critics who were calling—in vain, it would turn out—for agreement upon a *Schlußstrich,* or "end point," to all further uses of the files for screening purposes.[14]

In contrast, the passage of the StUG signified that events had been propelled in Gauck's direction. Over the coming decade, millions of public and private sector employees would be investigated for possible connections with the MfS, and at least fifty thousand would be dismissed from their jobs after their level of involvement in the ministry's activities was judged "unsuitable" (in the concise terminology of the German Unification treaty) to justify their retention. On an even grander scale, by 1999, nearly 1.6 million private citizens took advantage of the extraordinary opportunity to involve themselves directly in these processes. After decades of intimidation by the omnipresent but unseen hand of the Stasi, they could inspect their personal dossiers and come to conclusions on their own about how to react to revelations of friends, neighbors, colleagues, and even family members who had spied on them for the secret police.

Nevertheless, while it may appear in retrospect as if this victim-oriented approach to reconciliation was thoughtfully and deliberately selected by those at the helm of the new German state, a closer examination of the circumstances indicates that it was hardly a sign of rational decision making at work. Bonn's willingness to act upon the issue was a matter not so much of informed choice about Gauck's perspective as of a "giving in" to reality and a largely reluctant acceptance of the limits of the FRG's control. In fact, had western Germany's principal policy makers in the early 1990s been able to speak frankly about their wishes, they would have likely distanced themselves in one way or another from Gauck's approach. After all, given their western origins, most had not gone through the Stasi experience themselves. They did not know the pain and suffering of the East.

Furthermore, many western German politicians had well-founded reservations about allowing the Stasi issue to cloud the already enormously complicated task of reunifying Germany. Some figures, including even Chancellor Kohl, openly expressed the opinion that the lot of their eastern compatriots would have been easier had the MfS records never existed. For example, much like Schorlemmer, Interior Minister Wolfgang Schäuble conceded that he could not understand how eastern Germany would "really have a chance to win a better future" if it allowed itself to become stuck in this quagmire. Since families and friendships were being torn apart as a result of revelations from the files, he felt that "a considerable amount of the energy now being devoted to this task would be [better spent] by winning the future."[15]

Despite their inclinations, however, western officials evidently felt that they had no alternative but to climb on the bandwagon of scrutinizing the former victimizers and appeasing the victims. One factor behind their thinking had to do with decisions already reached. A half-year before the formal date of unification on October 3, 1990, the first free parliamentary (Volkskammer) elections of March 1990 were shaken by revelations that prominent figures from the movements that had overthrown the communist regime—among them, the co-founder of Democratic Awakening, Wolfgang Schnur; the eastern Social Democratic leader Ibrahim Böhme; and the Christian Democratic general secretary, Martin Kirchner—had been active informants for the MfS. More unsettling still, rumors spread at this juncture that even the GDR's new Christian Democratic prime minister, Lothar de Maizière, had been in the Stasi's employ. Under these conditions, the parties in the new parliament quickly caved in to public pressure to use the secret-police archives to screen their ranks for collaborators. Soon, the GDR government as well was vetting its employees.

Of course, in theory western Germany's leaders could have chosen to disregard, or at least downplay, these developments as they set the stage for the GDR's absorption into the FRG. However, given the extent to which these processes were already well underway, Schäuble and others concluded that they had little choice save to continue the screening procedures after unification. To do otherwise, they reasoned, would have been to fight an uphill battle with a population that already had ample misgivings about Bonn's intentions.

A second impetus behind the decision to take immediate action to use the files was provided by distinctly *eastern* concerns. Under any circumstance, ordinary eastern Germans were likely to be curious about the staggering amounts of information, rumor, and hearsay—on subjects ranging from favored work styles to dining habits, intimate encounters to hobbies—that the secret police had collected on their lives. As early as April 1990, one polling service found that an astounding 86 percent of the people it surveyed wished to see their dossiers.[16] Additionally, as the prospect of unification loomed just over the horizon, these feelings were joined with an even more powerful conviction in the East. Given the stories of human weakness and suffering behind these records, many easterners felt passionately that the fate of the files was their own affair. This was not a matter to be decided by the West!

Accordingly, in a burst of populist enthusiasm in summer 1990, the Volkskammer drafted a provisional law on the "protection and uses of the personal records [of the MfS]," that was specifically designed to ensure that this eastern perspective would be upheld in the inter-German negotiations. Reflecting western ambivalence on the question, the Kohl government was at first far from accommodating, and for a brief period in early September doubts arose about whether any part of the statute would be represented in the Unification treaty. Yet these developments simply had the effect of hardening the East's resolve to treat the files' fate as a litmus test of Bonn's intentions. The dissident Jens Reich summed up the defiant mood of his compatriots. "This is our dirty laundry and our stink," he declared, "and it is up to us alone to clean it up."[17] Finally, after a small group of oppositionists reoccupied the former Stasi headquarters to express their grievances, West German authorities relented and agreed to include many of the Volkskammer's original demands in the negotiations. Hence, contrary to Bonn's initial wishes, the government of unified Germany adopted the more ambitious and potentially more conflictual approach to the GDR's dictatorial legacy.

## Acting with a Double Vision

Against this background, it should not be surprising that numerous onlookers, from prominent legal theorists to former Communist Party notables, were quick to express the concern that this and other forms of coming to terms with the East German past would rapidly degenerate into an uncontrollable thirst for revenge and retaliation.[18] Would the activists who stood behind the opening of the Stasi files, they wondered, have the wisdom and courage to recall that the original purpose of their activities was to mend a broken society and not to fracture it anew? And what about the victims? In their passion to right the wrongs done to them, would they have the good sense to refrain from adopting the same intolerant attitudes and methods of their former oppressors?

Now that more than a decade and a half has passed since these fears were first expressed, the striking fact is how few of them ever came to fruition and, for that matter, how little social discord ever arose in the East. To be sure, this is not to say that there were no problems at all with the implementation of the Stasi-Records law or with the efforts of countless state and local governments, school boards, law associations, police departments, and private corporations throughout the 1990s to determine which of their employees had committed grave enough offenses that they could no longer be retained. Quite the contrary. As I have documented in *Judging the Past in Unified Germany,* the evidence available from subsequent court cases suggests that mistakes of all kinds were made in the handling of thousands of specific cases throughout the new *Länder.* In some, Schorlemmer's worries were evidently confirmed when MfS records were misread or misapplied to provide evidence of complicity that was manifestly lacking. In others, the agencies involved in ruling on collaborators' suitability to retain their jobs apparently utilized different, and even mutually contradictory, standards of judgment. In still others, overtly political motives conspired to tip the balance adversely between exculpatory findings and those of culpability.[19]

Notwithstanding these shortcomings, however, one is impressed by the extent to which the advocates of transitional justice, like Gauck, went out of their way to address the concerns of critics like Schorlemmer, even while steadfastly adhering to their expressed priorities. On this matter, a social scientist might say that the policy's implementers sought to define a manageable balance between the victim-centered and the inclusionary poles of reconciliation. I am prepared to concede the kernel of truth in his description, in the sense that everyday politics is always about compromise. But to my mind, a better way of characterizing the successful aspects of Gauck's and his colleagues' initiatives—and I will suggest something later about one evident failure—is that they came close to acting in the spirit of what Volf has termed "a double vision" of the challenges before them—that is, a way of viewing their objectives that took into account both their personal perceptions of what had to be done and those of the persons to be affected by these actions.[20] Whereas the social-scientific concept of balance might suggest that two distinct agendas had been weighed against each other, Volf would have us recognize that the attention to these contrasting attributes of reconciliation should occur simultaneously and as part of the same ongoing process.

If we treat Gauck as an exemplar of the FRG's policies over the first decade of unification, we can make a convincing case that a double vision of sorts played a role in his thinking. But this makes sense only if we are willing to expand Volf's understanding of the parties to be affected by the BStU's activities to a much broader audience than the Stasi perpetrators alone. One can understand why Volf would single out the accused victimizers for special attention given the threat that alienated elites can represent to the successful functioning of any new democracy. But the challenge of transitional justice is even more complex than that. I will suggest in the following paragraphs that the attempt to make determinations about guilt and innocence, punishment and inclusion, should be extended to a much broader swath of the German population. At least *two other groups* had reasons of their own for being concerned about the implications of Gauck's quest for justice. Their views, too, were relevant to the prospects for reconciliation in unified Germany.

The first group was the eastern German population itself, and in particular that broad, amorphous category of persons who could be easily classified neither as the victims of the secret police nor as the reputed victimizers in its employ. On the one hand, as we have seen earlier, Gauck viewed the East's exposure to the secrets in the Stasi files as a "therapeutic process." It would help to assuage the wounds of dictatorship by allowing ordinary citizens to confront the terrible truth about what had been done to them. But exposure to the files was equally important for another reason. Given the pressures of living and surviving under dictatorial rule, it could have the effect of confronting *them* with the corresponding harms and injuries, great and small, that they had inflicted upon others over the same period (97). In this case, even Schorlemmer would have agreed with Gauck. Such a recognition of one's own limitations was essential for the FRG's new citizens to come to grips with their own humanity.

On the other hand, Gauck must have been concerned about the danger of implying that the recognition of these all-too-human sins and foibles was tantamount to throwing virtually anyone who was not a certified victim of secret-police oppression into the same pot as the worst offenders. It was not the purpose of the BStU, he contended on numerous occasions, to meddle in the lives of the vast majority of easterners who had committed no greater offense than to make their peace with the realities of the communist system. Rather, his agency's sole objective was to use the files to identify those persons who, of their own knowledge and volition, had taken the extra, indefensible step of selling their honor to the MfS. "Accommodation [with the old regime] was normal," he insisted, "but over-accommodation, including working for the secret police, is not."[21]

Actually, German policy makers were forced to come to terms with this demand for differentiation from an early date, since they could scarcely avoid making a decision of some sort about how far they were prepared to take their campaigns for administrative screening. Technically, had they wanted to go beyond focusing on the MfS alone, there was nothing to prevent them from applying stringent loyalty tests to *anyone* who had been associated with the communist regime. If taken to its logical extreme, this step would have included the over 2.3 million members of the governing Socialist Unity Party (SED), the country's state bureaucracies, its armed forces, and its police. However, because such a policy could have led to the disqualification of as much as one-half of the GDR's adult population from ever serving in an official capacity in the unified German state, they prudently chose to limit their ambitions to the most egregiously problematic cases of secret-police collaboration. Unlike membership in the SED or service in the military, they reasoned, which had both been public facts in the GDR, the aspect of Stasi collusion that made it so unsuited to the task of building trust in a free society was that it was premised upon a deficit in personal integrity.[22]

The second group for which Gauck required a double vision was unique to Germany. This was composed of the western architects of German unification. Although one sometimes had to read between the lines to see it, this category included people like Kohl and Schäuble, who were inevitably concerned with the impact of others' agendas upon their priorities. As we have seen, many regarded the eastern interest in redressing ancient wrongs with misgivings. Not only would the attempt to identify the supposed perpetrators have complicated their efforts to proceed apace to unify the German people. In addition, they shared the critics' concerns about the ability of activists, such as Gauck, to abide by a course of moderation and, above all, the basic precepts of the rule of law.

In light of these concerns, Gauck's challenge was twofold. First, he had to convince his western interlocutors that despite their lack of a personal connection with the problem, special attention was required to address his region's need to confront the past directly. But second, he had to reassure the skeptics that this undertaking would be fully consistent with the tried and tested legal traditions of the FRG. On the first score, *Die Stasi-Akten* is practically a testament to the necessity of allowing the eastern German populace to deal with the legacy of dictatorship in its own fashion. This was really another way of saying that the East's march to democracy would be different from that of the West. If only a majority of westerners could be brought to understand, Gauck pled at one point, what it meant to experience the hopelessness, depression, and disillusionment of four decades of authoritarian rule! In any case, he advises, it would certainly not do to "treat the GDR's former citizens as though they had 40 years of the *Rechtsstaat* behind them." Nor, he added, would it help to pretend that the Stasi problem was resolved simply because its governing institution, the Ministry of State Security, had been overthrown (96–97). The issue was still very much alive in people's minds and in the presence of former secret-police operatives and informers in their daily lives.

At the same time, on the second count, *Die Stasi-Akten* shows that Gauck was at pains to convince his western counterparts that the resulting confrontation with the MfS records would not result in a "witch hunt" (92). To the contrary, while the Stasi's crimes had taken place under a dictatorship, they would now be handled by a fully functioning democracy. This fact signified that the eastern German populace would have a healthy alternative to using revenge as a means of expressing their pent-up anger and frustrations. The desire to see their former oppressors pay a price for their offenses would be properly channeled through the German *Rechtsstaat*'s impersonal norms of due process and proportionality.

In this spirit, Gauck underscored that the administrators of the BStU had no intention of applying a rigid definition of "guilt, complicity, and innocence" to the files. Although over 270,000 people had been associated with the MfS at the time of the GDR's fall in 1989 (counting both full-time employees and informants), this did not mean that all, or even most, of these individuals had to be lumped together as "perpetrators" or even that those who fell into the latter group should necessarily be punished. Gauck reassured his readers that the sheer complexity of the challenge meant that one would have to begin any investigation into the Stasi's activities by making crucial distinctions. The agency's low-ranking employees who had committed no wrong at all—the cooks and secretaries, soldiers and maintenance people—were not in the least the same types of people as the higher-ranking officers who had been chiefly responsible for its oppressive acts. Only the last were unfit for future public service (27).

Then, too, in the spirit of this paean to the rule of law, Gauck was careful to note that a balanced and fair-minded assessment of an individual's ties with the secret police should always take into account the specific circumstances that gave rise to the activity. Sometimes, he advised, personal crises led people of integrity to disregard their better judgment and consent to assist the MfS. On other occasions, the Stasi's psychological pressures to cooperate were so intense that it was hard to distinguish willing collaborators from unfortunate victims. In any case, for justice to be done, Gauck emphasized, one could only come to a single conclusion about the legitimate uses of the secret-police files: "a great deal of differentiation was necessary" (28).

Granted, as we have noted above, the different types of federal, state, and metropolitan agencies that were eventually charged with establishing guilt or innocence, suitability or unsuitability, were not always up to the challenge of reaching such differentiated judgments about the cases before them. Still, German policy makers could find solace in the fact that when mistakes were made the victims of their policies could, at least theoretically, seek legal remedies through their country's court system. Although this eventuality could hardly make up for the injustices done to them—in this case, ironically, by a new government under democratic auspices—the subsequent record was not all bad. The evidence suggests that by the end of the 1990s, hundreds of easterners had been reinstated in their jobs or received some form of compensation as a result of judicial findings overturning earlier rulings. Some courts called into question certain interpretations of the MfS files. Others demanded that more exacting standards be applied to such elusive concepts as "suitability" and "Stasi activity." In some cases, the courts took mitigating circumstances into account that tempered judgments of culpability.

Nonetheless, with respect to the final category of affected parties, the perpetrators themselves, it is hard to be as sanguine. This is not to maintain that Gauck and others had nothing to say to that particular group of persons who stood to have the most negative feelings about the issue of transitional justice. With respect to his leadership of the BStU, there is little to indicate that Gauck was driven by a personal animus to punish wrongdoers merely for the sake of imposing punishment. In fact, given the sober and methodical style that he brought to the agency's interpretation of its tasks as specified by the Unification treaty and the Stasi-Records Law, he was frequently criticized by eastern activists for being too slow to act upon opportunities to settle accounts with rights abusers and too attentive to legal niceties.

Additionally, in line with his message to western policy makers, Gauck goes to some lengths in *Die-Stasi Akten* to assure the potential targets of his policies that neither he nor his colleagues had any intention of using the Stasi's records as tools of "personal revenge or lynch justice" (92). In this regard, he should arguably be credited with responding to many of Schorlemmer's persistent worries about the files' exclusionary potential. By focusing on only the most culpable cases, Gauck seems to say, the practitioners of retrospective justice will free the great majority of easterners to enter their new society with their reputations intact. Likewise, he maintains, by carefully considering the context in which many Stasi-related offenses were committed, screening agencies, courts, and other administrative organs will give due recognition to the different circumstances under which eastern Germans lived and operated. In this fashion, they can pave the way for greater inter-German understanding.

In his own way, Gauck also responds to Schorlemmer's greatest concern that findings of complicity will lead to the permanent exclusion of some offenders from society's fold. According to Gauck the exposure of wrongdoing and clarification of murky events from the GDR past may actually constitute a blessing for the perpetrators. The chance to tell the truth, he contends, is simultaneously a chance to engage in a conscious act of self-liberation. For, as he expresses it, this situation forces one to make the hard choice between a life based on "a fearful strategy of covering things up and one based upon the risk of personal honesty" (100). The latter choice is the path of inclusion. "He who recognizes and admits to his complicity," Gauck emphasizes, "he who speaks out about the loss of self-worth that has come from his activities and who is willing to describe to others . . . his fears, his tears, and internal struggles, this person will surely not be treated as an enemy [in the new Germany] but will instead be accepted as a partner in dialogue" (100).

Perhaps Gauck thought he was doing the former Stasi agents and collaborators a favor by circumscribing their options in this fashion. Still, one cannot help noticing—and here, both Volf and Schorlemmer would undoubtedly agree—that there is one chapter missing from *Die Stasi-Akten*. For all of the deserved attention that the book gives to the needs of the victims and to their manifold concerns and considerations as they are brought face to face with the revelations from the files, Gauck's vision is incomplete. He fails to address the related trials and tribulations of those persons who must suddenly reckon with the fact that their darkest secrets and most inglorious failings have been made public for all to see. If Gauck is correct in anticipating that many will slowly come to understand the nature of their misdeeds, it is still unclear how this is to transpire. Who, for example, is to help them along this path? And, until they reach this stage of enlightenment, how can one guarantee that they are not overcome with bitterness, righteous indignation, and anger if they feel they have been wrongly singled out?

Admittedly, one can raise similar concerns on a larger scale about the Kohl administration's shortsighted handling of the problem. True, government officials could, and did, assure those classified as perpetrators that they enjoyed all of the protections of the rule of law. Also, the Bundestag and other agencies did on occasion implement concrete measures to limit the extent of sanctionable activities and to bring the vetting process slowly to closure. Yet one omission is telling. While both federal and state authorities were prepared to discuss at length strategies for dealing with the victim's experience with the Stasi question—general education sessions, legal counseling, rehabilitation, and even group psychotherapy[23]—they paid conspicuously little attention to the needs of that much smaller group of easterners who were to lose their jobs or, worse still, find their personal lives destroyed as a result of their past activities.

Most likely, decision makers in the Kohl government were reluctant to address themselves explicitly to the lot of the former victimizers, let alone to that of other representatives of the old SED regime. They feared angering the victims and alienating a potential source of electoral support in the East.[24] Still, it is worth reflecting on the possibility that this failure to articulate a more comprehensive vision of the Stasi's impact on the region was also a missed opportunity. After all, even if they had paid modest attention to the potential plight of the offenders, this would not have meant slighting the victims in any way. Their interests were clearly not being neglected. Nor would a more nuanced stand have signaled an obligation to modify their commitment to reviewing the democratic credentials of the MfS's former employees. These policies would have continued without interruption. What such a double vision could have added to the handling of this case, however, was the chance to convey a valuable message to all of their new-found eastern German compatriots. A robust and confident democracy could afford to show understanding and charity to all of its citizens, even to those with the greatest moral burdens.

In chapter 2 of this volume, Alan Torrance emphasizes the opportunity presented by such an attitude. If one avoids a rigid or overly legalistic approach to the pursuit of justice for the victims, it is possible to elevate to a guiding principle "the unconditional affirmation of [human] dignity." For a fledgling democracy, this approach is eminently preferable to a self-righteous demeanor that serves no one's interests. Predictably, given his views, Schorlemmer was more sensitive than most of his compatriots to this chance to "embrace" the wrongdoers. "The collaborators, too, are people," he reminded listeners, "to whom we all owe the human chance to find themselves and to come together again with their fellow human beings. They also need the chance to contribute their talents to the reconstruction of our country."[25]

## Anticipating Reconciliation after Dictatorship

In short, when we compare Volf's ideal image of the pursuit of justice after dictatorship with the putatively more realistic assumptions of social scientists, it is not self-evident that the predictions of the latter group are any more attuned than Volf is to the options facing the leaders of new democracies. As we have seen in the German case, social scientists may have overestimated the extent and reach of these options in the early days of transition. By the same token, if Volf's double-sided conception of reconciliation is correct, both they and the practitioners of transitional justice in the East may have then underestimated the importance of considering both victim-centered and inclusionary strategies within that narrower range of options that was truly available to the FRG.

In calling attention to these different degrees of freedom of maneuver, I by no means intend to imply that all, or even most, postauthoritarian regimes have been faced with the same challenges and the same circumstances as unified Germany. I suspect that one of the reasons social scientists have been so quick to generalize about the attractiveness of inclusionary forms of reconciliation is that many transitional states have found themselves, quite unlike the Germans, initially unequipped to confront former oppressors or to redress grievous wrongs. As a result of bargains struck at the initial moment of transition or the continued presence of threatening militaries, they have perforce begun the quest for reconciliation by accepting those aspects of the dictatorial past that cannot be changed and by searching for points of consensus. Yet as Volf has suggested and the German case will confirm, this does not mean that these regimes' chores are over. In view of where they have been and where they still hope to go, they can still discover that realism does not have to mean the abandonment of one's ideals and principles.[26] In this respect, the most realistic course for reconciling all elements of their society to living together is to combine their inclusionary foundations with the realization of some form of justice.

## Notes

1. Miroslav Volf, *Exclusion and Embrace: A Theological Exploration of Identity, Otherness, and Reconciliation* (Nashville, TN: Abingdon Press, 1996), 29.

2. For example, see Luc Huyse, "Justice after Transition: On the Choices Successor Elites Make in Dealing with the Past," *Law and Social Inquiry* 20, no. 1 (1995): 65.

3. José Zalaquett, quoted in Alex Boraine, *State Crimes: Punishment or Pardon?* (Wye Center, CO: Aspen Institute, 1989), 11.

4. Samuel Huntington, *The Third Wave: Democratization in the Late Twentieth Century* (Norman: University of Oklahoma Press, 1991), 231.

5. Karl Marx, "The Eighteenth Brumaire of Louis Bonaparte," in Karl Marx and Friedrich Engels, *Selected Works* (New York: International Publishers, 1968), 97.

6. Joachim Gauck, *Die Stasi-Akten: Das unheimliche Erbe der DDR* (Reinbek bei Hamburg: Rowohlt, 1991). Hereafter, citations to this work are given parenthetically in the text. For similar arguments, see Joachim Gauck, "Dealing with a Stasi Past," *Daedalus* 123, no. 1 (1994): 277–84, especially the following remark: "We will be in a position to forgive and forget only if we are given enough time and the right to heal our wounds, to calm our anger, and, yes, to curb our hatred. Reconciliation with such a past can only be achieved not simply through grief, but also through discussion and dialogue" (284).

7. Friedrich Schorlemmer, "Versöhnung heißt nicht 'Schwamm drüber,'" in *Weil das Land Versöhnung braucht,* ed. Marion Dönhoff et al. (Reinbek bei Hamburg: Rowohlt, 1993), 53–54.

8. Friedrich Schorlemmer, *Freiheit als Einsicht* (Munich: Knaur, 1993), 177. Quoted from an article in the *Bildzeitung,* October 5, 1992.

9. Ibid., 173. Cited from an article in the *Frankfurter Rundschau,* June 12, 1992.

10. Ibid., 176.

11. Ibid., 118. Cited from a 1992 Good Friday sermon in Nuremberg.

12. Ibid., 120–21.

13. Schorlemmer's reservations are outlined in his later book *Was ich denke* (Munich: Goldmann, 1995), 99–103.

14. See his interview with *Die Tageszeitung* on January 7, 1991, cited in Silke Schumann, *Vernichten oder Offenlegen? Zur Entstehung des Stasi-Unterlagen-Gesetzes* (Berlin: BStU, 1995), 130.

15. Wolfgang Schäuble, *Der Vertrag* (Stuttgart: Deutsche Verlags-Anstalt, 1991), 273.

16. Cited in Schumann, *Vernichten oder Offenlegen?* 16.

17. Cited in ibid., 111. From an interview in *Die Tageszeitung,* September 6, 1990.

18. For example, see Bernhard Schlink, "Rechtsstaat und revolutionäre Gerechtigkeit," in *Öffentliche Vorlesungen* (Berlin: Juristische Fakultät, 1996), 3–20.

19. See A. James McAdams, *Judging the Past in Unified Germany* (New York: Cambridge University Press, 2001), ch. 3, passim.

20. Volf, *Exclusion and Embrace,* 212–14.

21. Author's interview, Joachim Gauck, Berlin, June 11, 1996.

22. The German Unification treaty specifies two types of cases in which administrative disqualification may be considered, although it is not required: (1) participation in human rights abuses; and (2) evidence of Stasi activity. See Unification Treaty, Attachment I, Ch. II (B), §2 (2), August 31, 1990.

23. For a typical example of these concerns, see the 1996 report of the Berlin *Land* office responsible for Stasi-related questions, *Dritter Tätigkeitsbericht,* Drucksache 13/1395, pp. 10–16.

24. To the extent this was their strategy, it failed miserably. The postcommunist Party of Democratic Socialism (PDS) made surprisingly strong election showings

throughout the 1990s. The PDS was able to portray itself as a broadly inclusionary representative of eastern German interests.

25. Schorlemmer, *Freiheit als Einsicht*, 180.

26. On the similarities between these cases and the German case, see A. James McAdams, "Vergangenheitsaufarbeitung nach 1989: Ein deutscher Sonderweg?" *Deutschland Archiv* 36, no. 5 (2003): 851–60. An English-language version of this article appeared as "Transitional Justice after 1989," *Bulletin of the German Historical Institute*, no. 33 (Fall 2003): 53–64.

# CHAPTER SIX

# Restorative Justice, Political Forgiveness, and the Possibility of Political Reconciliation

## MARK R. AMSTUTZ

The extension of forgiveness, repentance, and reconciliation to whole nations is one of the great innovations in statecraft of our time.

—Walter Wink, *When the Powers Fall: Reconciliation in the Healing of Nations*

How should emerging democratic regimes reckon with the crimes and injustices of former governments? Should transitional regimes concentrate their limited political and economic resources on the consolidation of democratic institutions and the promotion of national reconciliation, or should they first seek strict justice and then attempt to promote political and economic development and national unity? If peace and reconciliation are viewed as legitimate regime goals, how should these objectives be pursued? Is the ethic of forgiveness applicable to politics, and if so, can it contribute to the resolution of deep political conflicts, the healing of collective injuries, and the restoration of communal solidarity? More specifically, can forgiveness play a role in transitional regimes in overcoming the suffering from state-inflicted crimes?

In the past two decades, emerging democratic regimes have pursued a variety of strategies in confronting the crimes and human rights abuses of former governments. These approaches have ranged from historical amnesia and denial to intermediary strategies of amnesty and truth telling to limited purges (lustration) and trials.[1] Democratic theorists generally agree that successor regimes are legally and morally bound to prosecute and punish persons guilty of criminal wrongdoing. According to Gary Bass, trials are a popular response to human rights abuses because they are perceived to be an effective way of carrying out justice and restoring the peace.[2] But trials may not always be feasible or even desirable. Since transitional regimes are concerned not only with retroactive justice but also with the consolidation of democratic processes and the promotion of national unity, legal retribution may not always provide the most effective way to satisfactorily address past regime wrongdoing. Thus, rather than pursuing retroactive justice through legal retribution, regimes may find it more helpful to place greater emphasis on forward-looking strategies that combine truth telling with initiatives to renew and reform cultural and institutional norms in order to promote national reconciliation.

The essays in this collection explore different moral, legal, and institutional resources available in promoting national reconciliation in the aftermath of deep injustices. Here I examine the potential role of political forgiveness in reckoning with gross human rights abuses of past regimes. While forgiveness is rarely practiced in politics, it nevertheless remains an important resource for confronting systemic wrongdoing. Because deep political cleavages frequently persist in transitional societies and because of the intractability of justice, collective forgiveness may provide an alternative means by which societies can pursue both national unity and the consolidation of democratic institutions.

This chapter has five parts. In the first part, I explore the nature and potential role of forgiveness and reconciliation in political life. I note that scholars and practitioners have been skeptical of their role in politics, commonly regarding these concepts as elements of personal morality. In this section I therefore explore how forgiveness and reconciliation can be appropriated in political discourse to confront and overcome the legacy of egregious human rights abuses perpetrated by a former government. In particular, I explore how communities might pursue political reconciliation through collective forgiveness.

In the next section, I contrast backward-looking retributive justice, which focuses on the legal prosecution and punishment of offenders, with restorative justice, an approach that emphasizes truth telling, moral accountability, and reconciliation. Although retribution, the prevalent state practice in confronting collective wrongdoing, is an effective strategy for implementing legal justice, it does not necessarily contribute to the healing of victims, the restoration of community life, and, most importantly, the consolidation of rights-based democracy. Moreover, since retribution assumes that reconciliation can occur only after legal justice has been achieved, such a paradigm allows little or no room for political forgiveness. The restorative justice paradigm, by contrast, emphasizes the renewing of relationships through reconciliation based in part on truth telling, contrition, and even forgiveness. The notion of restorative justice is important because it provides a potential strategy for healing social and political bonds. Although the restorative justice model does not explicitly incorporate forgiveness, the processes of interpersonal and intracommunity renewal are dependent in part on the capacity of individuals and groups to fulfill some of the elements of the forgiveness ethic.

In the next two sections I analyze the limits of retribution and the promise of restorative justice through two case studies. The paper's third part describes and assesses the "truth and justice" strategy pursued by the government of Argentina during the mid-1980s. Although the government's strategy succeeded in disclosing the widespread abuse of human rights and in prosecuting and briefly punishing top rulers, the government ultimately failed in its quest to promote national unity and to further institutionalize a rights-based democracy. Indeed, the retributive strategy not only failed to strengthen judicial institutions but also contributed to further polarization and political instability.

In the fourth section, I illustrate the restorative justice model by assessing South Africa's "truth and reconciliation" process. The fundamental aim of the South African Truth and Reconciliation Commission (TRC) was to encourage full disclosure of past political offenses in the belief that such truth telling would help foster national reconciliation. By emphasizing truth telling and the restoration and healing of victims, the South African model provided a context that facilitated perpetrators' admission of wrongdoing followed by victims' acknowledgment of offenders' confessions. The TRC process itself did not include political forgiveness. Whether offenders expressed remorse for their crimes and whether victims forgave their offenders was left to individuals themselves. All that the TRC model called for was truth telling and moral accountability, in the belief that the disclosure and acknowledgment of truth would create a moral basis for national reconciliation.

In the final section, I assess the extent to which Argentina's and South Africa's democratic transitions have promoted a peaceful, democratic transition and contributed to national unity and political reconciliation among former antagonists. Although assessing the Argentine and South African transitional justice experiences presents many difficulties, I suggest that South Africa's "truth plus amnesty" experiment appears to have been more successful in promoting values and actions conducive to forgiveness and national reconciliation than Argentina's "truth plus trials" model. While neither country has deliberately pursued policies of political forgiveness, South Africa's TRC process has established institutional practices and norms that have encouraged individual and collective forgiveness, thereby helping to promote national reconciliation.

## Forgiveness and Reconciliation in Political Life

Forgiveness is an interpersonal process by which ruptured human relationships are restored.[3] This interactive process between victims and offenders normally involves a number of elements. These include an offender's acknowledgment of wrongdoing, the expression of remorse for such wrongdoing, victims' empathy toward transgressors, and the lifting of debtors' deserved penalties. When transgressors and creditors carry out such behaviors, the moral inequality between them is reduced and mutual trust is encouraged. To be sure, offenders' repentance or victims' empathy alone will not ensure reconciliation. Nevertheless, authentic contrition can greatly facilitate the process of forgiveness.

In common usage the term *reconciliation* denotes the renewal of friendship or the reestablishment of community. From a religious, especially biblical, perspective, reconciliation implies the restoration of broken relationships— between God and persons and among humans themselves. Such a transaction is generally thought to depend upon the moral reconstruction of individuals and collectives through processes that may involve truth telling, the acknowledgment of guilt, repentance, mercy and compassion, and forgiveness. Forgiveness and reconciliation are therefore closely linked concepts, with the former frequently regarded as a necessary condition for full communal reconciliation.

The goal of forgiveness is the healing of persons and the restoration of relationships. Forgiveness is realized when victims stop demanding justice and give up anger and resentment so that transgressors may be given the opportunity to regain their place in the community. While reconciliation is the ultimate goal of forgiveness, partial forgiveness can take place without the restoration of communal relationships. Such forgiveness occurs when offenders' debts are released and victims' anger is healed without necessarily repairing the broken human relationships.

It is important to stress that forgiveness is a means of confronting moral wrongdoing, not a means of addressing strategic errors or unintended evil consequences. Forgiveness deals with serious wrongs by calling on transgressors to confront and acknowledge moral culpability and to repent through the implicit promise of not repeating the evil action again. For their part, victims refrain from vengeance and release debtors from some or all of the deserved punishment. By encouraging such actions, forgiveness fosters a context that encourages the moral renewal of persons and the transformation of enmity into community.

## The Nature and Potential Role of Political Forgiveness

Historically, legal and political philosophers have ignored the political dimensions of forgiveness. They have done so in the belief that the major moral purpose of the state is justice, conceived in terms of the protection of individual rights. Moreover, political thinkers have also neglected forgiveness because they have viewed it as a private, spiritual ethic. For them forgiveness is an aspect of personal morality to be applied among individuals in their private relationships, but it is not part of political morality. Accordingly, although individual victims can forgive, the state cannot.

In chapter 3 of this volume, Nicholas Wolterstorff argues that this view is unpersuasive. He claims not only that governmental forgiveness of offenders is widespread but that such public forgiveness may be easier to carry out than individual forgiveness. Political forgiveness is more feasible, he argues, because whereas personal forgiveness must overcome the moral emotions of anger and resentment, political forgiveness entails no such changes because states have no emotions. Moreover, since states have no mind, they have no memory and no capacity to remember or to forget. Accordingly, when governments forgive they are not required to transform the retributive motivations that fuel and exacerbate conflicts. Thus, when states forgive debts and abrogate deserved punishments — whether out of expediency, mercy, or for the quest of political reconciliation — they do so without having to overcome the anger and resentment that frequently impair interpersonal forgiveness.

Hannah Arendt was one of the first theorists to explore the potential role of forgiveness in politics. She argued that forgiveness was essential to communal life because it provided a means "to undo the deeds of the past." Although she credited Jesus with the discovery of this ethic, she believed that forgiveness, despite its religious origins, should not be restricted to the spiritual realm.[4]

More recently, Donald Shriver has argued that forgiveness—which he defines as an interactive process involving moral judgment of wrongdoing, the avoidance of vengeance, empathy toward offenders, and the renewal of human relationship[5]—is a legitimate ethic in domestic and international politics. Although Shriver's study has greatly encouraged the moral reassessment of the political role of forgiveness, his model has several limitations. First, Shriver fails to confront the inherent tension between justice and forgiveness, punishment and reconciliation. Second, because he presumes that justice and forgiveness are complementary processes, he neglects a distinctive feature of both popular and scholarly conceptions of forgiveness—namely, the cancellation of a deserved penalty.[6] Of course, Shriver omits this dimension of forgiveness precisely because the abrogation of deserved penalties would contravene claims of justice. Accordingly, Shriver's model emphasizes the restoration of relationships through the avoidance of vengeance and the encouragement of empathy, not the mitigation or cancellation of debts.

P. E. Digeser offers another important model of political forgiveness.[7] He conceives of forgiveness as involving, among other things, (1) a relationship between two parties—that is, between transgressors and victims; (2) a moral or financial debt owed by one party to another; and (3) a party with the authority to relieve an offender of a deserved debt.[8] Like Shriver, Digeser does not make remorse or repentance a part of his model. He omits these and other subjective elements because he seeks to develop a theory of political forgiveness based on purposive actions, not human motivations or sentiments. Although forgiveness is commonly viewed as a means to heal victims' anger and resentment, Digeser views forgiveness solely as a purposive human act that leads to the release of debts. He argues that offenders should receive what is their due but claims, contrary to the conventional wisdom, that retroactive justice is not the only, or even the most important, value in public life. On some occasions other values—such as the promotion of reconciliation and the establishment of domestic peace—may override the claims of corrective justice. As a result, forgiveness in political life may be morally justified under appropriate circumstances.

For Digeser, the major rationale for political forgiveness is that it may help promote peace and reconciliation. Even though forgiveness is not a necessary condition for political reconciliation, he claims that it can greatly contribute to the restoration of communal relationships. In particular, he suggests that political forgiveness can promote both the *process* and the *state* of reconciliation. It can contribute to the process of reconciliation by encouraging the restoration of relationships between transgressors and debtors and by fostering trust and understanding among antagonists. And it can promote the state of reconciliation by creating conditions that help to settle "the past" and open "possibilities for the future."[9]

Building on Shriver's sentiment-based model and Digeser's action-based approach, as well as other theological and philosophical perspectives, including those set forth here by theologian Alan J. Torrance (ch. 2) and philosopher Nicholas Wolterstorff (ch. 3), I conceive of political forgiveness as an interactive process in which the burdens of past wrongdoing are repaired, resulting in the healing of human relationships. To be successful, forgiveness depends upon a number of core elements, including consensus about past wrongdoing, remorse and repentance, renunciation of vengeance, cultivation of empathy, and mitigation or cancellation of a deserved penalty. Below I briefly describe each of these elements.

### Consensus on Truth

Forgiveness is possible if actors can agree on the nature of, and culpability for, past wrongdoing. As José Zalaquett, a leading Chilean human rights scholar and member of Chile's truth commission, has observed, truth must be deemed an "absolute value."[10] If consensus is to emerge, political communities must pursue an official accounting of collective wrongdoing. Although trials, religious institutions, and nongovernmental organizations can contribute to the task of truth telling about former regime crimes, government-sponsored truth commissions have proven to be the most effective way to pursue this task. Consensus on truth will necessarily imply agreement about which persons or communities are chiefly culpable for past wrongdoing. Shriver argues that when individuals and groups cannot agree that some past action needs to be forgiven, "forgiveness stalls at the starting gate." This is why he suggests that forgiveness must begin with "memory suffused with moral judgment."[11] Thus, if political forgiveness is to occur, culpable individuals and groups need to acknowledge their offenses.

### Remorse and Repentance

Contrition is also desirable in facilitating forgiveness.[12] To be authentic, repentance requires not only a change in attitude but also an implied promise that the evil action will not be repeated. Moreover, it assumes that offenders must be prepared to provide restitution of confiscated property and to provide financial reparations for victims' injuries and losses. Although forgiveness may be fulfilled without offenders' remorse in some circumstances, repentance greatly facilitates the process of reconciliation by helping to nurture norms and institutions conducive to a humane, harmonious society.

In his insightful essay in chapter 2 of this volume, Torrance distinguishes between legal and evangelical repentance. In the first type, forgiveness is made possible by the efforts to right the wrongs through remorse and contrition. By contrast, evangelical repentance, which is rooted in God's unlimited and unconditional love, is a result or manifestation of a prior, deeper commitment to community and human solidarity. Since believers are called to follow their heavenly Father, they are called, writes Torrance, to love and forgive without conditions, regardless of whether they are friends or enemies. Of course, authentic repentance, whether legal or evangelical, involves both contrition and transformation of commitments, but whereas in the legal model repentance occurs as a precondition for forgiveness and reconciliation, in the latter it occurs as a by-product of an all-embracing love and quest for communal solidarity.

*Renunciation of Vengeance*

Persons and groups that have suffered wrongdoing have a natural inclination to retaliate. But vengeance does not lead to justice or to the healing of victims' injuries. Rather, it perpetuates hate and enmity and provides the breeding ground for even greater evil. If the cycles of violence are to be halted, victims must refrain from retaliation and renounce vengeance.

*Empathy*

Victims must follow Saint Augustine's admonition to hate the sin and love the sinner. This means that people must treat enemies and offenders with dignity and respect despite the offenses that they have committed. Thus, if forgiveness is to occur, transgressors and victims must cultivate empathy and compassion toward the "other," viewing each other as humans worthy of respect. Although expressing empathy in interpersonal relationships is challenging, it is difficult to practice such attitudes collectively, especially since political communities tend to exacerbate human passions and evil.

*Mitigation of Punishment*

Forgiveness normally entails the reduction or annulment of a deserved penalty.[13] Although forgiveness does not require the full cancellation of punishment, debt reduction is generally a by-product of the forgiveness process in which victims (or their agents) respond with compassion to offenders' repentance and remorse. It is important to stress that while human forgiveness results in the reestablishment of a moral and social equality between victims and offenders, it does not eliminate offenders' moral guilt.[14]

The ultimate purpose of forgiveness is the moral healing of persons and the restoration of communal relationships. As noted above, reconciliation is partly the result of the interpersonal and intracommunity processes of forgiveness. Once moral equality is reestablished between victims and offenders, the possibility for restoring relationships among former enemies emerges. Of course, whether antagonists can move from enmity toward reconciliation will ultimately depend on whether offenders and victims voluntarily pursue actions that are conducive to the healing of relationships.

It is important to stress that the lifting of a deserved debt or punishment is a key element of political forgiveness. The mitigation of punishment is crucial because it encourages the healing of wrongdoers and helps restore broken relationships. At the same time it needs to be emphasized that justice is a central value of political life. Although forgiveness normally qualifies the norms of retributive justice, it does not fully override a state's obligation to prosecute wrongdoing. Still, when enemies seek to overcome past collective injuries through forgiveness, criminal justice procedures may be partially circumvented.

### The Nature and Potential Role of Reconciliation in Politics

As with forgiveness, scholars and practitioners have begun to explore the potential role of reconciliation in public life.[15] The growing interest in political reconciliation has been prompted by the large number of states that have replaced authoritarian government with participatory, elected government in the past two decades. As a result of these transitions, the new regimes have been confronted with the moral and political challenge of how to reckon with past regime wrongdoing while simultaneously seeking to restore and consolidate democratic government. Although a number of transitional justice models have emphasized the need for trials and truth telling, the initiatives that have received the most publicity are those that have sought to promote national unity and reconciliation through the discovery and disclosure of truth. Two important examples of this strategy are the transitional justice strategies of Chile and South Africa.

The Chile initiative, established by the democratic government of Patricio Aylwin in 1991, was based upon the premise that the consolidation of democracy could succeed only if the country carried out a program of moral and political reconstruction based upon two values—truth and reconciliation. As a result, the National Commission on Truth and Reconciliation was established to investigate major human rights crimes committed during the seventeen-year military dictatorship in the belief that the acknowledgment of past wrong-doing would contribute to individual and collective healing. South Africa used similar logic when it established the Truth and Reconciliation Commission four years later. The country's Interim Constitution of 1993, which established the basis for the commission, called for the establishment of a peaceful, demo-cratic society and the promotion of national unity, noting that the pursuit of these goals would require "reconciliation between the people of South Africa and the reconstruction of society."

But what does *political reconciliation* mean? When a war-torn, deeply frac-tured country pursues national reconciliation, what does such a process en-tail? Some scholars have suggested that reconciliation is an inappropriate po-litical concept because it has no clear, widely accepted definition.[16] The claim that reconciliation is an inappropriate political ideal because it is conceptually elusive has little merit, however. Many foundational political concepts are elu-sive and contested, yet political discourse depends upon them because they define fundamental elements of a good society. And such is the case with rec-onciliation, an ideal concept that identifies how alienation, enmity, and distrust can be transformed into social trust and communal solidarity. Others object to the idea of reconciliation because they believe that it is inconsistent with the demands of democratic government. Amy Gutmann and Dennis Thompson, for example, argue that a procedural democratic framework is far more hos-pitable to human rights than the intentional pursuit of social harmony. Ac-cording to them, the most desirable approach to promoting national unity is through "deliberative democracy" in which citizens can freely confront ongo-ing conflicts and disagreements within society.[17]

According to critics of reconciliation, the task of a humane society is not to prescribe beliefs and values for its citizens but to maintain procedural norms for structuring political decision making and regulating social conflict. Rather than seeking to build national unity through ideological indoctrination, po-litical liberalism assumes that the ideal community is one that protects indi-vidual human rights, especially personal liberty. According to this perspective, the challenge in creating and maintaining political community is not to impose peace through the propagation of values and beliefs but to resolve disputes and foster participatory decision making through discussion, debate, and negoti-ation. Such processes are of course feasible in stable, cohesive, and integrated political communities. But when societies are deeply divided along ethnic, religious, or ideological lines, democratic procedures may be ineffective in resolving social cleavages, religious and racial discrimination, and political animosity. The South Africa government did not establish national unity and reconciliation as goals for the TRC because it wanted to create an ideologically homogenous society. Rather, it established these aims because it assumed that democratic society was impossible without the development of further national solidarity, ethnic and political tolerance, and economic justice.

Conceptual confusion about reconciliation is also due to the failure to clearly distinguish between two of the concepts' key dimensions—scope and intensity. The first refers to the number of persons participating in the process of communal renewal and restoration, ranging from interpersonal reconciliation between two persons (micro) to international reconciliation between two groups or nations (macro). The second dimension, the level of intensity, refers to the degree to which animosity and distrust are transformed into cooperation and ultimately into deep social solidarity. The degree of reconciliation thus ranges from minimal (thin) to maximal (thick). If these two dimensions are combined, as in figure 6.1, reconciliation can be conceived in a multiplicity of forms.

Another reason for the confusion about reconciliation is that the concept is frequently associated primarily with people's feelings and emotions. Based

FIGURE 6.1. Reconciliation Based on Scope and Intensity

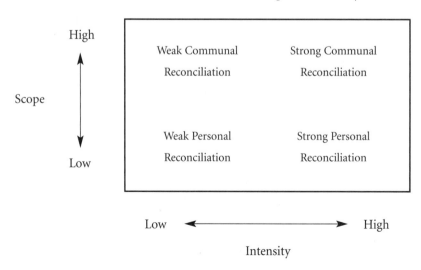

upon this perspective, reconciliation entails the replacement of negative feelings, such as anger, resentment, and alienation, with those that are positive, such as companionship, trust, and cooperation. Since collectives do not display feelings and emotions in the same manner as individuals, viewing reconciliation as the cultivation of positive feelings presents conceptual and metaphysical challenges for the incorporation of this idea into political discourse. Although collectives do not feel sensations like pain and anger, groups do in fact display attitudes and feelings. The media regularly report about distrust and anger among different racial, ethnic, and religious groups and about economic frustration between rich and poor peoples. What is one to make of such feelings and perceptions? Although discourse about the economic frustrations of the Third World and Muslim political animosity toward Western secularism and materialism may be conceptually nebulous and philosophically problematic, such discourse nevertheless describes, albeit imprecisely, the attitudes and dispositions of groups and nations. Interestingly, while scholars commonly question the legitimacy of communal expressions of positive group attitudes (e.g., compassion, generosity, repentance, and forgiveness), theorists and practitioners are eager to acknowledge the existence of negative collective attitudes, including enmity, hatred, and distrust.

## Justice, Reconciliation, and Political Forgiveness

As noted above, forgiveness involves the release of moral or legal debts. Since justice involves giving persons their due, forgiveness is likely to come into conflict with the quest for justice. Since justice and reconciliation are not necessarily complementary public goods, how should public authorities pursue justice and the restoration of community? Should justice be given priority, or should a government emphasize reconciliation through forgiveness? Below I briefly explore the interrelationship and relative priority of these goals and assess the challenge of reconciling forgiveness with justice. In the following section I further examine the relationship of justice to reconciliation and forgiveness through two alternative paradigms—retributive justice and restorative justice.

The conventional wisdom on transitional regimes is that governments should give priority to justice. This strategy is best summed by the claim "First pursue justice, then seek peace." Is the "first justice, then reconciliation" approach morally and strategically sound? According to Volf, such a strategy is neither realistic nor credible. It is unrealistic because relevant groups will always contest conceptions of justice, and even if justice could be defined impartially it is unlikely that it could ever be fully realized, since human actions are always approximations of ideal norms. Moreover, such a strategy lacks credibility because the pursuit of justice will not necessarily ensure the promotion of peace and reconciliation. If reconciliation is desired, argues Volf, strategies that explicitly promote the restoration of trust and communal solidarity will be necessary.[18]

The conventional wisdom also suggests that only individuals can forgive. Forgiveness is inappropriate in public life, so goes the argument, because collectives are not morally empowered to offer or receive forgiveness from another community. Is this claim warranted? Whether states can forgive or receive forgiveness will depend on several factors, including (1) the extent to which states are moral agents; (2) the capacity of public officials to carry out collective forgiveness; (3) the relationship of individual forgiveness to collective forgiveness; and (4) the capacity of political leaders, acting on behalf of a people, to initiate and lead a community in carrying out behaviors that foster forgiveness.

The first issue—the moral standing of political communities—concerns the extent to which collectives are responsible moral actors. Scholars generally attribute moral agency to groups and communities if they are joined by common purposes and have established decision-making structures.[19] Since political communities frequently fulfill these qualities through common national goals and through the decision making of authoritative governments, states may be presumptively regarded as political communities with the capacity for moral collective action. Whether governments are legitimate moral agents will, of course, depend on a variety of factors, including the character of the political regime, the extent to which decision-making authority is rooted in consent, and the degree to which public policies are consistent with common morality. But if states can be viewed as presumptive moral agents, then it may also be appropriate for them to carry out actions that lead to collective forgiveness.

The second issue concerns the authority to carry out political forgiveness. Can governments forgive and receive forgiveness? One of the widely accepted assumptions is that only victims have the moral right to forgive. As a result, it is commonly believed that collectives are not entitled to relieve individuals or groups of their deserved penalties or debts. Pricilla Hayner captures the conventional wisdom on political forgiveness when she observes that forgiveness and reconciliation are "deeply personal processes."[20] Governments may be able to show mercy and pardon offenders, but only victims have the right to forgive. Although forgiveness has been historically associated almost exclusively with the private and sacred realms, as noted earlier, the view that forgiveness is solely an aspect of personal morality is untenable. Even if forgiveness were solely a victim's prerogative, this would not necessarily prohibit collective forgiveness, since criminal wrongdoing results in injuries not only to individual victims but also to other persons and groups. Indeed, crimes can result in several levels of victimhood: those who have suffered direct wrongdoing (primary victims); family members and friends who have suffered indirectly from the crimes (secondary victims); and the society at large, which suffers from the indirect effects of lawless, unjust action (tertiary victims). Since crimes create a debt to the political community, the government may act to forgive the debt by pardoning offenders. Such action, as Digeser notes, does not necessarily erase the debt owed to a particular individual, but it does erase the public debt, thereby creating the possibility of restoring the relationship between the offender and the political community.[21]

The third issue relates to the relationship of individual forgiveness to collective forgiveness. Can a political community forgive an individual even if the victim is opposed to such action? And can individuals forgive when a state refuses to do so? To address such issues, it is important to distinguish between individuals and the communities of which they are a part. Using a framework devised by Tavuchis,[22] one can conceive of forgiveness at four levels: (1) a person forgives another person; (2) a person forgives a collective; (3) a collective forgives an individual; and (4) a collective forgives another collective. Political forgiveness is therefore a potential moral action by a community that is granting or receiving relief from a moral or legal debt. While a government cannot act as a moral agent for a specific victim, it can act on behalf of the community, forgiving either another individual (case 3) or another collective (case 4).

The fourth concern focuses on the capacity of leaders to initiate and sustain actions that are necessary for collective forgiveness. Can leaders express attitudes and implement policies that might contribute to communal forgiveness? And can leaders encourage citizens to develop attitudes and behaviors that contribute to national reconciliation? There can be little doubt that governments can implement initiatives that help to redress past injustices. For example, governments can express formal apologies and provide financial reparations as a way of redressing past wrongdoing.[23] One noteworthy recent illustration of a public apology was the official public expression of remorse by the U.S. government to Japanese Americans who had been placed in internment camps during World War II.[24] If governmental actions like apologies and reparations are to result in collective forgiveness, they must help transform citizens' attitudes and values. This means that the initiatives of leaders must contribute to the transformation of victims' anger and offenders' self-righteousness.

Thus, since groups and communities, like individuals, commit, or are victims of, moral offenses, and since governments are the authorized decision makers for collectives, political communities can in principle both grant and receive forgiveness. When wrongdoing is committed, moral and legal debts arise, fostering alienation among groups and rupturing relationships within communities. In seeking to restore relationships and to repair communal bonds, political communities may relieve transgressors' justified punishment or penalties in order to promote reconciliation. The lifting of deserved penalties is greatly facilitated when both offenders and victims agree on the truth of past wrongdoing and, more particularly, when offenders admit culpability and express repentance and victims renounce vengeance and express empathy.

## Retributive Justice versus Restorative Justice

Given the importance of justice in public life, I next examine two major approaches for reckoning with collective wrongdoing—retributive justice and restorative justice. Since retributive justice emphasizes justice as a precondition for reconciliation, it allows little room for forgiveness. The restorative justice framework, by contrast, emphasizes attitudinal and behavioral changes that are not only conducive to forgiveness but dependent on it in that their very success may depend upon individuals and groups fulfilling this ethic.

### Retributive Justice

Retributive justice assumes that a humane political community can be sustained only if wrongdoing is prosecuted and punished. According to this perspective, public crimes create state obligations for both parties in a conflict: victims must be given justice and perpetrators must be identified and held legally accountable. The retributive perspective assumes that when crimes occur justice is best secured through the prosecution and punishment of individual offenders. Most legal scholars justify retributive justice systems either in terms of their inherent rightness or in terms of their consequences. From a deontological perspective, punishment is a necessary moral response to criminal offenses. Utilitarianism, by contrast, justifies punishment as means to sustain a credible and effective criminal justice system. Retributive justice is also justified as a means to communicate moral values. Relying upon a hybrid Kantian-teleological approach, Hampton argues that punishment provides a method to assert the fundamental worth of persons. Since offenses threaten the fundamental equality of persons by uplifting offenders and deflating victims, punishment provides a means "to annul the offender's claim of superiority."[25]

Although the retributive justice model provides a legitimate and effective way of addressing individual crimes in a robust constitutional environment, the model is not well equipped to address past collective violence or systemic injustice. Indeed, the model suffers from a number of limitations. First, retribution focuses on the punishment of offenders and neglects the rehabilitation of victims and the restoration of communal relationships. Second, since legal retribution focuses on the culpability of individuals, it tends to underestimate, or even neglect, the role of institutions and the context in which offenses are committed. This is especially the case when confronting collective crimes committed during periods of domestic strife or as a result of brutal dictatorships. Third, since evidence of criminal wrongdoing is most easily secured for low-level officials, trials frequently focus on state agents who carried out gross human rights abuses and bypass the responsibility of decision makers. Thus senior officials who authorized programs and policies that led to criminal actions are spared accountability while persons who committed crimes are prosecuted and punished.[26] Fourth, legal retribution uses scarce political resources to confront past crimes rather than focusing on the future needs of society. Since transitional regimes tend to be politically fragile, the emphasis upon rectifying past wrongs may diminish resources available to confront other pressing societal needs. Bruce Ackerman writes that transitional regimes should concentrate their resources on the institutionalization of a constitutional order rather than seeking to correct past injustices. In his view, moral capital is better spent in educating people about the limits of the law than in correcting injustices perpetrated over a generation or more. "A few crude, bureaucratically feasible reforms will do more justice, and prove less divisive," he writes, "than a quixotic quest after the mirage of corrective justice."[27] Finally, trials can threaten and destabilize fragile regimes, especially when societies remain politically divided.

## Restorative Justice

Unlike legal retribution, which is concerned with punishment and the maintenance of a credible criminal justice system, the aims of restorative justice are to repair broken relationships. Whereas retribution focuses chiefly on objective wrongdoing, restorative justice emphasizes the transformation of subjective factors that impair community, such as anger, resentment, and desire for vengeance. Elizabeth Kiss identifies four elements of restorative justice: the restoration of victims' human dignity, accountability for offenses, restoring respect for human rights, and the promotion of reconciliation.[28] Since the first three behaviors are also emphasized in retribution, the distinctive feature of restorative justice is reconciliation. In the restorative model, reconciliation is conceived both as a process and as a condition. As a process, reconciliation is viewed as a means to heal broken relationships by replacing anger and enmity with empathy, tolerance and trust. And as a condition, reconciliation is conceived as a state of peaceful, harmonious relationships and as an environment where former enemies express mutual trust, demonstrate cooperation, and work out disagreements peacefully.

Although there is no single method by which enemies can be reconciled, the process of communal reconstruction is greatly facilitated by offenders' confession and apologies and victims' renunciation of vengeance and expression of empathy. Individual and collective forgiveness can also contribute to the renewal of communal relationships by facilitating the reintegration of offenders into society. Since accountability for past wrongdoing is crucial to the model of restorative justice, it is important to stress that forgiveness need not abrogate legal claims for punishment and reparations. Indeed, offenders should be prepared, as an expression of the authenticity of their remorse, to accept a state's legal punishment. Of course, whether restorative justice leads to the restoration of communal relationships will ultimately depend upon the mutual actions of transgressors and victims. Restorative justice can create the context in which communal bonds are repaired. Of course, whether individuals and groups succeed in the quest for reconciliation will depend greatly on people's moral courage in expressing attitudes and actions that are conducive to forgiveness.

Some scholars have criticized restorative justice for failing to appreciate the positive role of disagreement and conflict within society. Gutmann and Thompson, for example, argue that excessive concern with social consensus and political agreement can threaten a deliberative politics. As a result, they argue that societies should be guided by the principle of "the economy of moral disagreement," in which citizens pursue consensus where it exists and maintain mutual respect where it does not.[29] Others have suggested that restorative justice is problematic because it fosters "easy" reconciliation among antagonists, failing to come to terms with the past. Still others claim that the quest for national reconciliation places unreasonable burdens on antagonists, especially victims, by expecting them to express empathy toward former enemies.

Although these criticisms contain some truth, they exaggerate the claims and logic of the restorative justice paradigm. To begin with, restorative justice does not demand complete consensus. While "democratic reciprocity" is no doubt the preferred model for addressing domestic political conflicts, the reconstruction of a society following a civil war will require not only the institutions of deliberative democracy but also the cultivation of national unity. If deeply divided societies are to become humane societies, they need to embark on a radical program of moral, political, and legal reconstruction, such as that illuminated by the restorative justice model. Moreover, restorative justice does not disregard past wrongdoing, as critics allege. Rather, it seeks to confront the awful truth about past crimes and injustices by using the truth to foment changes in values and behaviors that increase the prospects for reconciliation. Finally, restorative justice is a demanding ethic that encourages enemies to confront their humanity. In particular, it calls on offenders to disclose their culpability and victims to show empathy toward perpetrators. In short, restorative justice seeks to achieve the requisite personal and communal reforms so that the burdens of legal retribution are reduced or even eliminated. It does so through the renewal of persons and the restoration of groups and communities through attitudinal and behavioral changes that increase the prospects for reconciliation.

To further explore the possible role of forgiveness and reconciliation in reckoning with the human rights abuses of former regimes, I next seek to illuminate the limits of retribution and the promise of restorative justice with case studies from Argentina and South Africa, respectively. Argentina's "truth and justice" strategy shows the limits of retribution, since the prosecution and punishment of some government leaders, far from promoting national reconciliation, encouraged further political fragmentation. South Africa's truth and reconciliation model, by contrast, has appeared far more promising. By pursuing a forward-looking strategy that emphasized reconciliation and the consolidation of rights-based democracy, the South African approach sacrificed some individual justice to promote national unity. Of course, the TRC did not explicitly call for forgiveness. But by pursuing unity and reconciliation through restorative justice, the TRC implicitly encouraged values and practices that made individual and collective forgiveness more feasible.

## Partial Retributive Justice in Argentina

### The Dirty War

During the late 1970s, the government of Argentina pursued an antisubversion campaign to rid the nation of leftist terrorism. When the military took power in 1976, urban terrorist groups had been carrying out daily killings and abductions.[30] Once in control of the state, military leaders, supported by business, religious, and professional elites, embarked on a covert war against terrorism. This campaign—dubbed the "Process for National Reorganization" and ostensibly aimed at restoring domestic order and protecting "Western, Christian civilization"—was carried secretly through terror tactics, including torture, kidnapping, and killings. It is estimated that from 1976 to 1980 more than nine thousand persons were killed through this antisubversion campaign.

In 1983 the military decided to return power to civilian authorities.[31] In the fall presidential elections, Raul Alfonsín, the Radical Party candidate, defeated the Peronista Party candidate, in great part because he had been much more vigorous in demanding trials for military leaders than his opponent. Throughout the campaign Alfonsín had repeatedly promised that, if elected, he would prosecute military and police officers responsible for crimes during this "dirty" war.[32] As a result, soon after assuming office, he established a presidential commission— the National Commission on Disappeared People (CONADEP), headed by novelist Ernesto Sábato—"to clarify the tragic events in which thousands of people disappeared." Fundamentally, the aim of the so-called Sábato Commission was to identify the fate of missing persons and to provide an official accounting of the nature and causes of the state's antisubversion campaign.

After collecting thousands of statements and testimonies about missing persons and investigating the role of military and police repression, CONADEP presented its findings to President Alfonsín in September 1984, publishing a summary of their report two months later under the title *Nunca Más* (Never Again). The report, which Ronald Dworkin called "a report from Hell,"[33] identified 8,960 cases of missing persons *(desaparecidos)* and some 340 detention/torture centers throughout the country. Although much of the report focused on the nature and targeting of the government's repression as well as the role of the judiciary during the dirty war, the study's most important contribution was to document the nature and scope of the state's criminality in carrying out its antisubversion campaign. As Sábato observed in the report's prologue, the military dictatorship established a campaign of repression that "brought about the greatest and most savage tragedy in this history of Argentina."[34]

The second part of Alfonsín's human rights strategy was the prosecution of senior military leaders. Since the military authorities had enacted a self-amnesty law shortly before transferring power, one of the first acts of the new government was to annul the amnesty decree. Additionally, the government amended the military justice system, giving civilian courts the right to review the judgments of military courts. Alfonsín then ordered the trial of the nine members of the three former military juntas. After the Armed Forces Supreme Council, the senior military court, found "nothing objectionable" about the junta members' actions, the case was transferred to the Buenos Aires Federal Appeals Court. The federal court found five of the nine military leaders guilty and sentenced the top two officers[35] to life in prison. Subsequently, additional criminal cases were begun against midlevel military officials that led to growing political instability. To contain the rising domestic turmoil, the government enacted two laws to limit trials—the Full Stop Law and the Due Obedience Law. The first measure halted all human rights claims against military and police officials; the second created a presumption that crimes by low- and middle-ranking officers had been carried out under orders from superiors and were therefore not punishable.

After assuming the presidency in mid-1989, Carlos Menem issued a decree halting all trials and freeing most imprisoned military officials and guerrilla leaders. In issuing his presidential pardon, Menem declared that "a permanent reconciliation among all Argentineans . . . is the only possible solution for the wounds that still remain to be healed."[36] A year later, the president issued another decree, pardoning the five senior military leaders who still remained in prison. Both of these actions, which were widely unpopular in Argentina, especially among human rights activists, reflected a failure of the government's retributive strategy. Thus, rather than promoting national reconciliation and contributing to the consolidation of constitutional government, the pursuit of legal retribution tended to undermine these goals.

## The Limits of Retribution

Samuel Huntington argues that the failure of Argentina to successfully prosecute top military leaders was due not to a flaw in the government's "truth and trials" strategy but to a failure in timing. "Alfonsín's failure to move quickly and decisively in 1984, when public opinion supported action," writes Huntington, "made human rights prosecutions the victim of changes in power relationships and public attitudes."[37] Others, especially human rights groups,[38] claim that the retributive justice strategy failed because the government did not carry out a vigorous and determined campaign to prosecute and punish all major human rights offenders. As a result, when political turmoil began to surface in 1986 and 1987, Alfonsín halted all trials, and when political instability persisted in the country in 1989 and 1990, Menem pardoned all guerrillas and state agents that were in prison or under investigation.

Jaime Malamud-Goti, one of Alfonsín's senior legal advisers, offers the most persuasive explanation for the failure of Argentina's retributive strategy. He claims that the trials, rather than strengthening democratic institutions and the rule of law, had the ironic effect of further polarizing society and eroding the authority of democratic institutions.[39] Malamud-Goti argues that the government's strategy of "corrective justice" was flawed in several respects. First, the state's prosecution of military leaders focused excessively on the offenses of perpetrators rather than on the restoration of victims and the creation of a rights-based democracy. Although he had favored trials when he was a presidential advisor, Malamud-Goti now questions that policy, claiming that "the advantages of corrective justice may be overridden by the drawbacks inherent to prosecution and conviction of human rights violators."[40] Second, Argentina's retributive strategy was flawed not only because it failed to foster a responsible rights-based civic society but also because it further undermined the authority of the courts. The courts, in being placed at the center of the transitional justice process, had to adjudicate a deeply political issue, one that continued to divide Argentine society.[41] Since courts' actions were widely perceived as serving the political interests of the executive, trials undermined their limited authority. Third, trials reinforced division and fragmentation by fostering a bipolar "us versus them" perspective and encouraging the illusion that those not prosecuted or found guilty were innocent. By defining culpability in narrow, legal terms, trials reinforced the unwarranted belief that criminal responsibility was limited to a small number of senior and midlevel military officials. Finally, since trials focused exclusively on top military leaders, they reinforced the false belief that the military was solely responsible for the crimes of the dirty war. And by reinforcing the "single-factor explanation" for state terrorism, trials contributed to the "reinvention" of history.[42]

The punishment of major offenses is important in establishing and sustaining a stable constitutional regime. But if trials are to contribute to the health of victims and the restoration of society, punishment should be justified not simply as desert but as a means to help institutionalize the rule of law and rights-based democracy. The Argentine experience suggests, however, that the pursuit of public truth about former regime abuses in a highly fragmented society may be difficult, if not impossible. More significantly, it suggests that the negative effects of trials in fragile democratic environments may outweigh the positive results. Thus, rather than contributing to the moral reconstruction of society, trials may "erode the very democratic authority they are devised to restore."[43]

## Partial Restorative Justice in South Africa

### The TRC Process

In February 1990, President F. W. de Klerk set in motion a reform process by un-banning the African National Congress (ANC) and other opposition political groups, releasing Nelson Mandela and other ANC prisoners, and partially lifting the state of emergency. Following two years of intense negotiations among the country's political elites, delegates to the Convention for a Democratic South Africa (CODESA) signed an Interim Constitution in November 1993 that established the basis for a transitional government. The transitional regime was given the task of establishing a permanent constitution and helping to create the preconditions for national unity. In confronting the injustices and human rights abuses perpetrated during the era of apartheid, the new regime had three basic options. First, the state could grant a general amnesty for all crimes and human rights abuses; second, it could carry out trials against all persons responsible for human rights crimes; and third, it could pursue an intermediary strategy, in between the extremes of impunity and comprehensive trials. This last alternative had the advantage of combining a backward-looking focus on truth telling and accountability with a forward-looking focus that encouraged the renewal of civic life and the promotion of national unity.[44]

South African leaders selected the third strategy, in great part because it reflected a political compromise among the major political forces in the country, and also because they believed that trials alone would not ensure the consolidation of democratic institutions and the promotion of national unity. The strategy they selected was based on the restorative justice paradigm that assumed "a need for understanding but not for vengeance, a need for reparation but not for retaliation, a need for *ubuntu* but not for victimization."[45] As conceived by South African leaders, the restorative justice paradigm involved a number of distinctive features. First, it called for a redefinition of crime that focused on personal injuries and human suffering rather than on impersonal rule breaking. Second, it emphasized reparations for victims and their integration into the fabric of communal life. At the same time, it called for the rehabilitation of perpetrators based upon full accountability for past offenses. Third, it encouraged direct conflict resolution among victims, offenders, and the community. At the same time it called for "a spirit of understanding" among former antagonists without necessarily mitigating or undermining offenders' accountability for wrongdoing.[46]

In 1995 the South African Parliament adopted legislation establishing the Truth and Reconciliation Commission (TRC). Fundamentally, the aim of the TRC was to uncover and disclose important facts about the crimes and injustices associated with the apartheid era in the belief that such knowledge would facilitate the democratic transition of South Africa and provide a basis for national reconciliation.[47] The truth that the TRC sought was of two sorts — factual and moral.[48] *Factual truth* consisted of empirical, objective evidence about past crimes and abuses that was gathered and corroborated through disclosure and investigation. *Moral truth,* by contrast, involved individual and collective acknowledgment of past wrongdoing. Although the disclosure of factual findings was vital to South Africa's democratic transition, the quest for moral truth through open hearings, public testimony, and the personal and collective acknowledgment of wrongdoing was even more significant to the healing and restorative processes.

The fundamental goal of the TRC was the promotion of national reconciliation. As conceived by South African authorities, reconciliation was viewed both as a goal and as a process. As a goal, reconciliation specified the desire for a unified, peaceful, and harmonious society. As a process, reconciliation specified the methods by which communal solidarity was to be pursued. Since reconciliation was viewed as a multidimensional process, the TRC believed that its promotion required reforms at the personal, interpersonal, intracommunity, and intercommunity levels.[49]

One of the key elements of the TRC process — and certainly one of the most criticized — was the provision of amnesty to offenders. Since such amnesty was conditional on offenders' confession, it was not a form of impunity. Rather, the offer of amnesty was conceived as a means to promote truth telling. According to the TRC parliamentary act, perpetrators who confessed their criminal activity were promised amnesty from criminal and civil liability, provided their confession was truthful and complete and the crime that had been committed was motivated by political objectives. The underlying assumption of the TRC process was that the moral reconstruction of society could be carried out only if apartheid-era crimes and gross human rights violations were disclosed and publicly acknowledged.[50]

## Assessing the TRC Model

Although it is premature to offer a comprehensive assessment of the TRC's effectiveness in fostering democratization and promoting national reconciliation, it is possible to offer some preliminary judgments about the South African experiment in pursuing reconciliation through truth telling. I first examine the merits of the TRC model and the restorative justice approach on which it is based and then offer some preliminary judgments on the TRC process itself.

Scholars and activists have raised a number of concerns about the TRC model, including (1) the legitimacy of the restorative justice paradigm itself, (2) the legitimacy of reconciliation as a goal of government policy, and (3) the relationship of truth to reconciliation. Some TRC critics have questioned the legitimacy of the restorative justice paradigm because they think the model undermines values, such as blame, resentment, and punishment, that are essential in building a stable, humane society. If societies fail to identify and condemn evil, goes the argument, the consolidation of a rule-based human rights regime will be thwarted. A society must pursue justice by prosecuting and punishing all persons responsible for human rights abuses. In particular, common morality and international law demand that crimes against humanity be punished, even when a former regime has enacted amnesty legislation designed to prevent such prosecution.[51] Other critics claim that fidelity to the law requires not only prosecution of crimes of violence but also the condemnation of the immoral laws and unjust structures and the prosecution of leaders who were responsible for their enactment. John Dugard, for example, critiques the TRC for minimizing the "memory of apartheid" by failing to hold leaders accountable for establishing the immoral rules of apartheid.[52]

Archbishop Desmond Tutu notes, however, that it would have been unwise, indeed impossible, to impose retribution, or what he terms "the Nuremberg trial paradigm,"[53] on South Africa. Not only did South Africa have limited resources for pursuing individual criminal justice, but, more significantly, comprehensive trials would have diverted political attention and economic resources toward past crimes and injuries without necessarily focusing on the development of democratic values and institutions. In Tutu's view, the forward-looking restorative justice paradigm offered the advantage of diverting scarce resources to the consolidation of democratic institutions and the promotion of national unity by balancing the claims of justice, accountability, stability, peace, and reconciliation.[54] Additionally, the paradigm provided a framework for advancing multiple goals simultaneously. According to Tutu, restorative justice helped promote "the healing of breaches, the redressing of imbalances, the restoration of broken relationships" by "seeking to rehabilitate both the victim and the perpetrator."[55] Richard Goldstone, a leading international judge and member of South Africa's Constitutional Court, also defended the restorative justice approach. He wrote: "[I]f the ANC had insisted on Nuremberg-style trials for the leaders of the former apartheid government, there would have been no peaceful transition to democracy, and if the former government had insisted on blanket amnesty then, similarly, the negotiations would have broken down. A bloody revolution sooner rather than later would have been inevitable."[56]

The second key issue concerns the legitimacy of reconciliation as a public policy goal. As noted earlier, some scholars argue that government should not promote national reconciliation deliberately. Rajeev Bhargava, for example, writes that rather than promoting reconciliation through public policies, societies should promote a limited public order—or what he terms "a minimally decent society." He claims that reconciliation is an excessively demanding political goal because it calls for, among other things, "a cancellation of enmity or estrangement via a morally grounded forgiveness, achievable only when perpetrators and beneficiaries of past injustice acknowledge collective responsibility for wrongdoing and shed their prejudices, and when victims, through the same process, regain their self-respect."[57] Crocker similarly argues that reconciliation is a potentially dangerous and undemocratic doctrine since it can threaten individual rights, especially human freedom.[58] Timothy Garton Ash has also questioned the celebration of the notion of "reconciliation of all with all," noting that such a concept is deeply "illiberal."[59] For Crocker, as well as for other scholars deeply committed to political liberalism, the only legitimate way to reckon with past atrocities is through "democratic reciprocity." But democratic procedures are not necessarily a means to create community. Indeed, democratic decision making is viable only in coherent, unified communities.[60] Thus the claim that reconciliation is inconsistent with democratic procedures derives from the unwarranted assumption that the deliberate pursuit of communal solidarity is contrary to political liberalism. But when societies are deeply divided politically, democratic procedures alone may not be sufficient to resolve disputes and provide effective decision making.

Is the multidimensional process of reconciliation, as conceived by the TRC, morally and politically misguided? Is the effort to overcome individual animosity and anger and collective distrust and enmity inappropriate? There can be little doubt that democratic procedures are a desirable way for managing conflict within stable, civic societies. But is democratic reciprocity the only way for emerging democratic regimes to reckon with the collective crimes of former regimes, especially in countries that remain unstable and deeply polarized? Given the fragmented nature of South African society and the long history of racial discrimination coupled with the institutionalization of racial separation during the apartheid era, the potential for major war among different ethnic and political groups was not insignificant in the early 1990s. Moreover, given the lack of democratic practice among black peoples and the large economic inequalities between racial groups, the development of constitutional, democratic institutions was not an inevitable by-product of political change. Therefore, a major task of the transitional regime of South Africa was to promote reforms that contributed simultaneously to justice, accountability, and reconciliation. And if these multiple, and at times conflicting, goals were to be advanced, an all-encompassing strategy had to be devised—one involving legal and political reforms coupled with social, cultural, moral, and spiritual changes. Elizabeth Kiss argues that the pursuit of reconciliation through restorative justice involved nothing less than the "moral reconstruction" of political institutions and human relationships. Given the demanding nature of this task, Kiss thinks that the TRC model depended upon "a leap of faith" in the possible moral transformation of both persons and institutions.[61]

Finally, theorists have expressed concerns about the assumed healing properties of truth. Truth commissions are based upon the premise that knowledge of the past, coupled with the acknowledgment of the truth, will contribute to the healing of victims, the promotion of peace, and the restoration of communal relationships. Building on the biblical admonition that if we know the truth, it will set us free (John 8:32), truth commissions, including Argentina's and South Africa's, have pursued truth in the hope that such knowledge would foster individual and collective healing.

But does truth telling lead to healing? In exploring the relationship of truth to reconciliation, it is important to differentiate between objective truth—the factual, empirical record about the past—and subjective truth—the perceptual, personalized understanding of the past. The first is propositional and concerns discovery and disclosure of facts; the second is dispositional and concerns the acknowledgment of empirical realities. If truth is to foster reconciliation, both types of knowledge will be needed. Indeed, knowledge of the past can contribute to political healing only when it is widely shared and when society as whole, but especially its victims and offenders, confronts the painful past by "working through" the legacy of suffering, anger, and guilt.[62] To be sure, truth telling may not be a sufficient condition to restore order and civility. But reconciliation is unlikely to occur if individuals and collectives fail to acknowledge responsibility for past wrongdoing.

## Assessing the TRC Process

The TRC formally terminated its work in 2001. The commission issued its principal findings in a five-volume final report in October 1998 and a sixth volume in March 2003 on the work of the amnesty and reparations and rehabilitation committee. While it is hazardous to offer judgments about the impact of the TRC, some preliminary observations about its role in South African society are in order. First, the TRC was successful in discovering and disclosing truth about gross human rights crimes perpetrated during the apartheid era. It succeeded in this task in part because of broad participation of citizens in the TRC's investigations. It is estimated that nearly 22,000 persons made submissions to the commission and more than 1,200 victims and their families testified in public hearings. A major innovation of the TRC was the inclusion of institutional group hearings. Institutional representation was thought to be especially important since apartheid crimes had been perpetrated with the tacit, if not explicit, support of a significant number of groups and institutions of civil society. Moreover, since the commission had refused to consider collective responsibility, the effort to hear from groups, including the media, business and labor, the legal profession, the armed forces, and religious communities, provided perspectives that greatly enriched the commission's analysis.

Second, despite opposition from some political groups, the TRC was also effective in engaging South African society. Several factors contributed to the commission's success, including (1) its nature, longevity, and public support; (2) the strong political backing for its work; (3) significant statutory authority; and (4) broad media coverage. Unlike most truth commissions, which are secret, short-lived, and underfinanced, the TRC was an open, lengthy, and well-staffed operation. Moreover, whereas executives have appointed most truth commissions, the TRC was established by the country's parliament, thereby enjoying significant political credibility. Additionally, the TRC had significant statutory powers, including the authority to issue subpoenas and to offer amnesty to offenders. Finally, since the TRC hearings were widely publicized in the media, South African people were confronted repeatedly with the truth of past regime atrocities, leading to a widespread collective awareness and acknowledgment of the pain and suffering inflicted by apartheid.

Third, the TRC helped to foster a foundation on which national unity and reconciliation could be promoted. It did so by emphasizing, among other things, truth telling, legal and moral accountability for past wrongdoing, empathy for perpetrators who acknowledged crimes, and the need for reparations for victims.[63] Given the deep political, economic, and racial cleavages institutionalized by the apartheid regime, the promotion of national unity would necessitate significant institutional reforms. Most importantly, reconciliation would require a significant transformation in the country's dominant moral values and cultural patterns. Perhaps Desmond Tutu's most important contribution as TRC chairman was his continued emphasis on the reformation of South Africa's moral order. He repeatedly reminded the nation that there could be no future without reconciliation and that this was possible only through moral reformation based on confession, mercy, and forgiveness. Some observers have criticized the TRC for not bringing about more change. One writer claimed, for example, that the TRC had contributed to truth but not to reconciliation.[64] Yet although South Africa has not become a unified, integrated ("rainbow") nation, it has made important changes that have contributed to increased communal solidarity.

South Africa remains a society divided politically, ethnically, and economically, but the TRC stands as the most successful truth commission to date. To be sure, much remains to be done to strengthen national unity and reconciliation. But critics who complain that the TRC has not promoted reconciliation are wrong, since a precondition for unity is truth telling. As Alex Boraine, the deputy chairperson of the TRC, has noted, "[W]hile truth may not always lead to reconciliation, there can be no genuine, lasting reconciliation without truth."[65] This point was reinforced by a *New York Times* editorial that lauded the commission's work as the most "comprehensive and unsparing examination of a nation's ugly past" that any truth commission has produced thus far. "No commission can transform a society as twisted as South Africa's was," the editorial goes on, "but the Truth Commission is the best effort the world has seen and South Africa is the better for it."[66]

## Political Forgiveness and the Promotion of National Reconciliation

While neither the Argentine nor the South African case fully applies collective forgiveness to past regime wrongdoing, each illuminates the limits and potential of forgiveness in pursuing the promise of reconciliation. In particular, Argentina in a limited way, and South Africa more explicitly, illustrate some of the important challenges in bringing the notions of forgiveness and reconciliation to the processes of regime change. In this last section I briefly assess the extent to which the transitional processes in Argentina and South Africa have contributed to the consolidation of a new political order through truth telling.

Perhaps the signal achievement of Argentina's "truth and justice" process was its success in disclosing information about the criminal nature of the government's antisubversion campaign. Through the truth commission's investigations and the public testimony of witnesses at trials, the government succeeded in discovering and disseminating factual information about regime atrocities. It did so through the truth commission's report *Nunca Más* (Never Again) but also through the disclosure of facts through trials. The government was also partially successful in translating factual or propositional truth into moral or dispositional truth. The wide dissemination of *Nunca Más* and the continuing media coverage of the human rights atrocities greatly contributed to the public's acknowledgment of the widespread abuse of human rights during the military dictatorship. In the 1990s, two accounts have especially contributed to the nation's acknowledgment of regime wrongdoing. The first occurred in 1995, when a retired Navy officer admitted that he had participated in throwing victims into the Atlantic Ocean from a military airplane. Horacio Verbitsky, a leading Buenos Aires journalist, used the confessions of this officer (Adolfo Scilingo) to write a book titled *The Flight*, which became an instant best seller in Argentina.[67] The second issue that has continued to keep the military regime's human rights violations on the conscience of the Argentine people is the ongoing effort to identify children of disappeared victims and to help them reunite with their blood families.[68] Since victims' children were turned over for forcible adoptions, the state has pressed charges against a number of senior military officers for their alleged role in this secret abduction campaign.

But if Argentina's "truth and justice" strategy contributed to the discovery and disclosure of truth, it was much less successful in developing consensus about past collective crimes. Most importantly, the Argentine strategy was largely unsuccessful in helping to heal the wounds of past crimes, to consolidate democratic structures, and to promote national reconciliation. Indeed, Argentina's strategy exacerbated political divisions and distrust, leading to a more polarized, fragmented society than when the country commenced its democratic transition in 1983. The lack of concern for forgiveness and reconciliation in Argentine society is captured by the motto of HIJOS, a leading human rights organization for children of the disappeared. Its motto is "We don't forget, we don't forgive, and we do not become reconciled."[69] Thus, while the retributive strategy resulted in numerous trials and the successful prosecution and punishment of the military's top leadership, the "truth plus trials" strategy failed to reform the nation's dominant political values and public institutions.

The focus on prosecutions also compromised the effort to gather information from the military and police about the killings and abductions carried out as part of the political repression. Ideally, a truth-seeking strategy should encourage perpetrators to disclose information about victims through anonymous channels. But Argentina's retributive strategy undermined such an effort. Fearing prosecution, military and police authorities, along with professional groups and business associations, chose, with few exceptions, to remain silent about human rights abuses. Even the leadership of the Argentine Roman Catholic Church failed to confess its complicity by remaining silent in the face of known atrocities.[70] Given the military's silence and denial about the dirty war, the truth commission was able to discover general knowledge about political repression (e.g., torture techniques, detention centers, abductions and killings) but was largely unsuccessful in uncovering facts about the abduction, detention, and death of specific persons. As a result, the emphasis on trials rather than on disclosure may have undermined efforts to bring closure to suffering and healing for victims. Perhaps the most important admission of culpability by a government official was expressed by the army's chief of staff, General Martín Balza, in 1995, when he confessed that the armed services had used inappropriate means in carrying out the dirty war. Balza noted that the army had used "illegitimate means of obtaining information, including the suppression of life."[71] Balza's statement, while falling short of full repentance, is significant because it represents one of the few admissions of wrongdoing by a senior government official.

Unlike Argentina's limited success in cultivating forgiveness, the South African "truth and reconciliation" process appears to have been far more effective in confronting the public with the moral tasks of individual and collective renewal. While the TRC did not require repentance or demand empathy, the commission's restorative justice framework encouraged offenders, victims, and the general citizenry to disclose truth and to confront personal and collective guilt in the belief that such confession would foster personal healing and the restoration of communal relationships. Since the TRC assumed that reconciliation depended upon truth, the TRC focused almost exclusively on the uncovering and public acknowledgment of truth. As a result, the TRC gave high priority to victims' stories and promised amnesty to perpetrators who confessed their wrongdoing.

Although the TRC did not explicitly call for individual or collective forgiveness, the restorative justice framework encouraged the partial or full implementation of some of the dimensions of forgiveness noted earlier. In particular, the TRC process emphasized truth telling and the mitigation of punishment, two core elements of forgiveness. The search for truth was viewed as an absolute value, and amnesty was regarded as a means to ascertain truth. Many religious, professional, and political leaders refused to participate in the truth-gathering process or to confront their individual and collective responsibility for past wrongdoing. Some political leaders, like former president P. W. Botha and Chief Mangosuthu Buthelezi, head of the Inkatha Freedom Party, refused to even acknowledge the legitimacy of the TRC. Botha, who referred to the TRC as a "circus," refused to comply with court subpoenas and was tried and found guilty of contempt of court.[72] Winnie Madikizela-Mandela, the former wife of Nelson Mandela and a leading political activist, similarly refused to acknowledge the TRC's legitimacy or to accept full responsibility for crimes and injustices carried out by her associates. Despite evidence that Mrs. Mandela had been involved in torture, abduction, and murder, she not only denied criminal wrongdoing but also refused to seek forgiveness from those she had wronged.[73] Some leaders grudgingly participated in the process. Mr. de Klerk, for example, testified before the TRC but refused to apply for amnesty, while Thabo Mbeki, ANC leader and deputy president (now president), testified and also completed an amnesty application, while remaining distrustful of the commission's work.[74] Nevertheless, the TRC succeeded in significant measure not only in developing a narrative about past human rights abuses but in confronting the South African people with collective wrongdoing.

It would have been easy for the TRC to serve as an instrument for the ANC, leading to the imposition of "victor's justice." Instead, the TRC pursued a broad, comprehensive strategy that emphasized the direct and indirect criminal culpability of all major political groups. This comprehensive perspective was captured by the major findings of the TRC's final report, which implicated virtually all sectors of society.[75] Not surprising, major political groups opposed the TRC's conclusions. Indeed, when TRC Chairman Tutu formally presented the commission's report to President Mandela, all political parties boycotted the ceremony. Moreover, several efforts were made to derail the publication of the commission's findings. For example, prior to the report's release former president de Klerk took the TRC to court, forcing the deletion of its conclusions about him. The ANC, too, took the commission to court in a last-ditch effort to halt the report's publication, but the judge refused to block its release. Once the report was published, Mbeki denounced it as "inaccurate" and contrary to international law.[76] Thus, unlike the Argentinean truth commission report, which focused criminal culpability exclusively on one group (the military), the TRC provided a more comprehensive and therefore more authoritative account about past wrongdoing.

Like forgiveness, the TRC process is based upon a seeming injustice— namely, perpetrators' release from a deserved punishment. Ignatieff aptly captures this perceived injustice when he observes, "[W]hen you trade amnesty for truth, murderers get away with murder."[77] But the apparent injustice provides a basis for another type of justice—one that is rooted in individual acknowledgment of wrongdoing and whose punishment involves the personal admission of culpability. Although such punishment may be less demanding than a sentence imposed by a judge, the admission of individual or collective culpability is a difficult act morally.

It is still premature to know whether the TRC model will ultimately succeed in consolidating democracy and promoting national reconciliation. Nevertheless, the evidence to date suggests that the TRC has contributed to South Africa's moral reconstruction through the disclosure and acknowledgment of truth and the priority given to the restoration of humane collective relationships. Although the TRC does not call for forgiveness, its emphasis on the healing of injuries and the restoration of relationships provides a unique context in which to explore the quest for reconciliation through the miracle of forgiveness. L. Gregory Jones has noted that the TRC process is "one of the most dramatic and hopeful signs of an authentically Christian contribution to political life to emerge in many years."[78] I agree.

# Notes

1. The literature on transitional justice is extensive. The best general introduction to this subject is Neil J. Kritz, ed., *Transitional Justice: How Emerging Democracies Reckon with Former Regimes* (Washington, DC: U.S. Institute of Peace Press, 1995). Vol. 1 deals with general themes, while vols. 2 and 3 explore country studies and relevant laws, rulings, and reports, respectively.

2. According to Bass, trials are regarded as the most effective response to collective crimes for several reasons, including (1) a belief that legal accountability helps to purge regimes from leaders who might impair the consolidation of democratic government; (2) a belief that punishment will deter future criminal wrongdoing; (3) the idea that legal accountability can help rehabilitate states by restoring credibility to the rule of law; (4) the belief that the individualization of culpability is necessary for justice; and (5) the belief that knowledge of the truth about collective wrongdoing is conducive to the social and political health of political communities. While Bass argues that each of these claims is plausible, none, in his view, has been fully corroborated by twentieth-century history. Indeed, he claims that only the fifth claim on truth telling is fully convincing. See Gary Jonathan Bass, *Stay the Hand of Vengeance: The Politics of War Crimes Tribunals* (Princeton: Princeton University Press, 2000), 286–310.

3. To a significant degree, the idea of human forgiveness is grounded in the concept of divine pardon. Just as God expresses unconditional love and unqualified mercy to those who repent of their sin, so victims of injustice are called to love and be compassionate to offenders.

4. Hannah Arendt, *The Human Condition* (Chicago: University of Chicago Press, 1958), 236–43.

5. Donald W. Shriver Jr., *An Ethic for Enemies: Forgiveness in Politics* (New York: Oxford University Press, 1995), 6–8, 30–32.

6. *Webster's Seventh New Collegiate Dictionary*, for example, defines forgiveness as (1) the giving up of resentment, (2) the giving up of a claim to requital, and (3) the granting of relief from payment.

7. P. E. Digeser, *Political Forgiveness* (Ithaca: Cornell University Press, 2001).

8. Ibid., 20 and 35. In addition to these three elements, Digeser's model of forgiveness includes four other features: forgiveness must be conveyed explicitly and directly to debtors by persons competent to offer it, motives and feelings must be disregarded in the act of forgiveness, moral reasons must be given for not pursuing punishment, and forgiveness may lead to the restoration of relationships among antagonists.

9. Ibid., 20–21.

10. José Zalaquett, "Truth, Justice, and Reconciliation: Lessons for the International Community," in *Comparative Peace Processes in Latin America*, ed. Cynthia J. Arnson (Stanford: Stanford University Press, 1999), 348.

11. Shriver, *Ethic for Enemies*, 7.

12. Scholars disagree on the priority of repentance in forgiveness. Some, like David Little, argue that a key element of forgiveness is repentance. According to Little's model, which is based on Jesus' parable of the unforgiving servant, forgiveness involves five elements: (1) a transaction between two or more persons; (2) a shared acknowledgment between the offender and victim about (a) culpability for wrongdoing and (b) a fitting punishment; (3) contrition and repentance on the part of the offender; (4) a merciful response by the victim, including the annulment of 2b; and (5) obligation of the forgiven offender to forgive others. See David Little, "A Different Kind of Justice: Dealing with Human Rights Violations in Transitional Societies," *Ethics and International Affairs* 13 (1999): 71. Others, like Digeser and Shriver, conceive of forgiveness as not requiring repentance. Elsewhere in this book, Alan Torrance suggests that Christian forgiveness is not dependent on prior repentance. He claims that evangelical repentance *(metanoia)*, rooted in the "transformation of the orientation of our minds," is carried out not to condition forgiveness but to express love. The Christian faith, he believes, calls on believers to forgive unconditionally.

13. In ch. 3 of this volume, theologian Nicholas Wolterstorff emphasizes this element by defining forgiveness as the voluntary "foregoing of claims of justice."

14. Miroslav Volf, following Nicolai Hartmann, argues that human forgiveness, unlike divine forgiveness, does not remove moral guilt. "To receive forgiveness," observes Volf, "is at the same time to admit to the deed and accept the blame." See Miroslav Volf, "Forgiveness, Reconciliation, and Justice: A Theological Contribution to a More Peaceful Social Environment," *Millennium* 29, no. 3 (2000): 875.

15. Some recent studies on the nature and role of reconciliation in politics include Raymond G. Helmick and Rodney L. Petersen, *Forgiveness and Reconciliation: Religion, Public Policy and Conflict Transformation* (Philadelphia: Templeton Foundation Press, 2001); Andrew Rigby, *Justice and Reconciliation: After the Violence* (Boulder, CO: Lynne Rienner, 2001); Gregory Baum and Harold Wells, eds., *The Reconciliation of Peoples: Challenge to the Churches* (Geneva: WCC Publications, 1997); and Walter Wink, *When the Powers Fall: Reconciliation in the Healing of Nations* (Minneapolis: Fortress Press, 1998). For a discussion of the reluctance of theologians to apply reconciliation to social and political issues, see Miroslav Volf, "The Social Meaning of Reconciliation," *Interpretation* 54 (April 2000): 158–68.

16. Tristan Anne Borer, "Reconciliation in South Africa: Defining Success," University of Notre Dame, Kroc Institute Occasional Paper 20:OP:1, March 2001. See also David A. Crocker, "Retribution and Reconciliation," *Report from the Institute for Philosophy and Public Policy* 20 (Winter/Spring 2000): 6.

17. Amy Gutmann and Dennis Thompson, "The Moral Foundations of Truth Commissions," in *Truth v. Justice: The Morality of Truth Commissions*, ed. Robert I. Rotberg and Dennis Thompson (Princeton: Princeton University Press, 2000), 35–36.

18. Volf, "Forgiveness, Reconciliation," 870–71.

19. Peter French distinguishes between two types of collectivities—aggregates and conglomerates. An aggregate collectivity is a group of people who are joined by

chance, not by common purpose. Because aggregates are not "intentional agents," they are not moral agents. Conglomerates, by contrast, are purposeful organizations whose members have joined together to advance shared interests through an institutional decision-making structure. Since conglomerates carry out purposeful actions on behalf of members, their actions bear moral consequences. See Peter A. French, *Collective and Corporate Responsibility* (New York: Columbia University Press, 1984), 5–18.

20. Pricilla Hayner, "In Pursuit of Justice and Reconciliation: Contributions of Truth Telling," in Arnson, *Comparative Peace Processes*, 375.

21. Digeser, *Political Forgiveness*, 121.

22. Nicholas Tavuchis, *Mea Culpa* (Stanford: Stanford University Press, 1991), 48. See also Digeser, *Political Forgiveness*, 110–11.

23. For an excellent overview of the nature and role of public apologies, see Tavuchis, *Mea Culpa*.

24. In 1989, President George Bush sent a letter of apology to each of the more than eighty thousand surviving internees. By the mid-1990s more than $1.6 billion had been paid out in reparations to redress this past injustice. For a discussion of the politics of repairing this past collective wrong, see Elazar Barkan, *The Guilt of Nations: Restitution and Negotiating Historical Injustices* (New York: W.W. Norton, 2000), 30–45.

25. Jean Hampton, "The Retributive Idea," in Jeffrie G. Murphy and Jean Hampton, *Forgiveness and Mercy* (Cambridge: Cambridge University Press, 1988), 143.

26. This anomalous situation was illustrated by the German government's prosecution of former public officials of East Germany (GDR). Not surprisingly, the first trials in the early 1990s were carried out against border guards, while failing to indict the vast majority of senior leaders of the GDR. In the end, a number of senior officials were prosecuted, including Egon Krenz, the state's last communist leader, who was sentenced for his part in the "shoot to kill" policy. And when the German government sought to prosecute Erich Mielke, the head of GDR's state security (Stasi), it did so for his alleged role in the 1931 murder of two policemen! See Tina Rosenberg, *The Haunted Land: Facing Europe's Ghosts after Communism* (New York: Vintage Books, 1995), 333–35.

27. Bruce Ackerman, *The Future of Liberal Revolution* (New Haven: Yale University Press, 1992), 72.

28. Elizabeth Kiss, "Moral Ambition within and beyond Political Constraints," in Rotberg and Thompson, *Truth v. Justice*, 79.

29. Gutmann and Thompson, "Moral Foundations," 22–23.

30. Estimates of the violence and destruction inflicted by leftist terrorists vary, ranging from six hundred to one thousand deaths during the 1970s. For a discussion of the impact of terrorism on Argentina, see Tina Rosenberg, *Children of Cain: Violence and the Violent in Latin America* (New York: Penguin Books, 1991), 121–23.

31. The military transferred power back to civilian authorities after it lost the 1982 Falklands/Malvinas War to Britain. In addition, the military's authority was damaged by its inability to devise a viable economic strategy to overcome inflation and recession.

32. According to Jaime Malamud-Goti, Alfonsín's commitment to trials and punishment for those responsible for gross human rights violations had a decisive effect on the election. See Jaime Malamud-Goti, *Game without End: State Terror and the Politics of Justice* (Norman: University of Oklahoma Press, 1996), 57–59.

33. Ronald Dworkin, "Report from Hell," *New York Review of Books,* July 17, 1986, 11.

34. *Nunca Más: A Report by Argentina's National Commission on Disappeared People* (London: Faber and Faber, 1986), 1.

35. The two leaders were Gen. Jorge Videla and Adm. Emilio Massera.

36. "Argentina: Presidential Pardons," in Kritz, *Transitional Justice,* vol. 3, *Laws, Rulings and Reports* (Washington, DC: U.S. Institute Peace Press, 1995), 529.

37. Samuel P. Huntington, *The Third Wave: Democratization in the Late Twentieth Century* (Norman: University of Oklahoma Press, 1991), 224.

38. The major human rights group that emerged during the dirty war was the Madres de Plaza de Mayo. This group originated when mothers of "disappeared" children began weekly marches in Buenos Aires's major city square. Subsequently, a related organization, the Grandmothers of the Plaza de Mayo, developed in order to publicize the secret, forcible adoption of children born in captivity.

39. Malamud-Goti, *Game without End,* 8.

40. Ibid., 9.

41. Ibid., 184.

42. Ibid., 187–88.

43. Ibid., 8.

44. Alex Boraine, "Truth and Reconciliation in South Africa: The Third Way," in Rotberg and Thompson, *Truth v. Justice,* 143.

45. This phrase is taken from the postamble of the Interim Constitution. According to the TRC Report, *ubuntu* is generally translated as "humaneness" and expresses itself in the phrase "people are people through other people."

46. Truth and Reconciliation Commission, *Truth and Reconciliation Commission of South Africa Report* (hereafter cited as *TRC Report*) (London: Macmillan Reference, 1999), 1:126–31.

47. The aim of the TRC was to promote truth in the belief that it would foster unity and national reconciliation. Some of the specific aims of the TRC included (1) uncovering the truth about gross human rights violations perpetrated during the apartheid era; (2) encouraging offenders to confess their crimes by granting amnesty to those who confessed; (3) encouraging a humane society by seeking to restore victims' human dignity through hearings and reparations; (4) fostering understanding and inhibiting vengeance; (5) preparing and disseminating a comprehensive report on the commissions' findings; and (6) making recommendations that would contribute to the establishment of a humane society and prevent the future violations of human rights. See *TRC Report,* 1:55.

48. Ibid., 110–14.

49. Ibid., 107.

50. By March 2003, when TRC released the sixth volume of its final report, the Amnesty Committee had granted amnesty to some 1,200 persons out of approximately 7,000 requests.

51. Although there is broad global support for the international law of human rights, significant disagreement among states persists on whether citizens may be prosecuted by foreign states for crimes against humanity—that is, torture, killings, and abductions. The 1998–2000 detention of Augusto Pinochet, the former Chilean dictator, by British courts in response to an indictment from a Spanish judge has significantly strengthened the legitimacy of foreign claims against officials responsible for major human rights abuses.

52. John Dugard, "Retrospective Justice: International Law and the South African Model," in *Transitional Justice and the Rule of Law in New Democracies*, ed. A. James McAdams (Notre Dame: University of Notre Dame Press, 1997), 284–86.

53. Desmond Tutu, *No Future without Forgiveness* (New York: Doubleday, 1999), 19.

54. Ibid., 23.

55. Ibid., 54–55.

56. Quoted in Boraine, "Truth and Reconciliation," 143.

57. Rajeev Bhargava, "Restoring Decency to Barbaric Societies," in Rotberg and Thompson, *Truth v. Justice*, 60.

58. Crocker, "Retribution and Reconciliation," 6.

59. Timothy Garton Ash, "True Confessions," *New York Review of Books*, July 17, 1997, 37.

60. D. A. Rustow has observed that the first step in establishing a democratic regime is the development of national unity. He argues that communal solidarity must precede the other three phases of democratization—namely, the acceptance of political conflict, the institutionalization of rules governing political conflict, and the habituation of political struggle. See D. A. Rustow, "How Does a Democracy Come Into Existence?" in *The Practice of Comparative Politics: A Reader*, ed. Paul G. Lewis and David C. Potter (Bristol: Open University Press, 1973), 120–30.

61. Kiss, "Moral Ambition," 80, 83.

62. Michael Ignatieff, *The Warrior's Honor: Ethnic War and the Modern Conscience* (New York: Henry Holt, 1997), 168.

63. For a discussion of the role of the TRC in promoting reconciliation, see Charles Villa-Vicencio, "Getting on with Life: A Move towards Reconciliation," in *Looking Back, Reaching Forward: Reflections on the Truth and Reconciliation Commission in South Africa*, ed. Charles Villa-Vicencio and Wilhelm Verwoerd (London: Zed Books, 2000), 200–207.

64. R. W. Johnson, for example, wrote upon the release of the commission's final report that the TRC "appeared to have done something for truth but very little for reconciliation." *New York Times*, November 3, 1998.

65. Alex Boraine, *A Country Unmasked* (Oxford: Oxford University Press, 2000), 341.

66. "South Africa's Stinging Truths," *New York Times*, November 1, 1998.

188 — *Mark R. Amstutz*

67. Horacio Verbitsky, *The Flight: Confessions of an Argentine Dirty Warrior* (New York: New Press, 1996).

68. In the 1990s, the dominant human rights issue in Argentina was the identification of children who had been forcibly taken from detained victims during the repression and given to military and civilian families. The Grandmothers of the Plaza de Mayo, a major human rights group, has spearheaded the search for kidnapped children and the quest of uniting such children with their blood relatives. To date, more than 250 adolescents and young adults have been identified, with many of them being reunited with their true families.

69. *"No olvidamos, no perdonamos, y no nos reconciliamos."*

70. For a critical analysis of the Catholic Church's role during military repression, see Emilio F. Mignone, *Witness to the Truth: The Complicity of Church and Dictatorship in Argentina* (Maryknoll: Orbis Books, 1986).

71. Marguerite Feitlowitz, *A Lexicon of Terror: Argentina and the Legacies of Torture* (New York: Oxford University Press, 1998), 223.

72. The judge gave Mr. Botha a suspended jail sentence and fined him roughly $1,600. The conviction was appealed, and in March 1999 the court upheld the appeal on technical grounds. For a discussion of the Botha trial, see Boraine, *A Country Unmasked*, 200–217.

73. In 1989, Madikizela-Mandela accused a Methodist minister, Paul Verryn, of sodomizing young men as a way of deflecting criticism she was receiving for the crimes and abductions carried out by her associates. The charge was, of course, false. During the TRC hearings, Mr. Verryn, now a bishop in South Africa, approached Mrs. Mandela and told her that he was eager to find a time and place to forgive her for her false accusations. Mrs. Mandela ignored the offer. See L. Gregory Jones, "How Much Truth Can We Take?" *Christianity Today,* February 9, 1998, 24.

74. Ken Owen, "The Truth Hurts," *New Republic,* November 23, 1998, 23.

75. Ken Owen, a journalist, summarizes the *Final Report*'s findings as follows: "No faction, neither oppressor nor freedom fighter, neither white nor black, neither suburb nor ghetto township, can entirely escape culpability for the gross abuse of human rights that took place during the long years of violent struggle against apartheid." Ibid., 21.

76. Ibid., 22.

77. Michael Ignatieff, "Digging up the Dead," *New Yorker,* November 10, 1997, 93.

78. Jones, "How Much Truth," 22.

# CHAPTER SEVEN

# Northern Ireland

*A Study of Friendship, Forgiveness, and Reconciliation*

## RONALD A. WELLS

In this chapter I will place the discussion of "forgiveness and reconciliation in politics" in the discrete reality of Northern Ireland. But before getting into the main point of the chapter we need to acknowledge the intellectual debt that all scholarly peace seekers owe to Scott Appleby. His recent book *The Ambivalence of the Sacred: Religion, Violence and Reconciliation* will help to reshape the subject this book seeks to illumine. If this chapter has value it is in specifying in greater depth the Northern Irish particulars of themes that Appleby displays on a larger canvas. As Appleby suggests, the instance of the search for peace in the Northern Irish "troubles" affords the observer a rare occurrence of a home-grown peace transformation that might actually work well. This is so because the institutional arrangements of many churches and para-religious organizations have been, in his terms, "saturated" with a will toward peace.[1] The obverse of "saturation" seems also to be true: the conflict is so intractable because dysfunctional behavior is not confined to the realm of politics but permeates the whole of Northern Irish life.

Appleby's notion of saturation is an important reality with which to begin our discussion. Other authors in this book discuss the roles of truth and reconciliation commissions in the attempts by various societies to deal with reconciliation of society after a long and bitter struggle. There will be no such commission in Northern Ireland, but that does not mean that truth is not being sought or that reconciliation activities are not happening. Rather, it means that the fabric of civil society is strong enough to encourage and enable discourse about forgiveness and reconciliation to go on without an ad hoc commission created for that purpose. Especially important, as will be detailed below, are the churches and para-church organizations that are uniquely positioned in Northern Irish society to foster reconciliation initiatives. Scholars who study politics often think that the "real" story of society can be told in terms of governments and their actions. Undoubtedly, that can be true; but it is also a specious truth. One of the main causes of prolonged and intractable conflict is precisely the inability of civil society to generate enough consensus to allow for governmental institutions powerful enough to provide social stability. Northern Ireland is such a case. Despite existing constitutionally within the nation that created the first Western parliament, the people of Northern Ireland have never known the proper working of democratic government. The Protestants of Ulster used their majority systematically to deprive the Catholic/Nationalist community of its civil and human rights. In the last few years since the peace agreement in 1998, we have seen just how weak the political institutions actually are. Therefore, it is all the more vital for us to stress the nongovernmental institutions of civil society—especially churches and para-church organizations— in the societal conversation about reconciliation. "Regular" political activity, and the establishment of strong political institutions, will be the result of, not the cause of, social consensus.

I will try first to untangle the various strands of interpretation, and the problems of writing, about this bitter conflict. Second, I will look again briefly at Irish history and present realities in terms of religion, arguing that a long-standing conflict like this, of largely religious cause, can be addressed in religiously curative terms only if there is a reformulation of the meaning of religion in that context. Third, most of this chapter will present the story of an extraordinary friendship—between Ken Newell, a Presbyterian minister, and Gerry Reynolds, a Catholic priest—that has had considerable impact on churches and society in Ireland. In the view argued here, such Christian friendships are the stuff of forgiveness and reconciliation. Even as a realistic observer acknowledges the challenges for the future of Northern Ireland, one is struck by the possibilities of where such gracious friendships might lead, often to the surprise and consternation of established political and religious leaders.

This is a historical essay. Historians deal in narrative and in analysis of narrative. It is the contention here that if societal healing is to occur, the old narratives must be confronted. A new set of stories of collective pasts must replace the old. The more theoretically oriented essays in this book discuss at length and with care the important concerns surrounding contemporary discourse on forgiveness, reconciliation, and peace building. This chapter need not restate those themes, but it does acknowledge them and, in a way, illustrates and demonstrates them. For example, Mark Amstutz (ch. 6) discusses the relationship between truth telling and forgiveness; we will find that theme illumined in the work of Ken Newell and Gerry Reynolds as they prod their respective communities to be truthful among themselves and discuss the hurts of the past with "the other." James McAdams (ch. 5) refers to competing theological approaches to reconciliation; we will see that echoed in the way Reynolds and Newell were able to work with Fr. Alec Reid and Rev Sam Burch. Alan Torrance (ch. 2) writes of evangelical repentance, as opposed to legal repentance; we will see that as the animating vision of Ken and Gerry, as they encourage their own communities of origin to appropriate fully the possibilities of restoring right relationships. Nicholas Wolterstorff (ch. 3) probes the links between forgiveness and justice; we will see this in the way the peace builders of Northern Ireland moved beyond stopping hostilities to lobbying the new governmental structures to implement strategies for a more just society. David Burrell (ch. 4) writes movingly about the various ways in which we can be empowered by encountering the spiritual gifts of "other" believers. As he notes, reconciliation with God is not really possible in the absence of reconciliation with each other. Gerry Reynolds and Ken Newell provide excellent examples of how delighting in the other's spirituality deepens one's own and leads to political reconciliation.

In the design of this book, this chapter is not a case study for theorizing done elsewhere. Narrative, and the analysis of narrative, is theorizing of a different kind. It may be informed by theology and philosophy (the subject here, after all, is religious actors trying to work out the gospel in a situation of conflicted history); historical analysis complements the other disciplines in welcoming theory grounded in an empirical reality.

## A History of "Troubles"

In all discussions of the Northern Ireland "Troubles," it is customary that writers depict the long-standing nature of the conflict. Especially if the writers are people of good will, they will go to great lengths to be fair to both sides, making the respective positions as plausible as possible. In some recent books in which peacemaking was the theme, the authors wrote with compassion and insight about the myths, the heroes, and the memories that have divided the two traditions in Northern Ireland along parallel, but hardly ever intersecting, lines. Such treatments, whether in scholarly or accessible books, have much to commend them. The authors' nonpartisanship is welcome in a situation often tinged with special pleading. This is especially important if the point of such writing is to illumine, even prophetically point to, Christian efforts to transcend historic differences and to look for common ground and peace.[2]

But we are left with a problem. If the writing about the Troubles is best when it is nonjudgmental, that otherwise winsome attitude often tends to legitimate these different viewpoints, at least to some degree. There is little room for the nonpartisan scholar or writer to express his or her own revulsion at the acts of violence that sicken all of us in the retelling. Little room is left for an author to say what a damnable business it has all been and to express dismay at how many people supported, in one way or another, the men and women who did the evil deeds. We show how plausible it was that, given a certain history and social location, otherwise-decent folk would join in the worst rhetoric of their community and continually retell the stories that depreciate the other side. This gives the writer little scope to be the prophet and say that all this sorrow and grief caused has just not been acceptable. In short, cannot the writer, even without giving up nonpartisanship, stand up and curse the makers of the troubles, mourn the victims, and point to the futility of it all?

I offer a qualified but determined "no" to the above question. I suggest that a scholar, to chronicle the efforts toward peace and reconciliation, must also evidence those qualities in writing. But if we can get to a "second naiveté" in this context, that will be a grace we receive only when we work through the difficulties that kept the people of Ulster mired in a seemingly intractable conflict, arguably the longest in Europe.

At the time of this writing, the cease-fires have largely held for seven years, and men and women on both sides have kept a kind of peace. The political process, launched on Good Friday, 1998, has lurched along, promising more than it has delivered. But as long as the process continues, we can take this moment of relative calm to look around and assess where we have come and how long the road ahead actually is. To move, on this narrow ground, from a culture of hatred and violence to a culture of forgiveness and reconciliation will take all the grace and wit the people of Ulster possess.[3] We who would go on the journey with them, and would tell the story of the peacemakers, must also adopt the long-suffering attitude of the Ulster people and settle in for a long journey that will not, and cannot, be quickly or easily accomplished.

Some commentators will not join us on the journey. They are thoroughly disgusted with the fruitlessness of the whole conflict; high-minded talk about forgiveness and reconciliation is not for them. Jonathan Stevenson, for example, has made an original contribution in his recent book about Northern Ireland after the cease-fires.[4] His bitterness and harshness are difficult for peace seekers to hear. One insists that the feelings he vents are most definitely not the last word. But, as peacemakers seek to spread *shalom* in contemporary Northern Ireland—and as scholars tell their stories—the feelings revealed by Stevenson cannot be easily discounted.

He interviewed a number of violent perpetrators of the Troubles as well as people who lost loved ones to the violence. For example, Ann McCann still mourns the death of her brother, Gerard, who was killed in the mid-1970s. When the cease-fires were announced and the peace process began, Ann experienced the euphoria most people did. But soon another feeling took hold, one of disgust that all the killing and suffering had been for naught. Listen to Ann McCann:

> I think when the troubles were continuing, and you switched on your television set every night and there was one atrocity after another . . . we often said, well, thank God Gerard died instantly. It almost made our situation not so bad. There was great joy about the ceasefire, but the sense of anger followed quite quickly—like what the hell was it for? Now, if I'm thinking that as a victim twenty-two years down the road, what must victims whose sons or husbands died earlier this year or last year be thinking?[5]

Jonathan Stevenson pushes us hard at this point, insisting that testimony like Ann McCann's must be heard and that it suggests a pattern of interpretation: "[A]dmit that the troubles do not deserve the label 'war,' that they arose out of a sectarian miasma, and that anyone lost was not martyred but wasted."[6] He seems particularly angry at the IRA, but his ire toward the paramilitary Loyalists is real enough. He relentlessly points out that not enough has really changed since 1969, in that neither side has altered the constitutional position of Northern Ireland or gained any territory. With barely veiled disgust, he writes, "Like Vietnam for the Americans, the fruitlessness of the conflict is hard truth for the Northern Irish. But unlike the mythologies of the past, the revelation might offer some lessons about the futility of runaway righteousness and hypersensitivity to history."[7] He goes on to discuss the tragic and poignant example of Gordon and Marie Wilson, to which we shall return, but which can be mentioned here to grant part of Stevenson's point. Mr. Wilson and his daughter were present at the War Memorial on Remembrance Day in Enniskillen in 1987 when the IRA exploded a bomb that left many killed and wounded at the scene. Marie was to die under the rubble.[8] Mr. Wilson, because of his high-profile "victimhood," was later asked to approach the IRA about renouncing the "armed struggle" and working for peace, and in a wonderful testimony to Christian grace he did so. All he got from the IRA was a statement that Enniskillen was a "mistake" but that the British were really to blame for being in Northern Ireland at all. Jonathan Stevenson closes his book by pushing the interpretive challenge to the maximum: "Wilson died in 1995. Marie's message, and his, is simply that the troubles were a pointless heartbreak unrepaid. This is a dignified and conclusive rebuke to the perpetrators. Even without contrition, ceasefires are welcome. Repentance is a bonus. Leave it at that."[9] No, we cannot "leave it at that." We cannot do so because we are interested in the future, in creating a culture of peace, which is more than putting a violent past behind us. For that sort of culture to come, a realistic assessment of the past is necessary, to be sure; but also necessary is a re-visioning of what life together in community might be like. Without such a vision, the great and painful cost of the Troubles would indeed be a "pointless heartbreak unrepaid."

Cecil Kerr, founder of the Christian Renewal Centre and one of the leaders in religious and political reconciliation, values very highly the applicability to the Northern Irish situation of the words of Martin Luther King: "He who is devoid of the power to forgive is devoid of the power to love. Forgiveness is a catalyst creating the atmosphere necessary for a fresh start and a new beginning."[10] This attitude is shared by many leaders in Northern Irish peace circles, such as: Ray Davey, founder of the Corrymeela Community; Michael Hurley, founder of the Columbanus Community of Reconciliation; Sam Burch, founder of the Cornerstone Community; Ken Newell and Gerry Reynolds, founders of the Clonard-Fitzroy Fellowship. Many other peacemakers in the various religious communities, less heralded than those named, would agree that the future turns on intentionally creating a culture of forgiveness and peace.[11]

To the realists like Jonathan Stevenson we acknowledge the difficulties of the past, and we do not suggest moving too quickly beyond those realities to which they relentlessly point. As scholars of those people and movements seeking the *shalom* of God in historically intractable circumstances, we admit that this is dicey business. But, along with Nobel laureate Seamus Heaney, we accept that "History says don't hope / On this side of the grave." Also with Heaney we believe that change is possible in human affairs and "that a further shore / is reachable from here."[12]

In the specific context of Belfast, in the mid-1970s—among the darkest days of the Troubles—a remarkable meeting was held at the Fitzroy Presbyterian Church. Organized by a committee, though energized by Cecil Kerr, representatives of all the religious traditions were invited to join the people of Fitzroy for an all-night prayer vigil for peace and reconciliation. Ken Newell wrote some verse for the meeting which those present said was deeply moving:

We are a people made one by the love of Christ, our Saviour and Lord.
We have been changed as a people by the grace of our Lord Jesus Christ.
Gone is the pride that desires to dominate;
Gone is the anger that wants to undermine.
By his Holy Spirit we want to listen to each other's hurts and fears,
And build together a community fit for all of us to live in,
Furnished with the generosity, justice and compassion of Jesus Christ.[13]

But the realist interpreters on Northern Ireland persist in asking us hard questions. It is argued that the application of religious principles in resolving community conflict turns on a prior acceptance of a religious component at the basis of the troubles. In short, what does Ken Newell's seeking "oneness in Christ" have to do with the socioeconomic realities people really fight about? So before we go on to discuss the ways in which religious solutions are desirable and possible we need to discuss briefly the senses in which the Northern Ireland conflict was, and is, a religious one. This is important to our argument because if the conflict is largely of religious cause it will admit more readily to a religious cure.

## Religion as Cause and Cure

In my insisting that most academics and journalists have wrongly resisted seeing what was right in front of them—that the Northern Ireland conflict was about religion—I am not saying that it was solely or merely about religion. To engage in a fully rounded analysis one must discuss politics, economics, social class, and gender. But the disinclination to see the explanatory power of religion turns on the secular construction of knowledge in the academy and the media, in which religion must be epiphenomenal in the modern world. In several other places, I and other scholars have argued with care and in detail the various ways in which religion was an important factor in the Troubles.[14] There is no need to repeat that here. But for present purposes a few points need to be made. Some scholars believe that religion, commonly defined (i.e., concern with doctrines and beliefs) is foundational to the social conflict in Northern Ireland, and there is much to commend that analysis.[15] But more nuanced work in recent years has located religion in its ethnic context. Indeed, in combining religion and ethnicity, some recent scholars believe they have enhanced religion's explanatory power in causing social dysfunction.[16]

In Northern Ireland religion energized ideologies about society, the nation, and "the other," but religion also became captive to those ideologies. In the conflict that broke out with renewed ferocity since 1969, religion provided a way to mark the boundaries of the mind and spirit as much as political boundaries did. It is important to recall that while these captivities to ideology had impact on all parties in Northern Ireland, they had more overtly negative impact among Protestants than Catholics. For the latter, religion helped to shape ethnicity in a defensive mode to explain its lack of social empowerment. For Protestants, however, it galvanized and energized a community toward a political program of dominance. It is important to note that when scholars advance religion's role in social dysfunction they usually conclude their analyses with a discussion of that kind of conservative Protestantism known as fundamentalism and/or evangelicalism.[17]

In discussing the relative "blame" one might adjudge to either religious side, Maurice Irvine has recently offered a most judicious assessment. In a dozen economically but sensitively written pages, he constructs a rather even balance sheet of remembered rights and wrongs perpetrated in the name of religion. But even the careful Irvine must come down somewhere, and the following riveting paragraph deserves quoting:

> While there are numerous obstacles to the dissolution of this communal division and to the growth of a normal integrated society in Northern Ireland, it is evident that the decisive one, that to which all others are subordinate, is the deep-seated hostility permeating the Protestant community to the Roman Catholic ethos. While it is not contested that there are some reasonable grounds for disquiet, it is argued that the virulence and

intensity of the sentiment in the Ulster psyche is far beyond anything that can be justified by events in the past or by the present sociological realities. This neurotic fear can probably not be eradicated or moderated by anything the Irish Catholic community can do; its irrationality renders it impervious to outside influence. Its removal, if this is ever to come about, must derive from within the Protestant community itself.[18]

In concluding this part of the chapter, one is afraid that evangelical Protestant readers of the above will say that academic liberals, attuned to the ecumenical movement, are ganging up on them again, and their defensiveness and resistance will once again stiffen. We can only say that we all need to hear another reading of the Gospel: precisely because religion was so important in causing conflict, a reconfigured religion is also vital in finding the way to peace. As we look to the Bible for guidance, we see that early in the story God seems to bestow his favor exclusively on a particular people. As the story unfolds, and especially after the resurrection of Jesus, we see that the good news from God is meant for all. Finally, in the last part of the Bible, the universality of God's grace is revealed. Those who name the Name, who will sing the praises of the Almighty in endless songs, will come from all tribes, tongues, and peoples. There will be, of course, the final boundary marking the faithful from the faithless— heaven and hell will exist—but the inhabitants of the two will not be chosen according to the human contingencies of politics, nationality, race, class, and gender.

All Christians share a common prayer, the Lord's Prayer. The Reformation did not change that. About the phrase "thy kingdom come," we do well to consult the Bible about what that kingdom will look like. We read that the kingdom will come in the morning, when time shall be no more, when all the tears will be wiped from our eyes, when the lion and the lamb will lie down together— when, in short, there will be *shalom*. In that time and place, God, it seems, will not prefer a certain race (whites will not be over blacks) or gender (men will not be over women), or nationality (English will not be over Irish), or social class (the powerful will not be over the meek and lowly), or denomination (Presbyterians will not be over Catholics).

Because the two readings of the Christian story are plausible, one can see the confusion possible: early in the story God's favor was exclusive, while in the post-Resurrection era God's favor is inclusive—some would say universal. It is not that God changes his mind but that the record we have of his revelation seems to develop over time. By the end of the Bible, it seems that God desires that all people come to him, to live in his favor and at peace with each other. This interpretation will cause its contemporary adherents to see their task of inclusion very differently from those who view their task as trying to maintain the boundaries between those chosen and those beyond the pale.

So do religious peacemakers actually make a difference? As many commentators have pointed out, it is impossible to demonstrate empirically the argument for peacemaking, namely that the violence of the Troubles would have been worse in the absence of such activity. For their part, religious actors are humble but persistent in their belief that they have had an impact. The experienced and much-respected Jesuit Fr. Michael Hurley insists that "the churches were once part of the problem; they are now part of the solution."[19]

## A Friendship for Peace

The remainder of this chapter will discuss the friendship of Ken Newell and Gerry Reynolds. A friendship such as theirs illumines both the truth about forgiveness and reconciliation that this book seeks to disclose and also the prophetic witness to the thorough transformation of persons and society demanded by a reading of the Gospel along the lines suggested above.

The friendship between Ken and Gerry emerged in the early 1980s. We should recall that this was a particularly low point in the history of the Troubles. Early in the premiership of Margaret Thatcher several signal events would put Northern Irish affairs on a downward spiral that would take many years to reverse. The demand by the Republican prisoners in the Maze prison (known in the Nationalist community as Long Kesh) that they be treated as political prisoners was rejected by Mrs. Thatcher, who advocated treating them like nonpolitical criminals. This dispute escalated into a hunger strike that brought a deep sense of polarization in Northern Irish life. In the end, ten Republican prisoners died on the hunger strike. The most notable was Bobby Sands, who died in May 1981, after sixty-six days on strike. Sands's memory moved deeply and quickly into the lore of Republicanism, and the ranks of the Irish Republican Army grew markedly. Mrs. Thatcher's triple rejection of the recommendations by the think tank called the New Irish Forum moved the IRA to try the spectacular bombing of the Conservative Party convention hotel in Brighton, England, a blast that missed the prime minister but killed five others. The early 1980s, then, was a particularly difficult time.

In 1981, Ken Newell was in his late thirties and only back six years from a missionary stint in Timor, Indonesia. With the encouragement of clergy senior to him, most notably the Presbyterian Alan Flavelle and the Anglican Cecil Kerr, as well as some elders and people of his own congregation, Ken had been leading Fitzroy since 1977 into interchurch and peacemaking activities in the immediate area of Queen's University, known locally and affectionately as "the Holy Land." He forged a strong friendship with Fr. Denis Newberry, a curate in St. Malachy's Catholic Church, very near to Fitzroy. Together they organized annual Christmas carol services in each other's churches, as well as other informal occasions for fellowship. These activities were unprecedented, and they generated an ethos of tolerance and acceptance in the local area.[20] Unknown to Ken, the priests of the Redemptorist order at the Clonard Monastery in West Belfast, a Republican stronghold, were also—at the same time—thinking and praying about how they might be more active in promoting peace and reconciliation, first among their own parish people and then in the wider community.

In April of the hard year of 1981, the BBC in Northern Ireland, Radio Ulster, asked Ken to take "Thought for the Day," a short program of religious reflection. Ken did so and spoke for several days on the beatitudes. In this last program—broadcast when Bobby Sands was well into his fatal hunger strike—Ken spoke on the passage from Mark's Gospel, "Blessed are the peacemakers for God shall call them his children." He noted that Robert Kee's excellent series on Irish history was just then running on BBC television and that the secular viewpoint drawn from that series would offer little hope that the Irish people, especially the Northern Irish, would be able to escape the vicious and violent cycle of history. Ken also spoke of recently having attended a charismatic, ecumenical meeting in Belfast, at which several tapestries were displayed. One was quite moving to him. It portrayed two people, one clad in orange, and another in green, engaged in an embrace. Though engaging and embracing, the two figures were still clearly distinct and still clearly represented their own particular traditions and cultures. The seven hundred people at this large meeting were then asked to find, and embrace, a person from "the other" community. This, in Ken's memory, was an appropriate sign of hope for peace among Ulster's peoples.[21] Although Ken Newell spoke these words in 1981, they prefigure a compelling reformulation of "embrace" in the work of Miroslav Volf, whose 1995 article "A Vision of Embrace" soon found its way into the peace-oriented discourse in Northern Ireland.

In an embrace I open my arms to create space in myself for the other. Open arms are a sign that I do not want to be by myself only, an invitation for the other to come in and feel at home with me. In an embrace I also close my arms around the other. Closed arms are a sign that I want the other to become a part of me, the other enriches me. In a mutual embrace none remains the same because each enriches the other, yet both remain true to their genuine selves.[22]

The day after Newell's radio address his phone rang. The caller was a young American, Greg Hendrickson, who asked for Ken's text. When Ken asked why, Greg disclosed that he was working as an intern for Fr. Christopher (known as Christy) McCarthy at Clonard Monastery, hoping to set up Bible studies and prayer meetings for people in the "renewal" movement, Protestants and Catholics alike. Ken met Fr. Christy a few days later. The two discussed the idea of a friendship-in-mission between Fitzroy and the Church of the Most Holy Redeemer, attached to the monastery. The Clonard-Fitzroy Fellowship began in principle.

Fr. Christy was a generation older than Ken, but the two hit it off quite well, and their partnership gave renewed energy to the vision of cross-community Bible study first envisioned by McCarthy. Fr. Christy was to die about a year later. It took a little time for Clonard to reposition itself with regard to this cross-community work. Early in 1983, Ken went up to Clonard and approached Fr. Gerry Reynolds, a Redemptorist priest only recently arrived at Clonard from his home area in County Limerick, in the Republic, about renewing the fellowship. Gerry later recalled his walking in the garden with Ken, wondering what he, a rather retiring priest from the South, was getting himself into with this big, gregarious, and voluble Ulster Presbyterian. Just then, the Angelus bell sounded, and Gerry took that as a sign from God that he and Ken should go forward in faith.[23]

Over the next two decades their friendship would deepen, and the influence of this unlikely pair would broaden. They brought along with them on their journey the worshiping congregations at Fitzroy Presbyterian Church and in the Church of the Most Holy Redeemer at Clonard Monastery. Out of the credibility of that slowly built friendship between two men and their communities wonderful works of forgiveness and reconciliation would come, first in small acts of kindness and then on the larger political scene. Twenty years ago no one could have imagined, for example, a contingent of Presbyterian evangelicals having a retreat on Celtic spirituality along with Catholics priests and laity. By 1996 it was a normal occasion to have an impromptu meeting at a Presbyterian elder's home to discuss the pain and social anguish of the Drumcree standoff about Orange marching. The credibility of the fellowship was seen in representatives from both constituencies going both to the offices of Mary Robinson, president of the Republic, and to those of the Orange Order, to witness to their common resolve for peace. As signs of their oneness in Christ, Ken preached at the Great Novena at Clonard and Gerry officiated at a foot washing at Fitzroy (in lieu of full communion).

Gerry Reynolds and Ken Newell are not theoretical people. While surely thoughtful and intellectually capable, both men are prepared to act on what they call their biblical faith without having worked out all the details of engagement. As they were later to say, they believed it was time to declare the cold war between the churches to be over and to say in public that each saw in the other friend—and in his denomination—the real presence of Christ. As much in having a cup of tea with an inarticulate old person in the church hall of the other denomination as in talking substantial politics with "terrorists," the two friends, in their own self-estimates, were doing the work of forgiveness in politics and ecclesiastical reconciliation. In fact, for Gerry and Ken, the notion for "forgiveness in politics" never existed as a discrete area: the "religious" and "political" concerns were always closely related. As Fr. Gerry remarked to me, "The church was the sacrament and the source of unity in society." For them, it was almost as if politics was religion by another name or means, because the goal was the same, namely to end the violence, to bring peace, and to cultivate an ethos of forgiveness and reconciliation throughout Ulster. Over the next pages we will first follow the more religious track. Then we will introduce a new character, Fr. Alec Reid, who helped move the religious for Ken and Gerry to the overtly political.

We look first at Ken Newell's attempt to bring his own denomination, the Presbyterian Church in Ireland (PCI), into the whole discussion about forgiveness and reconciliation. Ken was not the first member of the Presbyterian clergy to try to nudge the PCI in a more tolerant and cooperative direction, as the prior work of J. Ernest Davey in theological education and Ray Davey in community outreach recalls for us. But Ken was among the first prominently placed clergy from the evangelical wing of the PCI to do so, especially in the deeply troubled context of the 1980s. During that decade, Ken worked with like-minded colleagues on two very important meetings that were to have lasting consequences.

In June 1983 the PCI General Assembly had its annual meeting in Dublin. Ken, through his own experience of growing up in Belfast with virtually no contact with Catholics, was aware that many other Presbyterian clergy and elders lived out their lives in a similar atmosphere of emotional "apartheid." Most had never sat in the same room with a Catholic bishop or theologian and listened to him explain his faith or his perspectives on political and social issues. Ken felt called to risk a great deal of his credibility in calling a side-meeting at the Abbey PCI congregation in Dublin. The speakers at the meeting were Rev. Alan Flavelle—an evangelical theologian of note and a leading light among an older generation of PCI clergy for the cause of reconciliation—and Cahal Daley, then the Roman Catholic bishop of Connor and Down (later to be car-dinal). The hosts for the evening were three former moderators: Dr. Austin Fulton (1960), Dr. John Davey (1962), and Dr. W. A. A. Park (1965). Some two hundred Presbyterian clergy (instead of Ken's projected fifty) came over from the General Assembly on a cold, wet night to participate in the first-ever wor-ship service in Ireland at which a Presbyterian and a Catholic leader preached. Moreover, about fifty Catholic clergy attended, through the invitation of Paddy Monaghan, later to be the leader of the Evangelical-Catholic Initiative. The sub-ject under discussion that night was "Ministering the Peace of Christ." Those in attendance were apparently a bit nervous and awkward at first, but the at-mosphere soon changed to respectful listening and serious engagement. It was a good evening for all concerned to have the ecclesial distance bridged in a graceful way.

For Ken Newell, though, the risky service in Dublin was only the beginning: it would bring a new reality home to the Protestant heartland in Ulster if they could do it in Belfast. This was upping the ante very steeply. In 1986 Ken orga-nized another meeting, this time in the hoped-for friendly confines of his own congregation at Fitzroy. Once again the Catholic representative was Bishop Daley, a person much loved among Catholics and also respected among Prot-estants because of the prelate's consistent criticism of the IRA's violence. This time the Presbyterian speaker was Dr. Robert Dickinson, the moderator of the PCI. This service would be the first ever in Irish history in which a Catholic bishop and a current Presbyterian moderator worshiped and preached together.

The right wing of Ulster Protestantism would not allow this meeting to pro-ceed unchallenged. Extremely conservative Protestants, associated mainly but not exclusively with the Rev. Ian R. K. Paisley, brought several kinds of protests. Pickets protesting boisterously were outside. Security was very tight when the moderator and the bishop, who had to endure name-calling as they negotiated pickets, arrived. About a dozen protesters gained seats inside and shouted dis-ruptions as the service proceeded, and they had to be removed forcibly by ushers and in some cases by plainclothes police. Others approached the communion table and clung to a leg while protesting this meeting of the righteous with the "Antichrist." Ken later recalled: "It was an astonishing night. The fact that it took place at all spoke volumes about the determination of the peacemakers not to yield to the threats of those who have nothing to offer in building a better future." The storm was weathered and another milestone was marked: it was the first meeting of its kind in Ulster, but it was also the last in which the forces of reaction associated with Ian Paisley would try to disrupt an ecumenical gathering.

The participants at the tumultuous 1986 Fitzroy meeting were keenly aware that a new wind was blowing in the religious life of Northern Ireland, and they were eager to keep it going. Under the leadership of Gerry Reynolds and Ken Newell, they conceived of an annual meeting in which all manner of theological questions dividing Protestants and Catholics could be discussed. The priests and lay brothers of Clonard Monastery offered the hospitality of St. Clements, their retreat center on the Antrim Road, on the north side of Belfast. Each year since then, hundreds of clergy—though slightly more Protestants than Catholics—have met to discuss all the main subjects of dispute between the two theological expressions and to try to find as much common ground as possible. The participants have found these meetings, known as the Evangelical-Roman Catholic Theological Conferences, very helpful, and they have gone a long way toward breaking down the spirit of sectarianism in Northern Irish religious life, at least as regards the clergy.

Although this chapter is mainly about Gerry Reynolds and Ken Newell, we must diverge a little to discuss the person who gave energy to the two and whose work for peace behind the scenes is largely unsung. He is Fr. Alec Reid of Clonard, a man from County Tipperary who has served the people of West Belfast since the late 1960s. He has never given a public interview and has always avoided the public view. But all close observers agree that he has been the eminence in the background who has given courage and vision to politicians and clergy alike in support of the peace process. He has also done some of the hard thinking that has given political energy to his activist comrades. There are only two known occasions when Fr. Alec went on the public record. In view of his enormous influence on events, it is worthwhile for us to pay close attention to what he wrote and said; in an article in the *Irish Times* in the mid-1980s and in a lecture at the interclergy meeting at St Clements, we get insights into how clergy and people, like the Clonard-Fitzroy Fellowship, were able to conjoin the religious and political tracks toward reconciliation.

First, the *Irish Times* piece, in which Fr. Alec wrote:

We must begin by lifting our eyes to a vision of the peace we want to create. That, in general, can only be a new political situation where the people of Ireland, in their Nationalist and Unionist traditions, are living together in friendship and mutual co-operation for the common good of all, and where the people of Ireland, and the people of Britain, are living together in the same way.

How to make this vision a reality is, therefore, the great question on which all our peace-making energies and abilities must focus. For those who believe in the Christian message of justice and love . . . this means that the principles of peace are essentially the principles which respect and correspond to the human dignity and human rights of all the people. . . . Rooted in the God-given dignity of the human person, these principles define the "narrow road" which leads to political salvation. Any road defined by policies which lack respect that is due to the dignity and the rights of people must, therefore, be seen as the "broad road" which leads to political destruction. Here, those who believe in the Lord Jesus must be prepared, like His first followers, to leave "all things," all their partisan and sectarian attitudes, and follow Him down the road of democratic justice and charity to whatever political destination it may lead.[24]

It was this sort of straightforward political theology that guided Fr. Alec to work secretly to patch up the differences with the Nationalist, Republican movement, especially between John Hume of the moderate Social Democratic and Labour Party (SDLP) and Gerry Adams of Sinn Fein (SF), and then in helping to turn SF/IRA toward the peace process (of which more below). For now, though, let us continue to follow Fr. Alec's thinking, as revealed in the only public lecture he is known to have given—at the Ninth Annual Evangelical-Roman Catholic Theological Conference at the Clonard's St. Clements Centre. For Fr. Alec, the beginning point was an incarnational theology, the idea that what he named "the serving Christian" must be a pastoral agent of the Holy Spirit "in the midst of the conflict, in all its flesh and blood reality, in order to know the conflict from within and to see all the moral issues." He reminded his audience at St. Clements that "Jesus lived among us fully and unreservedly" and that "he came to create a companionship between God and people, and among peoples." For Reid, drawing upon linguistic roots, companionship is more than friendship or fellowship: companions are people who eat bread together. Jesus used the table of food to foster this type of companionship, and he was willing to risk this companionship with all those willing to share his company. For Fr. Alec, "[T]he serving Christian [in a situation of conflict] must engage in sustained, direct dialogue with all participants. Thus, it is by listening in the midst of conflict that we hear the way forward, and we hear the words of Jesus from whoever speaks the words of peace."[25]

Alec Reid knew what it meant to be in the midst of conflict. From the mid-1980s onward he took a determined view never to condemn anyone but to be available, as he said of Jesus, to all who would risk his companionship. Although his spiritual leader, Cardinal Daley, was regularly condemning the violence, and specifically the IRA, Fr. Alec would not do so. He knew that, on a given Sunday when he looked out on his congregation at Most Holy Redeemer Church at Clonard, he saw IRA people, some possibly on active service in the armed struggle and surely those who supported the armed struggle. He was absolutely determined to be their priest and not condemn them; but he was equally determined never to condone the violence and to try to find a way to end the killing. He was credible in the eyes of all, not because he vacillated, but because he saw his Christian role as the interpreter of each to all.

The credibility of Fr. Alec can be seen in one of the most extraordinary scenes in the entire history of the Troubles. In March 1988 there were a series of events that would, for a moment, catapult this quiet priest into the world spotlight. That month began with an "active unit" of the IRA being spotted in Gibraltar. Although Mairead Farrell, Danny McCann, and Sean Savage were on an assignment of murder and mayhem among the British forces in Gibraltar, they were, in fact, unarmed at the moment that British forces in plainclothes shot, some would say murdered, them (three bodies received a total of twenty-nine hits). The three were brought back to Belfast (with Fr. Alec accompanying the bodies on the road from Dublin) and given a solemn IRA funeral at the Milltown cemetery, the near-sacred burial ground of the Republican movement. But in the midst of it a Loyalist terrorist, Michael Stone, attacked the funeral party with guns and grenades, killing three people and injuring dozens more. Three days later, there was another funeral at the same West Belfast cemetery, this time for one of Stone's victims. The atmosphere was already supercharged with tension, both because of legitimate grief and because of Republican fears of another attack like Stone's. A bizarre event then occurred that broke the tension and unleashed blind fury and mob savagery (an army helicopter was hovering above, and the following scene was captured on videotape). A car drove into the funeral cortege. In it were two off-duty British soldiers, Derek Woods and David Howes, one showing the other, a recently arrived recruit, around Belfast. The IRA escorts for the funeral cortege, fearing it was another attack, surrounded the car and encouraged the crowd to overwhelm it. The soldiers were dragged from the car, partially stripped and beaten. There were then driven away in a taxi to a vacant lot, where they were beaten again, this time quite severely. They were then shot and left to die. Someone had the grace to call for a priest. In the nearby crowd was Fr. Alec Reid, the priest everyone knew would come, no matter what. As the journalists Eammon Mallie and David McKittrick recall the scene, Fr. Alec "knelt down in the dirt beside the spread-eagled, semi-naked body of one of the soldiers. Although he knew there was little or no hope, he bowed, and, amid the mud and the blood, attempted to give him the kiss of life. . . . Fr. Reid leaned down and pressed his mouth to that of the soldier; when he straightened up, after his hopeless effort, his lips had the soldier's blood on them." A fellow-journalist, Mary Holland, also on the scene, later wrote: "His courage and compassion redeemed us all. It sent one image of Ireland across the world that spoke human pity in the face of death rather than the savagery of the mob." Mallie and McKittrick continue: "In that ghastly tableau, Fr. Reid was also the picture of helplessness, a living symbol of the impotence of organized religion and indeed of rational argument in the face of a merciless, determined gunman. Many would have given up; yet the same priest, spurred on by this awful experience, was able to play a hidden but vital part in bringing about the IRA cessation of violence in 1994."[26]

The religious and political tracks were beginning to converge for all concerned in the late 1980s. Events often pushed participants in directions, or to degrees, that they had not fully expected. For example, the episode on November 8, 1987, at Enniskillen, in County Fermanagh, was another turning point (we have noted this, in another connection, above). On that Sunday morning, crowds of people, mostly Protestants, were gathering to participate in the Day of Remembrance for war dead. Gordon Wilson, age sixty, and his daughter, Marie, age twenty, just home for the weekend from her nursing job in Belfast, stood with friends and neighbors. Without warning the IRA detonated a bomb containing forty pounds of gelignite. It took down the wall of the community hall where the device had been hidden, and it killed outright the three couples standing near the Wilsons: William and Agnes Mullan, Kitchener and Jesse Johnston, and Wesley and Bertha Armstrong. Gordon and Marie were buried in the rubble, unable to move. Many people later commented on the deeply affecting quality of Wilson's account on the BBC, describing how he and his daughter lay trapped in the debris, holding hands and talking. After a while, she said, "Daddy, I love you very much," and then she fell silent. Gordon Wilson survived but Marie did not. He deeply touched many people by giving the wonderful testimony that he bore no ill will to the murderers. His testimony is as moving now as it was then: "I bear no ill will. That sort of talk is not going to bring her back to life. She was a great wee lassie . . . , and she's dead. . . . Please don't ask me for a purpose. I don't have an answer but I know there has to be a plan. If I did not think that, I would commit suicide. It is part of a greater plan, and God is good and we shall meet again." Ken Newell was later to say that, in Wilson's testimony, "Christ came back to Enniskillen."[27]

The next Sunday, November 15, 1987, Ken Newell changed the sermon he had intended to give at Fitzroy Church. This was a strategic decision, for not only was his own congregation to hear the sermon, but it was to be broadcast across the whole community on Radio Ulster. He now knew that his congregation — and, he hoped the religious listeners of Ulster, and possibly the Republic too — would be ready to have contemporary politics engaged from the pulpit. For him, the Enniskillen tragedy changed everything, and it required from him a more direct response, to let the light of the Gospel shine on political aspects of the Troubles.

Everyone in Fitzroy Church, and those listening across Ireland, expected Ken Newell to condemn the violence. He did, in no uncertain terms. In fact, he expressed his horror at the sight of the events on television. But then he moved to another angle of vision. He said it was relatively easy to condemn violence when it comes from the other side and is against our side. "But when it comes from those whose political aspirations we have some sympathy with, it is amazing how in the back of our minds we find ways of condoning it, at least just a little, or so we think. The tragedy of Enniskillen must surely now have destroyed all such mental maneuvering; all justifications for violence, all sympathy with those who act violently, from whatever source, died in the carnage around that War Memorial last Sunday."

Instead of taking the easy and understandable route of simply blasting the IRA, Ken focused the light of scrutiny also on himself and on his fellow Protestants who were listening to the broadcast. It was not an easy issue to raise, the whole matter of the Protestant "ascendancy" in Northern Ireland. It was precisely this set of attitudes and realities that Protestants must learn to repent of when remembering Enniskillen.

After a past filled with centuries of violence and a present with thousands of broken hearts, I have a deep longing for peace; the Troubles have changed me, and Enniskillen has pushed that change further. I am a Protestant, but with no desire to see a Protestant Ascendancy; I am British in my political identity but with the highest regard for the richness of Irish heritage; I am a Presbyterian who enjoys deep and loving relationships with many of my Roman Catholic brothers and sisters in Christ. And after Enniskillen, the only ascendancy I am interested in is that of Christ's love and justice, and his reverence for life. In this I know I am not alone. But that can only be achieved if, after Enniskillen, we now—as one people—close our minds completely against the way of violence.

Ken surely must have startled some of the listeners on the BBC, perhaps more than his own people at Fitzroy, who knew him better. The conclusion of the sermon pushed Protestants quite hard in terms of what they had to do if they were to remember Enniskillen rightly: that is, stopping simply pointing the finger of blame at others and finding the way in which each might contribute to the welfare of all. And Ken would not let his hearers be content with a safe but unengaged spirituality:

While prayer is vitally important, it is no longer enough to pray without action; it is no longer enough to pray without repentance for the distances we have created among people in which suspicion and mistrust can grow; it is no longer enough to wait for God to send revival when what He clearly demands in scripture right now is the forging of new, healthy relationships and positive Christian attitudes without which this community cannot survive and without which we have no future.

Ken was aware, as he said in the sermon, that the Troubles had changed him, especially with respect to political consciousness. He was listening to the concerns of the Nationalist community through his contacts at Clonard and elsewhere and had become aware of the thorough pattern of discrimination and hardship that the minority community had experienced. While he was aware that his own community might not appreciate it when he spoke up, he felt it was his duty to tell the truth about some of the less acknowledged aspects of the realities of Northern Irish political life. At the meeting of the General Assembly of the Presbyterian Church of Ireland in June 1993, Ken substantially ruffled some feathers when in the course of debate he asserted that there had been "long term discrimination against Catholics in public sector employment" in Northern Ireland. He referred directly to the former Unionist prime minister, Sir Basil Brooke, to suggest that discrimination against Catholics was "embedded in the Unionist political leadership." Another delegate at the meeting interrupted Ken and challenged him on the accuracy of his comment about Brooke, to which Ken spiritedly replied: "It is sin, it is evil, it is wrong. You need to stand up and say it." When this was reported in the press, several people commented on Ken's statements. Most notable was praise from Oliver Kearney, chairman of the public advocacy group Campaign for Economic Equality, who said it was a "courageous and honorable declaration," which was the first time "that a senior Presbyterian clergyman publicly acknowledged the endemic nature of anti-Catholic discrimination, and identified it as 'evil and wrong.'" What is clear in Ken Newell's engagement with political concerns, and equally clear in what we will say about Gerry Reynolds, is the desire to connect religious beliefs with social justice, while never associating that with a particular political movement or party.[28]

Alec Reid knew Ken, of course, but the Presbyterian was more the friend of Fr. Alec's colleague Gerry Reynolds. It was through Gerry that Alec was kept abreast of Ken's thinking. Alec also saw Ken occasionally when the latter would visit Clonard with the Clonard-Fitzroy Fellowship. So, in late 1989, when Fr. Alec's secret diplomacy within the Republican movement was beginning to bear fruit, he knew where to go, and to whom, when the time was right to bring Protestants into a wider dialogue.

Early in 1990, Fr. Gerry told Ken that there was an element within Sinn Fein that wanted to make contact with Protestant, Unionist people. Ken was asked if he would be interested in participating in talks. He agreed. This was a high-risk venture for Ken because he knew he might be meeting face to face with people who might have ordered the maiming of members of his congregation or the killing of members of his own denomination. Further, it was politically risky because the official line from London and in Unionist circles in Ulster was that there could be no talks with Sinn Fein until its comrades in the IRA declared a cease-fire. Ken later disclosed that if his church people had known of his involvement in talks with Sinn Fein during 1990–93 (the IRA cease-fire did not come until 1994) "I would have been in real trouble and would have been basically blown out of the water of my congregation and been demonized."[29] Ken took steps to protect himself in the potentially vulnerable position in which he found himself by inviting one of the senior Fitzroy elders, Denis Boyd, who was clerk of session, to participate in the dialogue with him.

Not only did this wise step bring a lay dimension to the heavily clerical discussions, but after the IRA cease-fire was announced in 1994 Ken and Denis were able to break the news of their involvement to the elders before everything became public knowledge.

The talks with Sinn Fein were, of course, the most important, but there were other tracks of talks going on too—for example, with the Protestant paramilitaries of the Ulster Defence Association (UDA). The religious actors in these talks varied, but there was a core group that almost always included Alec Reid, Gerry Reynolds, Ken Newell, Rev. Sam Burch (a Methodist, and leader of the Cornerstone Community), and Dennis Boyd, Ken's clerk of session at Fitzroy. The first year of engagement with Sinn Fein was very difficult for Ken. He later recalled that he was quite "frosty" with the president of Sinn Fein, Gerry Adams. Ken later said that he probably "sounded like a broken record as I repeated my viewpoint about ending the violence."[30] But Fr. Alec and Fr. Gerry encouraged their Protestant friends to keep at it. Gradually each told his own story of growing up in Ireland and how each had conformed to his own community's narrative. Further, each apparently began to understand more about the other than he had thought possible. Ken could now begin "to listen to the pain on the Republican side, of people who grew up a mile and half from me, but, in terms of their feelings, were on a different planet from me." Gerry Reynolds may have seen all this a bit sooner than Ken, because he went into the talks quite sure that both sides had only a partial claim to truth and that the role of the serving Christian was to affirm what one could in all positions. In time, Ken did come to see that too. By the end of the first year, late 1990, Ken said, "As I listened, I heard that they too had a compelling story of anger, injustice, and suffering."[31]

Meetings with Sinn Fein were frequently opened with prayer or a moment of quiet reflection, and sometimes with a Bible reading too. Ken recalls vividly the first meeting at Clonard with Gerry Adams and his colleagues and some bodyguards. Fr. Gerry Reynolds opened his Bible and read from Psalm 85:8–13. The passage spoke powerfully to a situation dominated by violence and pointed the participants toward the peace and hope that faith in God makes possible and that human action makes real. Some phrases from the psalm began to etch their way into the consciousness of those present: "Let us hear what God the Lord will speak to his people, to his faithful, to those who turn to him in their hearts." Further in the passage we read Gerry's goal for the meeting: "Steadfast love and faithfulness will meet; righteousness and peace will kiss each other." The meetings were often very businesslike; Sinn Fein might present a position paper, and the peace builder might make considered responses (often led by the much-respected Fr. Alec Reid).

But while Ken Newell was grateful for the insights gained, by mid-1992 he reckoned that the talks were stalled and going nowhere positive, that Sinn Fein was not prepared to budge. The IRA's campaign of violence was unabated, and its political wing was not willing to indicate much about stopping it. Reluctantly, Ken felt that, in the absence of Sinn Fein's willingness to commit itself to a process of conflict resolution by first establishing a cease-fire, he should withdraw from further discussion. At this critical turning the two Clonard priests were an inestimable influence in two respects: they kept the pressure up on Sinn Fein, and they continued with Ken and the others in the parallel talks with Protestant paramilitaries, held at Fitzroy and at the Columbanus Community of Reconciliation.

Reid and Reynolds persisted with Gerry Adams and the Sinn Fein leadership, focusing on two points: that while the IRA could not be defeated militarily, neither was it going to drive Britain out of Ulster; since a negotiation must come someday, Sinn Fein was going to have to deal with Unionists at the end of the day. In the lights of these realities, the priests insisted, if Sinn Fein could not deal with the likes of their friends, Ken Newell and Sam Burch, it could never deal with mainstream Northern Irish Protestants. The exact workings of the collective mind of Sinn Fein on this are not known, but the result was that in early 1993 Gerry Adams told Reid and Reynolds to come back to the talks with their Protestant friends. Fr. Gerry had great but guarded hopes for this new round of talks. Ken did too and noted immediately the change of mood as Gerry Adams welcomed him back. Among the peacemakers, Ken was first to see the change, in the warmth of genuine friendship and human concern he received from Adams. In Ken's own words, and inimitable way, he later told me: "The emotional warmth of the meetings began melting the iceberg of traditional responses. How do you destroy an iceberg? If you ram it, as in a ship, it will sink you. But if you gently nudge it towards warmer waters, it will eventually melt."[32]

The other talks accelerated then too. The same peacemakers were also meeting with the UDA. The then-leader of the Columbanus Community of Reconciliation, Sr. Roisin Hannaway, offered her building as a venue. She later told me that she did so in full awareness that she might be inviting an IRA attack on the building if it became known that Ray Smallwood and Gary McMichael were in the building. She was, understandably, frightened by the prospect of violence, but with the encouragement of Gerry, Ken, Alec, and Sam (as well as her own community members and leadership, particularly by that tower of strength, Gemma Loughran), she welcomed the UDA to the house on the Antrim Road.[33]

The pace toward peace quickened in 1993, and in 1994 the IRA declared a cease-fire that was soon matched by the UDA. The leadership of the two paramilitary forces have not always been able to control their own men on the ground, and several excesses have happened despite the cease-fires. In due course, the two leaderships have policed their own turfs and exacted reprisals against recalcitrants on their own side. Peacemakers may not like this aspect of intracommunity violence, but they have learned to accept it as an earnest of the respective leaderships to maintain the cease-fires. This rough consensus was strained to near the breaking point when, just as the cease-fires were taking hold, a still-unspecified group of Republican paramilitaries assassinated Ray Smallwood, with three shotgun blasts, outside his home in Lisburn, County Antrim. No one has been able to solve the puzzle of this murder. Smallwood had been an active paramilitary in his time. For example, he was part of a UDA hit squad that shot, and nearly killed, the celebrated Nationalist Member of Parliament, Bernadette Devlin (McAliskey) in 1980. During his lengthy jail term for that attempted murder Smallwood apparently renounced violence and embraced religion and politics, and by 1993 he was the political spokesman for the Ulster Democratic Party, the political wing of the UDA—that is, a direct equivalent of Sinn Fein/IRA. It was obviously not in the interest of Sinn Fein, just moving from the armed struggle to politics, to countenance this murder of a leading Unionist who was thinking along the same lines. As said, no one has satisfactorily explained this, other than to observe that both IRA and UDA leadership cannot always control the men nominally under their command.

This serious impasse was overcome both because of the genuine movement toward peace on all sides and because of the quick thinking and courageous acting of the religious peacemakers, now informally known as "the cross-community group," namely Reid, Reynolds, Newell, and Burch. A strong bond had developed between them and Smallwood, and the latter's sincerity about peace had made a deep impression on them. They were very saddened by this murder. The two priests in the group, best connected to the Republican movement, were known to have complained bitterly to Sinn Fein/IRA about it. They went down to Lisburn on the night of Ray Smallwood's wake. It was a very important gesture and symbol that Fr. Gerry and Fr. Alec attended the wake without their Protestant colleagues. Present at that wake were many of the heavyweights of Protestant paramilitary activity (especially John White, the known and convicted assassin of the assistant of former SDLP leader, Gerry Fitt). Gary McMichael, the new leader of the UDA, welcomed them all.[34]

Several weeks later, when the whole clergy group was to meet Gary McMichael and other UDA leaders in Lisburn, Ken was aware that the latter were still grieving Ray Smallwood's death. He believed that it was wiser to acknowledge those feelings than to go right into political discussions. He asked everyone in the room, about eight in all, to stand for a moment of silence and prayer for Smallwood and his family. Ken recalls that "of all the occasions when we met with paramilitaries, this was the most moving and miraculous." Gerry recalled that it was Ken who asked everyone to stand and asked him to pray; Gerry does not recall exactly the words he said, but he is sure that the prayer arose out of the anger, pain, and hurt of the occasion. He said he had "the sense that was very significant in our lives; here was God in the midst of life."[35] Whether Fr. Gerry's prayer was the reason we do not know, but we do know that there was no UDA violent response to Smallwood's murder and that, under Gary McMichael's leadership of the UDA, the cease-fire has held.

From 1994, when the first cease-fires were first declared, to Good Friday, 1998, when the peace agreement was signed, the political process has moved forward. That story has been told in detail elsewhere, so there is not need for us to reiterate it here.[36] But, for our purposes, one or two words need to be said. The cross-community group did not retire from activity when political leaders began to talk directly and openly. Be it recalled that in a democracy, political leaders can go only so far without taking their constituencies with them; conversely, if a constituency seeks change, political leaders must respond or lose their positions. So, even as one might laud the determined work of John Hume, David Trimble, Gerry Adams, and George Mitchell on the ground, and the good support of Tony Blair, Bertie Ahern, and Bill Clinton, if the political process is to succeed it needs broad and deep public support. As Scott Appleby has noted, "[T]op-down structural processes devised, negotiated and implemented in the political area are unlikely to succeed in the absence of parallel and coordinated cultural initiatives designed to build the social infrastructures of peace." As in the image of "embrace" discussed above, a community need not disown its entire particular past; it need only reframe it toward mutual accommodation, forgiveness, and reconciliation. As Appleby says well, "[L]asting peace is impossible without a change of hearts and minds, without a new story to replace the old."[37]

Gerry Reynolds and Ken Newell are still involved in many sorts of reconciliation activities. In November 1999 and in May 2000, for example, when the peace process had slowed to a snail's pace, and when the new assembly was threatened with failure, Ken and Gerry organized a group of clergy to support the peace process. The form of it was an ad in the three newspapers, the *Belfast Telegraph,* the *Belfast News Letter,* and the *Irish Times.* Some five hundred Protestant and Catholic clergy paid ten pounds and signed their names to the following:

*Faith in a Brighter Future*
We, the undersigned, are men and women committed to Jesus Christ, and wish to share our deep convictions at this time. We believe that in the providence of God, Protestants and Catholics, Unionist, National-ists and others have been placed here together. For generations we have lived mainly in separation, rivalry and conflict. In these last few years the opportunity has been given to us to travel together in a new direc-tion in order to create a healthier and more harmonious society. Many of us have begun this journey. It has involved us in painful change but also in new challenges and enriching friendships.

The political process is just one expression of this journey, but a vital one. The difficulties we face are real, but one way or another we have got to overcome them. There can be no turning back. This week is a signifi-cant moment. Our doubts and fears must not be allowed to strangle our vision. We are committed to continuing this journey towards the heal-ing of our society.

When asked about this activity on a radio interview, Ken and Gerry told not only of the ad campaign but of marching up to Stormont, the seat of gov-ernment in suburban Belfast, to lobby the politicians further. Over a hundred clergy turned up to encourage their leaders to go forward. The clergy believed they were trying to do in church and society what the politicians were trying to do in government, namely to find the way forward to peace and reconcili-ation. When the interviewer asked how the politicians responded, Gerry and Ken observed that, without boasting, the clergy leadership was "a serious and intellectually-capable group" whose views the politicians seemed to value. Ken and Gerry thought they were seen not as religious lightweights but as "serious Christians committed to an inclusive society."[38]

The two friends have not retired from political engagement, as witness the ad campaigns and the lobbying, but they are now content to leave the actual daily work of politics to elected officials of the various parties. The overall goal of Reynolds and Newell was forgiveness, reconciliation, and healing in all areas

Ulster life. It was always out of this comprehensive "religious" vision that their "forgiveness in politics" activities took place.

Their faithfulness over the long haul was duly noted in 1999, when they received a singularly important award. They were awarded, on behalf of the Clonard-Fitzroy Fellowship, the Peace Prize for 1999 from Pax Christi, the peace movement of the Catholic Church, with headquarters in Brussels, Belgium. Pax Christi awards a Peace Prize annually to people and groups working on a grassroots level for peace. This was the first time the award had been given to someone in Ireland and, in the person of Ken Newell, to a Protestant. As the award formally read, "We are delighted that the 1999 Peace Prize is going to the Clonard-Fitzroy Fellowship. Their work in building the Kingdom of the prince of Peace in the traumatized community of Northern Ireland has been a shining example and a beacon of hope."[39]

This award gave Gerry Reynolds and Ken Newell a higher public profile in Ireland, both North and South (the award was presented in Dublin, not Belfast), than either of the two men had ever imagined or even hoped for. They consider themselves pastors in divisive circumstances in which they try to portray the gospel of *shalom*. But now they are listened to and respected on many levels because of the award. Even in their new celebrity they continue to push the pace of change in Northern Ireland. Their religious establishments may not always like what they do and say, but they are taking a large number of people with them on the journey of trust and peace.

Gerry and Ken have become very close friends, and by transcending their religious and political points of origin they encourage others to think that a "kingdom vision" does actually mean that we act differently toward and with each other. Their political goals of forgiveness and reconciliation were always an aspect of the larger transformation of the spirit they sought for Ireland. For them, and for many Christians they have touched, worship is one of the activities that characterizes the Christian life; redeemed people lead a eucharistic life. Thus, when they attend worship at each other's churches, the pain of the separation between their denominations is often difficult to bear. Being separated at the communion table is particularly hard for people like Ken and Gerry, two comrades with a sacramental vision for worship and life who have come so far together over so many years.

Gerry Reynolds had attended worship services at Fitzroy many times and had been present when Holy Communion was served. He had always let the elements pass him, even though he felt the grace of the fellowship present in them. It deeply affected and troubled him, and he wept unashamedly many times. But in November 1999, just two weeks before going down to Dublin to receive the Pax Christi award, he could no longer live with this deep contradiction in his life. He reckoned that his place in the fellowship of Fitzroy was so solid and his companionship with the people there so complete that either he must participate in Holy Communion there or leave Fitzroy altogether. In mid-November 1999, he did partake and believed that he experienced grace in a way hitherto unknown to him. He told this story in an interview broadcast all over Ireland (on the RTE, the Irish equivalent of the BBC), saying that his "participation is for the theologians to sort out elsewhere, but it is where I am on the journey." The interviewer asked Fr. Gerry if this is how and where he *does* his theology. Gerry agreed, contrasting "the ecumenism of the battlefront and the ecumenism of the salon. For me not to partake two weeks ago would have been to make a mockery of the cross of Christ."

In the same RTE interview Ken Newell told of a similar story of pain and breakthrough. He related having recently been one of several Protestant speakers at a Catholic charismatic service. Aware of the provisions of canon law, and not wanting to embarrass anyone, he removed himself to the far side of the platform when the Eucharist part of the service came, "so no one would see how lonely and isolated I felt." He said he felt "like it was a Christmas party and that I had been put outside in the snow." Well, it seems there was a "wee lady" there who went forward and received her wafer but did not consume it. Instead, she walked around to where Ken was sitting. (As Ken recalled: "I'm 6'3", and sitting down, and she's 4'10" standing up, so we're eye to eye.") She broke the wafer in two, and gave half to Ken, saying, "Ken, the body of our Lord Jesus Christ, broken for you." Ken was, uncharacteristically for him, left speechless; but he later was to say that, on that day, he had experienced a grace hitherto unknown to him.

As the theologian Miroslav Volf observed, in the Eucharistic feast we enact the memory of each other as those who are reconciled to God and to each other in Christ. Another peacemaker in Belfast, and a good friend of Ken and Gerry, could not agree more; but her agreement comes instead from the deep sense of loss about the way Catholics and Protestants are separated and segregated at the table. Sr. Roisin Hannaway, S.S.L., leader of the Columbanus Community for most of the 1990s, feels the pain very deeply both in excluding Protestants from her own church's Eucharist and from absenting herself from the invitation to the table of Protestant churches.

The situation angers me, makes me scream inside. I complain to the Lord that it is dreadful, intolerable, unbearable and unchristian, that it is not what God desires. . . . It hurts people who want to love one another and to be at one. . . . There are days when my sense of justice is offended: I look around the [Columbanus] Community chapel aware of the haves and the have-nots, those who are being fed and those who are hungry; and I wonder if we are not sometimes celebrating the Eucharist with bread taken from the poor.[40]

Sr. Roisin is helpful in detailing the ways in which the spirit of reconciliation is the main meaning of the Eucharist. In sum, it is a reconciliation that transcends dogma and doctrine and embraces all Christians; that involves forgiveness and pours the oil of compassion on the wounds of humanity; that deprives no one of the bread but brings all to the table of life; that gathers all of creation with the bread and the wine into the web of life to await the final liberation.[41]

On the Feast of Columbanus (November 29) in 1999, Gerry Reynolds was welcomed to the Columbanus Community on the Antrim Road by Roisin Hannaway. He gave the homily to the community on that day, in which he told the congregation of being profoundly moved by a celebration of the Eucharist he had attended in a congregation of the Church of Ireland. With respect to that experience he formulated three questions that pushed the argument about the Eucharist to a new level of intensity. His questions were these: (1) Does the Father in heaven give to them the True Manna, the living bread from heaven that we believe he gives us the Eucharist? Or does he give them something less? (2) Does Jesus, our crucified and risen Saviour, become really present to give them the fruits of his passion as they celebrate the Holy Communion in memory of him? Or do they have to settle for something less? (3) Is the Holy Spirit poured out upon the bread and the cup of wine they drink to hallow them and make them the Body and Blood of Christ for their spiritual nourishment? Or do they invoke the Holy Spirit in vain? As Gerry commented, "When I lived in the Republic of Ireland, I never had to ask myself such questions. But now friendship and faith oblige me to face them."[42]

It is this sort of vision and articulation of eucharistic grace that keeps Ken Newell and Gerry Reynolds going and their friendship so strong. Now approaching retirement, the two comrades look back with humble pride and satisfaction on how far they have come together. They are, however, still deeply troubled by the continuing scandal of the disunity of the churches. The process of societal forgiveness and reconciliation that has had such a good start in Northern Ireland still has a long way to go politically, but perhaps more so religiously. One wonders how much more can be done in other areas of society when the churches, long dominant in Ulster life, still allow some of the faithful to continue to tell bad stories about other persons and denominations. In the view of Ken and Gerry, which I find compelling, church people were important in the breakthrough that began the peace process; but unless church people enter into honest dialogue with one another at the local level they will impede the growth of peace. As the two friends said in another place, "Our doubts and fears must not be allowed to strangle our vision."

## Reconciliation?

There is one final set of questions to be discussed in the Irish context. They refer to the questions and concerns with which we began this chapter: Is all this talk of changed lives, forgiveness, and reconciliation indeed all talk, or can it really happen? What are we to do with the memories of hurts and injustices that trouble our several communities? Can our narratives and those of our former enemies really be reconciled? These are questions articulated in various ways by other authors in this book.

An original Irish contribution to that discourse admits that we, in our own power and in our own time, probably cannot overcome the weight of the past. But in God's power to redeem history and in his timelessness, we may be able to do so. In this regard, the work of Fr. Gabriel Daly on the reconciliation of memories is of great importance, and it accords well with the work of Ken Newell and Gerry Reynolds, as well as with the concerns of the other contributors to this book. In Daly's view, for forgiveness to "work" from the present to the past we must be able to transcend our own time and place. Daly has made a valuable contribution in his explication of Iris Murdoch's novel *Bruno's Dream*.[43] Readers meet Bruno at the end of his long life, in which religion has not played a part. He is thinking back over his unhappy past and especially his failed marriage to his late wife, Janie. Bruno was unfaithful to Janie once, and she reproved him for it for the rest of their lives and resolutely refused to forgive him. Over the years she called him to her room to berate him. One day toward the end, she called him to her room. He sensed—rightly, as it turned out—that this would be the last time. He didn't go because he did not want to hear Janie reprove him with her dying breath. The decision has haunted him ever since. As the novel ends we find Bruno aware of his own imminent death. He still longs for Janie's forgiveness but fears he will be cursed instead. With the clear-sightedness that only impending death can give, Bruno sees that if something really matters at the end of his life it must be the only thing that truly matters about that life. Now he longs for a forgiveness that he fears it is too late to find:

> "If only it could work backwards, but it can't."
> Some people believed that too. That life could be redeemed. But it couldn't be, and that was what was so terrible. He had loved only a few people and loved them so badly, so selfishly. He had made a terrible muddle of everything. Was it only in the presence of death that one could see so clearly what love ought to be like? If only the knowledge he had now, this absolutely nothing-else-matters, could somehow go backwards and purify the little selfish loves and straighten out the muddles. But it could not. Had Janie known this at the end? For the first time Bruno saw it with absolute certainty. Janie must have known. It would be impossible in this presence not to know. She had not wanted to curse him; she had wanted to forgive him. And he had not given her the chance.
> "Janie, I am so sorry," murmured Bruno. His tears flowed. But he was glad that he knew, at last.[44]

Gabriel Daly brings out the meaning of this story to demonstrate the transcendent nature of history and eschatology. Forgiveness must collapse the structure of time and space; indeed, it must, as Bruno hopes, "work backwards." As Daly writes, "It has to embrace the offence, the offender and the offended. . . . Forgiveness, in short, is both a symbolic mediation of God and a transcendent experience arising out of human limitations. . . . Historically the past is closed, eschatologically it remains open."[45]

Earlier in this chapter we referred to the "kingdom vision" of those who say the prayer of the kingdom they hope will come, in which God's peace will reign. It is when we see that eschatological vision that we all will offer and receive forgiveness and reconciliation. It is from the testimony of those who Ken and Gerry call "icons of grace," those who have received and extended that sort of peace, that we can see our memories changing.

One final story concludes our study. The story comes from remarks made at a public hearing held by Sinn Fein in the period between the cease-fires in the mid-1990s. One who spoke to the Sinn Fein leadership on that day in March 1995 was Dr. William Rutherford, a retired surgeon and an elder at the Fitzroy Presbyterian Church. He came to the meeting on the urging of his minister, Ken Newell, with whom he had participated in several reconciliation initiatives in

Belfast. Rutherford reminded the assembled Republicans of a day ten years earlier, in 1984, when Loyalist gunmen had wounded the president of Sinn Fein,
Gerry Adams. Adams had been rushed to the Royal Victoria Hospital at which
William Rutherford was the surgeon on duty. He led the team of surgeons that
saved Gerry Adams's life. He implored the members of Sinn Fein to let that be
the model of where the Republican movement might go: even as he had helped
to save and heal Adams's body, now let Adams lead Sinn Fein into the political
process that would heal Northern Ireland. The moment was a poignant one
and was widely reported in the press the next day.[46] Since that time, Sinn Fein
has entered the political arena and become part of the peace process that was
launched on Good Friday, 1998.

Forgiveness, peace, and reconciliation are still a work in progress in Northern Ireland, but one can look forward with some confidence. The Good Friday Accord enjoys majority support throughout Northern Ireland. Moreover,
ideas and initiatives that foster forgiveness and reconciliation are deeply embedded in many of the institutions of civil society. Whether they can provide
the basis for stable political institutions is a future for which Christian peacemakers hope.

# Notes

1. R. Scott Appleby, *The Ambivalence of the Sacred* (Lanham, MD: Rowman and
Littlefield, 2000), 236–39.

2. E.g., ibid.; Ronald A. Wells, *People behind the Peace: Community and Reconciliation in Northern Ireland* (Grand Rapids, MI: Eerdmans, 1999).

3. A. T. Q. Stewart, *The Narrow Ground: The Roots of the Conflict in Ulster* (London: Faber and Faber, 1977).

4. Jonathan Stevenson, *"We Wrecked the Place": Contemplating an End to the Northern Irish Troubles* (New York: Free Press, 1996).

5. Ibid., 256.

6. Ibid., 257.

7. Ibid.

8. Ibid., 258.

9. Ibid.

10. Quoted in Cecil Kerr, *The Way of Peace* (London: Hodder and Stoughton,
1990), 186.

11. See Wells, *People behind the Peace.*

12. Seamus Heaney, *The Cure at Troy* (New York: Farrar, Straus and Giroux, 1991), 77.

13. Kerr, *The Way of Peace,* 169.

14. David Livingstone and Ronald A. Wells, *Ulster-American Religion* (Notre Dame: University of Notre Dame Press, 1999); Steve Bruce, *God Save Ulster: Religion and the Politics of Paisleyism* (New York: Oxford University Press, 1989); Duncan Morrow, *The Churches and Inter-Community Relationships* (Coleraine: Centre for the Study of Conflict, University of Ulster, 1991); Richard Jenkins, *The Sectarian Divide in Northern Ireland* (London: Royal Anthropological Institute, 1986); Martha A. MacIver, "A Clash of Symbols in Northern Ireland," *Review of Religious Research* 30 (1989): 360–74.

15. John Hickey, *Religion and the Northern Ireland Problem* (Dublin: Gill and Macmillan, 1984).

16. Steve Bruce, *The Edge of the Union: The Ulster Loyalist Political Vision* (Oxford: Oxford University Press, 1994); Brian K. Lambkin, *Opposite Religions Still? Interpreting Northern Ireland after the Conflict* (Aldershot: Avebury, 1996).

17. Lambkin, *Opposite Religions*; Wells, *People behind the Peace*; Appleby, *Ambivalence of the Sacred*; Maurice Irvine, *Northern Ireland: Faith and Faction* (London: Routledge, 1991).

18. Irvine, *Northern Ireland*, 192.

19. Quoted in Appleby, *Ambivalence of the Sacred*, 191.

20. Ken Newell, conversation with the author, March 17, 2001.

21. "Thought for the Day," BBC Radio Talk, April 11, 1981.

22. Miroslav Volf, "A Vision of Embrace: Theological Perspectives on Cultural Identity," *Ecumenical Review* 47 (April 1995): 394. The insights in this article soon became part of the peace discourse in Northern Ireland and were included in the analysis in the pamphlet "Doing unto Others," by the Faith and Politics Group, Belfast, 1997.

23. Gerry Reynolds, conversation with the author, March 19, 2001. Unless otherwise indicated, the material to follow comes from interviews between the author and the principals, Gerry Reynolds and Ken Newell, on various occasions in the period 1998–2003.

24. "Clonard and the Work for Peace and Reconciliation in Northern Ireland," retrieved June 30, 2005, from the Clonard Monastery Web site: www.clonard.com/cunity.htm.

25. Alec Reid, "The Serving Christian in a Situation of Conflict," paper presented at the Ninth Annual Evangelical-Roman Catholic Theological Conference, Clonard's St. Clements Centre, St. Clements, September 14, 1993.

26. Eammon Mallie and David McKittrick, *The Fight for Peace: The Secret Story behind the Irish Peace Process* (London: Heinemann, 1999), 1–2.

27. Ken Newell, *Forgiveness in Conflict Resolution: Reality and Utility, The Northern Ireland Experience* (Washington, DC: Woodstock Theological Center, 1997), 57–59.

28. Ken Newell, sermon, BBC Morning Service, November 15, 1987.

29. On November 18, 1999, Ken Newell and Gerry Reynolds submitted to a lengthy interview in the Belfast Office of Radio Telefis Eierran, the Irish equivalent of the BBC, hereafter referred to as the RTE Interview.

30. Ibid.

31. Ken Newell, conversation with the author, March 17, 2001.

32. Ibid.

33. Roisin Hannaway, conversation with the author, June 20, 1997.

34. Gerry Reynolds, conversation with the author, March 19, 2001.

35. RTE Interview.

36. Mallie and McKittrick, *Fight for Peace*; Wells, *People behind the Peace*; George J. Mitchell, *Making Peace* (New York: Knopf, 1999).

37. Appleby, *Ambivalence of the Sacred*, 170.

38. RTE Interview.

39. Pax Christi International, "Press Communiqué," Brussels, November 13, 1999.

40. Roisin Hannaway, "Eucharist and Reconciliation," in *Reconciliation in Religion and Society*, ed. Michael Hurley (Belfast: Institute of Irish Studies, 1994), 190.

41. Ibid., 193.

42. Gerry Reynolds, Columbanus Day Homily, in possession of the author.

43. The following discussion is drawn from Daly's "Forgiveness and Community," in *Reconciling Memories*, ed. Alan D. Falconer (Dublin: Columba Press, 1988), 99–115.

44. Iris Murdoch, *Bruno's Dream* (London: Penguin, 1970), 266–67.

45. Daley, "Forgiveness and Community," 102–3.

46. "Adams Surgeon Urges Work for Peace," *Belfast Telegraph*, March 5, 1994; "Surgeon Makes Plea for Peace," *Irish Times*, March 5, 1994.

# Conclusion

*Reconciliation and Realism*

## R. SCOTT APPLEBY

The authors of this book might reasonably expect that few of their colleagues read it. Consider how other social scientists, for example, might respond to a text dedicated to treating utopian ideals—Forgiveness! Reconciliation! Peace!—as if they were viable political concepts capable of effective application in "the real world." The historian in me, searching for cases in which the practice of forgiveness and reconciliation among erstwhile combatants led to the cessation of hostilities and to something approaching "peace," knows that such examples are few and far between and that the advocates of reconciliation typically relied upon the power of the state to arrange and manage the process and to secure the peace.[1] Even theologians and philosophers, more accustomed to translating abstractions into precepts, might blanch at the notion, advanced here by Nicholas Wolterstorff (ch. 3), that the modern nation-state is an appropriate practitioner of "forgiveness."

Yet the editor, a political scientist, has succeeded in forging a fellowship of purpose among the philosophers, political scientists, theologians, and historians who contributed to this volume. He encouraged them to provide intellectual foundations for extending the scholarly and political discourse *beyond* the debate between *Realpolitik* and *Moralpolitik*—that is, beyond the camp of those who see the world, politically, as a struggle between sovereign nation-states that act only to preserve or increase their power and those who believe it possible and desirable for nation-states to conceive of their interests as compatible with—as even being served by—an international order based on a universal code of human rights conditioning the exercise of state sovereignty. Daniel Philpott is convinced that the assumptions and terms of this debate are already exhausted, inadequate to the political reality facing the world fifteen years after the end of the Cold War and five years after September 11, 2001.

What has changed? To be a realist today is necessarily to engage the question of human dignity in a new way. Distance from one's adversaries and the anonymity it brings are no longer possible in societies rendered irreversibly multicultural by east-to-west and south-to-north migration, and in a world shrunken by globalization and scarred by dozens of face-to-face shooting wars that are waged by militias and peoples unconstrained by superpowers threatening one another across continents and oceans, above the fray. Today the human face of suffering caused by war and oppression is unmasked; the possibilities for vengeful retaliation are innumerable; the social-psychological dynamics of conflict are undeniable. Any political leader, diplomat, or policy maker who fails to account for "the human factor" in postwar political and social reconstruction is doomed to preside over unending, often bloody reminders that deadly political conflict today is personal and communal as well as global.

None of the contributors to this volume believe that the sovereign nation-state is going away or that the building up of international law and human rights does not remain an urgent necessity in curbing the raw power of the militarized state. But neither do they believe that humanity can continue to suffer the spirals of revenge and retaliation unleashed by abundantly armed tribal, religious, and ethnic as well as political enemies. Increasingly, the international order, as well as the previously inviolable borders and sovereignty of even the strongest nation-states, is at risk. New instruments are required for managing deadly conflict and recovering from its depredations.

The authors of this volume argue eloquently that a social process leading to reconciliation is one such political instrument, and an indispensable one at that. Taken together, their essays cohere around the following theme: introducing "God" explicitly into our thinking about transitional justice, democratization, human rights, and the state's role in fostering social harmony clarifies and sharpens the assumptions, terms, and goals of the ongoing debate about reconciliation in societies recovering from violent conflict. Indeed, one's view of what is ultimately meaningful in life powerfully shapes one's positions on a range of discrete questions, from the precise role of trials, punishment, and other forms of retributive justice to the proper function of the state in restoring the rights and status of victims. "God," in short, makes a difference. How so?

The theologians, Christians who practice Christian theology, would seem to have the shortest distance to travel in addressing the question. Reconciliation and its prerequisite, forgiveness, are theologically resonant terms in the Christian tradition. Jesus Christ, one who prayed that God forgive his tormentors, enjoined and embodied reconciliation with enemies. Huddled behind locked doors after his crucifixion, the apostles, who had abandoned or denied Jesus at the time of his arrest, sentencing, and death, were suddenly confronted by him. Rather than rebuke them, he offered a word of reconciliation: "Jesus came and stood in their midst and said to them, 'Peace be with you.' When he had said this, he showed them his hands and his side. The disciples rejoiced when they saw the Lord. Jesus said to them again, 'Peace be with you'" (John 20:19–21).

The Christian Bible offers a more complicated picture of the role and place of reconciliation, however, than conveyed in this passage and in the injunctions to forgive one's offenders and love one's enemies. Elsewhere in the text of the New Testament, the earthly, pre-Resurrection Jesus, bound by the exigencies and moral ambiguities of life on earth, and struggling for justice in a world of corrupt political and religious leaders, seems to limit the scope of forgiveness and reconciliation to the company of believers and to legitimate discrimination against unbelievers. "Do you think that I have come to establish peace on the earth? No, I tell you, but rather division. From now on a household of five will be divided, three against two and two against three; a father will be divided against his son and a son against his father, a mother against her daughter and a daughter against her mother, a mother-in-law against her daughter-in-law and a daughter-in-law against her mother-in-law" (Luke 12: 50–53; cf. also Matt. 10:34: "Do not think that I have come to bring peace upon the earth. I have come to bring not peace but the sword.") One might fairly conclude that "peace" is an eschatological promise rather than a mundane reality, a state of being reserved for heaven and embodied only by the *risen* Lord. His apostles, like all historical actors, remain mired in a world that deserves "not peace but a sword." Jesus as the ultimate political realist.

Given this kind of ambiguity and ambivalence in the sacred texts of Christianity, the task of identifying "the theological grounds of advocating forgiveness and reconciliation in the sociopolitical realm"—the title and subject of Alan Torrance's essay in this volume (ch. 2)—requires the construction of a nuanced and elaborate argument. Torrance provides one.

Readers versed in Christian theology will appreciate the logic and depth of Torrance's "exposition and interpretation of Christian thought" as it applies to his subject. Those who get their theology from the Sunday homily, or from casual reading and conversation—a set that includes, one presumes, the majority of the statesmen, policy makers, diplomats, academics, and media professionals that make up the audience for this book—will find it fresh, challenging, sophisticated, and anything but "straightforward," as Torrance describes the exercise. In explicating the theological meaning of reconciliation, the author first distinguishes Christian understandings of the Jewish concepts of covenant, *torah,* and righteousness from their distortion, during the course of Western Christian history, into the categories of contract, law, and justice. Central to this distinction is the mutual unconditionality of the covenant between God and God's people, a covenant set within a filial—rather than a legal—relationship. Torrance then provides a succinct primer in basic Christian soteriology, or theology of redemption, as it unfolded in Saints Paul and Augustine, in Luther and Calvin, in Kierkegaard and Rahner, and, most recently, in the work of the author's late father, James Torrance: grace is prior to justification; human faithfulness is inspired by a prevenient divine love, not by acts of repentance designed to earn a forgiveness that has already been given in Jesus Christ; Christians readily forgive others because they have been forgiven by God.

This is a distinctively Christian and eschatological vision. Christians are blessed with "a self-giving desire to make amends of a kind that legal repentance (the desire to satisfy legal conditions for contractually conceived ends) could not conceive." Christian practice therefore bears no resemblance to "the contractual, self-oriented categories of means and ends characteristic of the secular world." Christians are bound to forgive "seventy times seven, as the one true human, the *eschatos Adam* [Jesus Christ], forgives seventy times seven."

Herein lies the challenge to anyone who would find not merely a common thread but an underlying unity in the various meanings and applications of "reconciliation" proposed in this volume and, indeed, increasingly present within the world of politics. Torrance's forceful statement of a *Christian* concept of reconciliation raises two major questions faced by theorists who would extend the concept beyond the Judeo-Christian categories of covenant, *torah,* and righteousness.

First, on what grounds can we expect "reconciliation" to be meaningful, much less fruitful, in the political order of non-Christian societies? If reconciliation is to be defined as "the restoration of right relationships"—with "right relationships" understood according to God's will for humanity as revealed in Jesus Christ—are we not left with an unavoidably condescending stance toward other faith traditions? More than forty years ago, the Roman Catholic theologian Karl Rahner, striving to preserve Christianity's exclusive truth claims while affirming the spiritual truths and moral wisdom upheld by other faiths, coined the term "*anonymous Christians*" for Buddhists, Jews, Hindus, et cetera, and atheists alike who, notwithstanding their explicit truth claims or denial thereof, live a morally exemplary life of self-gift inspired by the Holy Spirit. Such people, Rahner wrote, thereby participate, outside their conscious awareness, in what Torrance calls (following St. Paul) the *koinonia*, or communion that God establishes with humanity.[2]

Few, if any, Christian theologians writing today, however, would dare to reduce Buddhism, Judaism, Islam, or secular humanism to an underdeveloped, imperfectly articulated version of Christianity. The awareness that each tradition offers its own distinctive and irreplaceable contributions to the store of human wisdom and practice of peace raises the question of whether "reconciliation" can serve as a cultural basis for personal or political practice in non-Christian or post-Christian societies.

The second fundamental question is posed by Torrance's claim that Christian revelation "is an event in and through which our understanding and perception of God and humanity, our language and our categories of interpretation, are transformed . . . *such that they are no longer 'schematized' by the secular order*" (emphasis added). Must the secular order itself, then, be transformed if the concept of reconciliation is to have meaning and applicability within the secular realm? Can we realistically expect such a transformation? Under what conditions would Christian sensibilities regarding reconciliation permeate and be appropriated by the non-Christian worlds?

Perhaps we find in the recent attempts to foster social reconciliation and explore its relevance to political culture precisely the kind of heightened awareness of the contours of human suffering that constitutes the beginnings of such a transformation. If so, the case for such a change in political and cultural attitudes will have to be articulated and documented by anyone who seeks to demonstrate the applicability of the theologian's descriptions of a renewed spiritual awareness to contemporary conditions "on the ground."

In various ways the authors of this volume address these two fundamental questions. Their answers provide a foundation for a coherent theory of reconciliation that both bridges and transcends the personal and the public, the theological and the political.

## Among the Religious

How universally resonant is "reconciliation" as a religious concept? The question must be addressed first within Christianity itself, given the historic tension between justice and forgiveness in the development of Christian "public theology." From St. Anselm to Gustavo Gutierrez, Christian thinkers have emphasized the priority of justice and liberation, relegating reconciliation and forgiveness to an individualized realm of private morality. Against this tendency Torrance invokes the recent work of Miroslav Volf, the Croatian theologian who believes that forgiveness is intrinsic to the creation of a just society.

Yet a public ethic of forgiveness raises thorny questions. How can anyone, save the victim, "forgive" acts of irreversible evil (e.g., the murder of a child)? Indeed, "keeping faith with the dead" would seem to require an ethic of retaliation. Even God has no right, some would say, to forgive evil acts perpetrated against a human being, whose freedom and dignity are irreducibly personal and thus unique. If God has no right, certainly the nation-state may not presume to involve itself in the dynamics of forgiveness.

Such questions are important but penultimate. The prior question is whether forgiveness for putatively unforgivable acts is a worthy goal, apart from whether the theologians deem it so. In short, on what grounds are we to listen to the theologians who urge radical forgiveness as a political practice?

If *theology* is to serve as the foundation for a public ethic of justice, then one must eventually address the problem of God. All talk of divine forgiveness, grace, and reconciliation rings hollow to those who do not believe in God, or who differ dramatically on what is to be signified by the word "*God.*" Accordingly, a Christian theology of reconciliation that would escape sectarianism and effectively address a pluralist society must achieve a minimal consensus: "*God*" signifies "that which is real," or "the way things are." In the traditional formula: theology presupposes ontology. Language about "God" is always also language about "Being." The nature of Being determines the truth of all realms of existence, from the religious to the political. If people seek to achieve justice, they must know what is just in the order of Being.

The great contribution of religion is precisely to reveal to the world the nature of reality, "the way things are." God-talk does this in a richly evocative manner. Hence Torrance immerses the reader in first-order religious language— in discussion of incarnation, "the *eschatos Adam,*" "Christ's vicarious humanity, together with the pneumatological element intrinsic to it," and "the Christian epistemic base" of forgiveness. Christianity, he avers, claims a special insight into

God. The Incarnation of God—the ultimate reality, the "ground of Being"—in Jesus Christ revealed both the irreversibility of God's communion with and "commitment to" humanity and the unconditional dignity of the human person. In this event we witness the definitive confirmation of the unity of humankind, and of humankind's communion with God (with "that which is real").

Sin against a fellow human being is therefore always also a sin both against the human community and against God (that is, against the reality in which we all move and live and have our being). In this respect only God is in a position to forgive in a manner that upholds the eternal, unconditional dignity of the victim. But the human community is called nonetheless to replicate that divine forgiveness in the temporal realm.

This is a tall order, to say the least. Scandalously, it would seem, divine forgiveness encompasses the victimizer as well as the victim. There is a sort of divine logic to this imperative to love the enemy as well as the friend, one acknowledges. If human dignity—even the dignity of the perpetrator—is rooted in God, in ultimate reality, it can be eradicated neither by the commission of evil acts nor by victimization at the hands of evildoers.

What, then, would it mean for the human community to replicate divine forgiveness? At the very least, it would mean that measures in the political order that fail to honor the irreducible dignity of every person would fail thereby to be just.

Most serious Christians, one assumes, would subscribe to this statement of the inherent relationship between God, forgiveness, and justice in the world. But how persuasive is it to non-Christians? A sectarian, exclusivist expression of Christianity as "the one true religion" stands little chance of serving as a compelling theological basis for political realism. Only a truly universal Christianity can do so—a Christianity that proclaims the truth about the dignity of the human person *and* engages the truth claims of every religious and philosophical tradition that purports to describe reality.

Each tradition, Christianity included, speaks of the universal from a particular set of historical perspectives. The hope for a common foundation for human values lies in the unity of reality itself. Many gods must ultimately be reconciled in the one God, in the one reality. In this process the religions and their various gods strive to contribute to the common perception, naming, and apprehension of the one.

Although Torrance does not invoke the language of "Being" or "reality" per se, he certainly does claim that the Incarnation of God in Jesus Christ discloses the radical truth about the human person, namely that every person is loved by God and redeemed from sin—reconciled—in the depths of his or her humanity. For Torrance "human dignity" is not an ideal or goal set apart from, or standing above and judging, Christian revelation; rather, it is a truth and reality derived from the encompassing truth about God revealed in Jesus Christ. "Human dignity" is second-order language, the application of Christian doctrine to the social and political order.

Yet Torrance is presumably concerned about the relationship between Christianity's truth claims and the beliefs and convictions of people who do not speak "first-order" Christian language; certainly, this volume must be so concerned if it is to advance reconciliation as a political instrument in communities that are religiously diverse. Any theology that would lend itself to an inclusive politics of reconciliation in a pluralist society must, like Torrance's interpretation of Christianity, demonstrate its relevance to the question of human dignity, which we have identified as the primary geopolitical question of our time.

Accordingly, we must ask whether the creedal specificity of Torrance's discourse invites an inclusive—ecumenical, inter-religious, religious-secular—understanding of forgiveness and reconciliation in the political order. We must ask, that is, whether Christianity, as Torrance interprets it, can participate in a public philosophy that both grounds sociopolitical efforts at political reconciliation in religiously plural societies and remains true to Christian convictions.

Torrance does not directly address this practical, political question. Yet it seems consistent with Torrance to affirm that Christianity, properly understood, welcomes and critically weighs the testimony of every human witness to the nature of divine reality and human dignity. On the one hand, Christianity proclaims that Jesus Christ is the perfect, unsurpassed self-revelation of God. This could be read as a highly particularistic claim that seems to regard only one historical starting point and one social form of revelation as valid. On the other hand, one must consider the Christian philosophical notion that God is the ground of all Being—a notion that has been embraced strongly by Roman Catholic philosophers working within the Thomist tradition. I argue that this approach, in which Christian revelation discloses the fundamental truth about reality, also recognizes that every concrete statement about God is analogical and thus relatively inadequate as an exclusive, absolute statement—or woefully inadequate, as the *via negativa* practiced by Christian mystics would have it. It follows that no one historical expression of the divine self-gift, however transparent, excludes others: access to "ultimate reality" (God, the sacred, etc.) is available throughout history and in different social contexts. Would Torrance agree that each religious and philosophical tradition contributes its own insights and specific formulations to the cumulative record of the human encounter with ultimate reality—with God?

Such a rigorously formulated affirmation of pluralism as a foundation for religious contributions to the common good is the sine qua non for religion's peaceable participation in any politics of reconciliation. This principle should govern the state's effective and prudent "consultation" of religions and religious actors. Public officials concerned with achieving "transitional justice" in a rightly ordered society, that is, would be wise to pay heed to the publicly responsible and representative religions to which their citizens adhere. For those religions provide a guide to the depths of human "being," even though that "guide" is encoded in the particulars of the individual's creed, race, religion, or nationality.

The other Abrahamic religious traditions, Judaism and Islam, are Christianity's surest partners in testing the proposition that reconciliation, or a culturally analogous practice, is a requirement of justice in the political order.[3] The complementarity of Jewish, Muslim, and Christian perspectives on the question of forgiveness and reconciliation is the thesis of David Burrell's essay in this volume (ch. 4). Burrell's contribution is useful to our theoretical task, not least because he provides a compatible alternative to Torrance's theological method. Where Torrance writes on a theoretical and conceptual level and ranges across generations, Burrell focuses on concrete contemporary societies that are in transition away "from regimes that managed to shred the very fabric of that society," often by using religious "identity markers" to divide people. In so doing he explores Christian warrants for engaging the religious "other" in order to bring one's own understanding of God closer to perfection. The presence of "other-believers," he writes, "can help the faithful in each tradition to gain insight into the distortions of that tradition: the ways it has compromised with various seductions of state power, the ways in which fixation on a particular 'other' may have skewed their understanding of the revelation given them."

Burrell's critical insight, however, is the recognition that theological and philosophical concepts, however refined, are lifeless without their incarnation in practices. Practices, more than shared ideas, create relationships across religious and personal borders, and Burrell sketches several analogous practices— the call and response of prayer, the rituals of mourning, acts of mercy and charity—familiar to the three Abrahamic traditions. Echoing Torrance while applying his insights to the world of action, Burrell sees these practices as the basis for what he calls "a relational ontology"—that is, a way of being that opens each believer to the other and thereby creates the conditions under which forgiveness, atonement, and reconciliation, despite their different roles and resonances in the Abrahamic faiths, may nonetheless become elements of a shared practice and discourse across the faith communities.

Marc Gopin, among others, has explored and retrieved the practices within each Abrahamic tradition that might constitute a platform for new, intercommunal practices of forgiveness and reconciliation. If a sustainable peace is to become plausible in societies emerging from deadly conflict, Gopin argues, religious leaders must cultivate practices of "holy remembering," "holy repentance," and forgiveness within their own communities and *across* religious communities. Such practices, that is, must not be presented as exclusive of the religious other but must somehow raise the visibility of the suffering that occurs in every community besieged by deadly conflict. In the absence of such practices, the ideas of reconciliation, repentance, and forgiveness gain little traction in a pluralistic political order. The cultivation of such practices, by contrast, helps to create "a culture of reconciliation"—a society in which the symbols and discourse of healing, justice, and forgiveness are sufficiently pervasive to influence the political climate in the direction of peace building.[4]

The experience of Northern Ireland illustrates one kind of possibility. The history of the implementation of every politically negotiated pact during the course of "the Troubles," up to and including the Good Friday Accord of 1998, suggests that top-down structural processes devised and implemented by political elites, if they are to take root and succeed in the long run, must be complemented by the mobilization of cultural actors at the grassroots level. Early attempts to manage the conflict through structural political and economic measures failed, in part because they were not accompanied by the kind of cross-community partnerships described by Ronald Wells in this volume (ch. 7). The politically effective friendship between a Redemptorist Catholic priest, Fr. Gerry Reynolds, and Ken Newell, a Presbyterian minister, reminds us that Northern Ireland has produced more than its fair share of "religious militants"—not only violent extremists, however, but also entire networks of people, working at different levels of society, who are committed to the peaceful transformation of a society trapped in the unrelenting cycles of a centuries-old conflict. In such settings lasting peace is impossible without a change of hearts and minds, without a new story to replace the old. Wells narrates one such story, of religiously motivated peacemakers, exemplified by Reynolds and Newell, who have established programs to enhance dialogue between Catholics and Protestants, promote common education, and foster joint economic programs. Rejecting partisan constructions of the past, most of them based in religious-nationalist mythology, is central to these enterprises.

Peacemaking of this sort is not utopian; while it strives to create a sense of a "community beyond communities," it does not ask people to abandon the particular in deference to the universal. While religiously motivated peacemakers are striving to build a societal network of associations across confessional boundaries, they seek, not to undermine confessional ties, but to foster different styles of religious expression emphasizing forgiveness and reconciliation rather than revenge and the nourishing of grievances. In that respect, the religious and cultural approach to conflict resolution has long understood that Northern Ireland desperately needs a politics of forgiveness.[5]

A politics of forgiveness finds its cultural foundation in a remythologizing project—the replacement of narratives of righteous revenge with stories and practices that can bind together two historically divided peoples in a new pattern of active tolerance. The dismal state of public education in Northern Ireland—for example, the prohibitive class structure of the system and the low incidence of "mixed" (i.e., Catholic-Protestant) schools—has been an enormous impediment to the realization of this goal. The debunking of ideologically loaded "histories" is therefore a priority of educators who are challenging the manipulation of religious symbols by sectarian propagandists, textbook writers, and others who seek to reinforce and augment destructive cultural myths.

Unfortunately, the myths are deeply ingrained. The situation becomes all the more complicated when multiple religious traditions are locked in a struggle for political power and sovereignty over sacred sites. In Northern Ireland, the Catholic-Protestant divide is sometimes bridged by the invocation of symbols and teachings of a shared Christianity. In a pluralistic religious setting such as the Middle East, the internal divisions within any faith tradition are complicated by the presence of competing religious traditions and sacred narratives. In contemplating the possibilities for building a culture of reconciliation, one would think the situation utterly hopeless.

Yet Burrell and Gopin's research on constructive Jewish-Christian-Muslim relations in the Holy Land suggests the power of "relational ontology"—the way in which our common humanity, in its irreducible dignity, is being revealed, reinforced, and celebrated in new cross-cultural myths, rituals, and ceremonies (e.g., groups of bereaved Jewish, Muslim, and Christian parents come together to mourn the violent deaths of their children). The acknowledgment of this underlying humanity—of what Torrance would call our mutual participation in God, or "Being itself"—is a potentially powerful source of unity, forgiveness, and reconciliation.

## Religious and Secular

Far from being utopian, such theological principles and religious practices have much to offer in the arena of statecraft. A viable theory of reconciliation in the public realm emerges from and responds to the experiences of states that have attempted to incorporate truth telling and forgiveness into the process of democratization. Accordingly, the growing literature on transitional justice, authored in the main by political scientists and human rights and legal scholars, borrows generously from the language of social ethics and theology. One reads of the importance of "communal solidarity," "national reconciliation," and "a politics of forgiveness."[6] In part the new lexicon reflects an awareness that "the secular" and "the religious" are not separate, isolable sectors of contemporary societies but rather modes of public presence, overlapping and interacting in dynamic and mutually transformative patterns. Seldom does "the secular" eliminate "the religious" in society; rather, secularization shifts the social location of religion, influences the structures it assumes and the way people perform their religious functions, or forces religion to redefine the nature, grounds, and scope of its authority. Even in secularized or secularizing societies where people come to interpret the world without constant reference to religious symbols, religion is displaced rather than destroyed, as believers transfer religious loyalties to the nation, "the people," or other objects of unconditional devotion.

Missing from much of the literature on transitional justice is the kind of second-order reflection, provided in the current volume, on the social benefits of "restorative justice, political forgiveness, and the possibility of political reconciliation"—the title of Mark Amstutz's chapter (ch. 6). Amstutz explores the extension of forgiveness, repentance, and reconciliation beyond the grassroots religious and ethnic communities, "to whole nations."

Both Amstutz and James McAdams, who contributes the volume's chapter on reconciliation in unified Germany (ch. 5), grapple with the thorny practical political questions surrounding the recent attempts of emerging democratic regimes to reckon with the crimes and human rights violations of former governments. In particular, the authors address the difficult task of combining truth telling and retributive justice with forgiveness, inclusion, and restorative justice. Are legal remedies, including trials and punishment, the most effective way of ensuring the restoration of order and the rebuilding of economic and civic associations? Should the state (or civil society) attempt to heal collective injuries caused by dictatorial regimes and to build "communal solidarity"? Is "political forgiveness" a means to reckon with gross human rights violations of past regimes?

In pondering these questions Amstutz draws on the experiences of Argentina and South Africa, while McAdams, as mentioned, examines the case of unified Germany. Amstutz and McAdams are concerned with *evaluation* of the disparate processes, and their approach is both scholarly and "interested"— that is, informed by a profound, if unspoken, set of assumptions that cohere in most respects with the Christian universalism delineated above. Amstutz, for example, citing the failure of Argentina's efforts, under the leadership of President Raul Alfonsín, to consolidate democracy and heal the nation following the trauma of the "Dirty War" against leftists, pins the blame squarely on a "strategy of retribution" that failed fully to consider the dignity of the victims. Rather than promoting national reconciliation and contributing to the consolidation of constitutional government, he argues, the pursuit of legal retribution undermined these goals.

At the heart of Amstutz's argument is the conviction that a viable democracy requires a cultural as well as a political-legal foundation and, more pointedly, that the cultural foundation must be built on the principle of the inherent dignity of the individual. Communal solidarity and a stable regime of human rights depend on the honoring of this cornerstone value. Thus, invoking the critique of Jaime Malamud-Goti, one of Alfonsín's senior legal advisers, Amstutz rejects the notion that the military trials failed because they were badly timed. Rather, the trials mistakenly focused on the offenses of the perpetrators rather than the restoration of victims and the creation of a rights-based democracy, relied too heavily upon the courts and legal system to adjudicate profound political and moral issues, and limited the culpability to a small number of senior and midlevel military officials.

By contrast, what Amstutz calls "the partial restorative justice model" followed by South Africa's Truth and Reconciliation Commission defined crime in such a way as to focus on the suffering of the individual victim, emphasized reparations for victims and their integration into communal life, called for the rehabilitation of perpetrators based upon full accountability for their past offenses, and encouraged direct conflict resolution among victims, offenders, and the community.

Amstutz believes that the Argentinian approach failed because it ignored or trivialized the sentiment and convictions of the people, who identified with the victims. In that failure, he notes, lies an important lesson for political leaders who would otherwise be insufficiently attentive to the cultural and social foundations of emerging democracies. The South African process was considerably more successful, Amstutz argues, because it recognized that "democratic decision making is viable only in coherent, unified communities." The TRC boldly attempted to advance the consolidation of a unified, multiracial South African community by sparking a multidimensional process of justice, accountability, and reconciliation. Such a process, the commissioners argued, would best honor human dignity—the dignity of the perpetrator as well as the victim. To some observers this goal was morally correct and courageous. To others, it was blasphemous, disrespectful of the victims, and destined to lead to greater acrimony and social division.

The disagreement runs deep. Many responsible scholars and public officials are concerned that the momentum to integrate forgiveness and reconciliation into the public process of transitional justice is a recipe for disaster. The presence of these critics' voices in the current volume is one of its major strengths. McAdams provides the reader with a window on the debate by explaining the opposing views of Joachim Gauck and Friedrich Schorlemmer on the question of whether the files of the former East German secret police (the Stasi) should have been opened and used to assess the democratic credentials of hundreds of thousands of public officials. Whereas Gauck favored opening the files, identifying the perpetrators and specifying what they had to do in order to be reintegrated into society, Schorlemmer emphasized the role of the victims in rebuilding the torn social fabric and political order. McAdams, citing Miroslav Volf, concludes that "these contrasting attributes of reconciliation should occur simultaneously and as part of the same ongoing process." For McAdams, including the victims as well as the collaborators in the process of evaluating the past and pursuing justice is "the most realistic course." In this way what Avishai Margalit calls the weight of "moral witness" is incorporated into the process.[7]

Amstutz underscores the contested nature of reconciliation. In advancing his own position, which seems to me grounded in what Burrell calls "a relational ontology," he rebuts a variety of views that contrast sharply to his own. These include Rajeev Bhargava's argument that reconciliation is an excessively demanding political goal that increases fragmentation and threatens the achievement of "a minimally decent society"; David Crocker's contention that reconciliation threatens human freedom and individual rights; and Timothy Garton Ash's claim that reconciliation is a deeply "illiberal" idea. In each of these minidebates, Amstutz argues, in effect, that his is the more realistic position—the position, that is, which conforms most closely to "the way things are" in societies poised between tyrannical regimes and democracy.

Critics of reconciliation such as Amy Gutmann and Dennis Thompson, for example, argue that the task of a humane society is to maintain procedural norms for regulating social conflict and structuring political decision making. Society, according to this view, should not prescribe beliefs and values for its citizens but simply resolve disputes and foster decision making through ordered discussion and debate. In response Amstutz suggests that democratic procedures alone may not suffice in societies that have experienced ethnic, religious, or ideologically driven wars. Democratic society may be impossible, he writes, without the development of further national solidarity, ethnic and political tolerance, and economic justice. Along the way he invokes cases that support this conclusion.

Daniel Philpott (ch. 1) devotes an entire, rich essay to answering the charge that political reconciliation is illiberal. While Philpott acknowledges and explores the several points of tension between liberalism and a political philosophy that would privilege reconciliation, he locates a basis for the compatibility of the two, "not [in] the balance of consequences, but [in] deep principles of justice that political reconciliation itself instantiates." What are these deep principles of justice? Philpott does not identify them but mentions the "restoration of people and relationships. . . . restoring and affirming the dignity of those whose human rights have been violated" and the promotion of "the reciprocal, deliberative, democratic conversation between equals that, for [certain scholars], is the heart of a just, liberal democracy."

The next step seems to me an effortless one. Restoration of people, relationships, and the dignity of those whose human rights have been violated—these goals embody the foundational ideal of liberal democracy as well as the highest teaching of Christianity. One must honor the irreducible dignity of the individual, regardless of race, creed, or religion. Might Judaism and Islam, along with other indigenous religious (and cultural) traditions, be recruited to endorse this putative foundation for just relations in a civilized society? The present volume fails to wrestle with this central question, Burrell's affirmations notwithstanding.

My elaboration of Philpott's (qualified) defense of the compatibility of reconciliation and liberalism is based on two particularly noteworthy aspects of his essay. First, he cites to his advantage scholars such as Gutmann and Thompson, whose specific prescriptions for political reconciliation and understanding of its benefits (and limits) differ from his own. Second, he suggests, correctly in my view, that these "deep principles of justice" are the surest common ground underlying the various pragmatic considerations and disagreements of the experts. These principles, however, while clearly recognizable to Christian theologians, are not readily available to liberals, in part because "the liberalism of the Enlightenment and later periods offers little role for divine restoration."

Yet secular as well as religious figures invoke "the deep principles of justice," albeit through a different discourse and symbol system. Human rights, accountability to the other, hospitality to the stranger, forgiveness itself—all exist along a continuum of meaning and affirmation of human dignity. What religion and theology bring to the debate is insistence on the depth dimension, the immutability and "eternal nature" of these principles. They are much more than procedural methods or pragmatic political concessions. To the degree that liberals consider God relevant for the political order, Philpott notes, "it is as the Creator of the natural law in which that order is rooted." Yes, and what a profound relevance it is. I have argued that Christian theology is useful to the debate on political reconciliation to the extent that it sheds light on the nature of reality itself (of which "the natural law" is considered an accessible manifestation). The same must be said of other theological, cultural, and philosophical traditions: their political "utility" rests precisely on the resonance and validity of their "cosmology" or "ontology"—their ability to describe reality, and especially the human condition, in its depth dimensions. Political systems that ignore or misconstrue human dignity and freedom face the rising tide of democracy from a position of weakness.

In sum, theology, by disclosing and providing insight into the ontological basis of human dignity, is the surest foundation for correct and politically effective thinking on "deep principles of justice" such as the inviolability of human rights. But any particular theology must be evaluated in conjunction with other religious claims and insights, each of which is ultimately put to the litmus test: Does it contribute to our understanding of the depths of human dignity? Do we recognize in the theological insight or religious practice a truth about the human person and the human community that previously escaped articulation, public expression, and political response?

## The Godless State?

These criteria are put to the test in Nicholas Wolterstorff's essay (ch. 3) on the place of forgiveness in the actions of the state. In his discussion of the nature of forgiveness, Wolterstorff, a professor of philosophical theology, moves effortlessly between the language of rights and the language of religion. Forgiving, he argues, consists in "an enacted resolution to forego, actively or passively, at least some of the goods to which one has a retributive right." Invoking Christianity, he notes that Jesus teaches that his followers have "an imperfect duty" to forgive their enemies—an obligation to forgive, that is, even though their enemies have no *right* to forgiveness. Repentance, however, Wolterstorff continues, citing the New Testament, gives the wrongdoer the right to be forgiven. Whether the state, in addition to the individual Christian, must acknowledge that "right" is left as an open question.

Nonetheless, Wolterstorff asks: Can and should states forgive individuals? Yes, he answers, listing the many ways in which states do, in fact, practice forgiveness (albeit, indeed, a kind of incomplete or partial forgiveness)—out of financial expediency, mercy, the need for social order, the social contribution of the offender, and so on. In some cases, as in South Africa, he notes, states offer forgiveness (beginning in amnesty) in a move toward the ultimate goal of reconciliation.

There is far more to Wolterstorff's closely reasoned essay, but his theoretical assumptions are particularly relevant for our discussion of a theory of political reconciliation. Wolterstorff, the *Christian* philosopher, borrows some of his central assertions about the desirability of political forgiveness from Jesus' teachings in the New Testament. Notwithstanding the historical appeal one might make to the Judeo-Christian foundations of the Western legal system, this seems to be a remarkably religious move. Yet Wolterstorff, the Christian *philosopher,* appeals primarily to human reason and common human experience. Many of his arguments are pragmatic, in the sense of being appropriate to an accurate assessment of human behavior: What kinds of human reactions and sensibilities must the state take into account? What policies satisfy the need for stable human community and political order? What might ensure the long-term good of the people, and of the state itself?

Indeed, the central question of Wolterstorff's essay is whether it is ever "*a good thing* for the state to forgive." His notion of "the good," however, is derived not only from observation of human society but also from explicit insights and teachings revealed by a religious tradition. A Christian notion of human dignity informs and deepens his claims about the proper role of the state in practicing forgiveness. In the end, one is left with the question of how a "godless state"— a state that does not establish its laws and procedures in dialogue with the deepest insights about the human person—can achieve a just and politically effective transition to democracy.

Along the way, we have noted that ideas and precepts alone may not suffice to galvanize a religiously pluralist society toward a process of reconciliation. Thus it is significant that Wolterstorff invokes "practices" as well—in his case not the ritual practices of culture and religion but the everyday practices of people engaged in personal and communal negotiation, forgiveness (or refusal to forgive), and reconciliation. An accurate assessment of "what people do" is part of the calculation that goes into good governance, of course. It is also a bridge across cultures, ethnic groups, and religions, whose practices both reveal and shape "who they are."

Among the important contributions of this volume on political reconciliation is the calling of attention to this organic connection between moral agency, the truth about the human person, religious insights into both, and the relation of all three to prudent, just, and politically effective processes of transition toward democracy. If their efforts to sketch this connection inspire others to explore it more deliberately and comprehensively, the authors of this volume will no doubt be delighted that their colleagues have read it.

## Notes

1. See, *inter alia,* A. James McAdams, ed., *Transitional Justice and the Rule of Law in New Democracies* (Notre Dame: University of Notre Dame Press, 1997); and Priscilla Hayner, *Unspeakable Truths: Confronting State Terror and Atrocity* (New York: Routledge, 2001).

2. Karl Rahner, *Theological Investigations,* trans. Cornelius Ernst, vol. 5 (New York: Crossroad, 1974).

3. Buddhism, Hinduism, and Confucianism, among other religious and ethical traditions of Asian origin, take a fundamentally different view of ontology and the sacred,

seeing a far less direct (or no) causal chain or organic relationship between temporal justice, human agency, and ultimate reality.

4. Marc Gopin, *Holy War, Holy Peace: How Religion Can Bring Peace to the Middle East* (New York: Oxford University Press, 2003).

5. R. Scott Appleby, *The Ambivalence of the Sacred: Religion, Violence and Reconciliation* (Lanham, MD: Rowman and Littlefield, 2002), ch. 5.

6. See the survey in Gregory Baum and Harold Wells, *The Reconciliation of Peoples: Challenge to the Churches* (Maryknoll, NY: Orbis Books, 1997).

7. Avishai Margalit, *The Ethics of Memory* (Cambridge, MA: Harvard University Press, 2002), 147 ff.

# Index

Party of Democratic Socialism (PDS), 148n24

Patterson, Orlando, 17

Paul, 49, 50, 80, 82nn15–16, 85n48

Pax Christi award, 215

penalty. *See* punishment

Peter (apostle), 98

*Phaedo* (Plato), 71–72

Phelps, Terri, 125

Philpott, Daniel, 237–38

Pinochet, Augusto, 3, 187n51

Plato, 71–72, 85n48

*Political Forgiveness* (Digeser), 94–95

political reconciliation: defining, 13–15, 127–29, 160–62; dimensions of, 15–19; as modern philosophy, 11–13; practices of, 19–25; with restorative justice, 166–68; theology's role summarized, 224–40; with truth telling, 38–39, 159–60. *See also* forgiveness *entries*

political reconciliation, liberal arguments: overview, 6, 11–13, 40–42, 237–38; pragmatism, 35–38; public-private actions, 27–30; public reason, 30–34; punishment, 26–27; restorative-oriented, 38–40; social unity, 34–35

pragmatism argument, 35–38

Presbyterian Church of Ireland (PCI), 201–2, 208–9

prodigal son parable, 56–57

Protestant *vs.* Roman Catholic communities. *See* Northern Ireland

Psalms (book of), 210–11

public-private arguments, 27–30, 69–73, 163–65

public reason argument, 30–34

punishment: and accountability, 22–24, 25, 26–27; as duty, 94; and forgiveness, 63–65, 158–59, 165; as lose-lose, 98–100. *See also* retributive justice

Qur'an, 118, 120–21

Radio Ulster, 199

Rae, Murray, 53–54

Rahman, Fazlur, 120–21

Rahner, Karl, 227

Rawls, John, 30–31

reconciliation. *See* forgiveness *entries;* political reconciliation *entries;* Truth and Reconciliation Commission (TRC)

Reich, Jens, 139

Reid, Alec, 203–6, 209–12

relational ontology. *See* interfaith encounters

reparations, 23–24, 164–65, 185n24

repentance: evangelical *vs.* legal, 6, 53–58, 78–81, 82n20; and forgiveness, 97–98, 101–2, 157–58, 183n3, 184n12; as reconciliation practice, 24

resentment and forgiveness, 92–94

resolution and forgiveness, 95

restitution rights, 111n7

restorative justice. *See* political reconciliation *entries*

retributive justice: Argentina's example, 168–72, 179–80, 235; defining, 91; as lose-lose, 85n53, 98–100; and pragmatism arguments, 35–38; predicament of irreversibility, 60–61; restorative justice compared, 152–53, 165–68; scales myth, 61–63, 65, 68, 83n31, 83n33

retributive rights, 91–94, 104–5, 107–8

revenge, 60–61, 68–73, 83n32, 158

Reynolds, Gerry, 200–203, 209–18, 232–33

righteousness, 50, 52–53

Roberts, Robert, 101

Robinson, Mary, 201

Roman Catholic *vs.* Protestant communities. *See* Northern Ireland

Romans, 82n20, 118

# DANIEL PHILPOTT

is associate professor
in the department of political science
and the Joan B. Kroc Institute for International Peace Studies,
University of Notre Dame.